doing business in asia

in

asia

a cultural perspective

robert burns

doing business in asia

a cultural perspective

 LONGMAN

An imprint of
Addison Wesley Longman

Addison Wesley Longman Australia Pty Limited
95 Coventry Street
South Melbourne 3205 Australia

Offices in Sydney, Brisbane and Perth, and associated companies throughout the world.

Copyright © Addison Wesley Longman Australia Pty Limited 1998
First published 1998

2 3 4 5   02 01 00 99

Cover designed by Lyndell Fynney
Cover photographs reproduced with permission of the International Photographic Library
Designed by Jan Schmoeger/Designpoint
Edited by Margaret Trudgeon
Set in 10.5/12 pt Apollo
Printed in Malaysia, VVP

Tables 12.2 and 12.4 reprinted with permission from *Human Resource Planning*, vol. 14, no. 1 (1991). Copyright 1991, by The Human Resource Planning Society, 317 Madison Avenue, Suite 1509, New York, NY 10017. Phone (121)490–6387, Fax (212)682–6851.

National Library of Australia
Cataloguing-in-Publication data

Burns, Robert, 1939– .
Doing Business in Asia: a cultural perspective.
Bibliography.

ISBN 0 7339 0193 X.

1. Business communication - Asia. 2. Business communication - Cross-cultural studies. 3. Intercultural communication - Asia. 4. Business travel Asia - Guidebooks. 5. Asia - Social life and customs. I. Title.

395.52095

Contents

Introduction

THIS TEXT provides a first reference point for Western business people visiting or temporally residing in major Asian countries, providing assistance on the nuances and subtleties of cultural behaviour, ideology, expectations and values, and the impact of these issues on business activities, whether they be marketing or buying products, developing bilateral trade, arranging a joint venture, studying, establishing an overseas outpost of an organisation, or whether the endeavours are short-term or long-term.

In the current economic crisis, where reduced purchasing power is decreasing market size, it becomes even more imperative that organisations fully understand the cultural and social mores that surround doing business in particular Asian countries, in order that they do not get shut out in the intense competition that will exist for the limited Asian dollar.

This text rests on the assumption that to operate effectively in another culture it is essential to have some understanding of that particular culture, as it impacts both on the purpose of the endeavour and on day-to-day activities. Preparation ahead of time is the best approach and this text will provide the means of doing that. This is not to say that actual experience (on-the-job learning, often from mistakes!) has no place, since no amount of preparation can cover all eventualities.

However, the basis offered by this text may prevent the failure of a project and provide some indication to the hosts that an attempt is being made to understand and work within what is to them accepted cultural practice. Some *faux pas* are inevitable and courteously forgivable; total ignorance or a deliberate 'in our country we do it this way' approach will lead to polite indifference and an inability to operate. Whether we are dealing with negotiating, managing or marketing, the success of an organisation depends on how effectively its staff can exercise their skills in a new location. Job-related expertise is certainly necessary, but so also is the individual's sensitivity and responsiveness to the new cultural environment. It is an erroneous assumption to believe that if a person is successful at home, success is guaranteed overseas. Most overseas failures are not due to technical/professional incompetence or defective products, but to a failure to understand how to operate at a personal level in a different culture.

The text does *not* deal with those technical aspects of business and management such as structuring MNOs, international tax law, sourcing international finance, or the specific laws in each country that govern the establishment of companies and the import/export of products etc, which are so admirably covered in a plethora of business texts. The ethos of this text is socio-psychological, directed towards cross-cultural understandings and facilitation. The content will focus on providing cultural information that can be applied; it is not an analysis or synthesis of academic/research type material, although occasional reference will be made to some research findings about cultural differences.

While the text is a necessary inclusion in the kitbag of any Western person sent on an overseas activity in Asia, it is particularly relevant for Australian business people. Australia, whether under Labor or Liberal management, or whether perceived as part of Asia or not, is physically located close to a major world market containing more than half of the world's population and which has moved in the main from undeveloped to developing and developed status. After 200 years of being distracted by its links with distant Europe, Australia has realised that it is perched on the rim of the most exciting economic region of the world. Trade and business relations with the region were strongly promoted under the former Keating administration and will continue to develop at an exponential pace. APEC is no longer a fledgling body but developing into a force for multinational trade and tariff removal in the region. APEC has also brought Australia into the regional consciousness. Sixty-one per cent of Australia's exports already go into the region with Australia basically functioning as the region's quarry. Six of Australia's top ten trading partners are in Asia. Some Asians do suspect that the Australian motive for neighbourly zeal is more to do with money than neighbourliness. Therefore, an appreciation of cross-cultural matters becomes increasingly important as the *'team Australia'* approach to winning trade relations and regional acceptance in Asia gathers momentum.

At a conference on trading with Asia convened by the Department of Foreign Affairs and Trade (DFAT), 16 June 1996 in Canberra, Senator McMullan indicated that cultural issues were a vital element of the government's commitment to building a 'team Australia' approach and that Australian companies needed to become more open and responsive to Asian practices and sensitivities. As a result of the conference it was recommended that a body be established to provide a forum for the provision of cross-cultural information and understandings, and for developing cross-cultural strategies covering exporting, off-shore operations, and strategic alliances, particularly for small to medium business enterprises. It could also serve as an advisory body for the delivery of cross-cultural curricula.

Given this scenario, more and more Australian companies, particularly small and medium ones, will be active in Asian countries, alongside other major Western players. However, it is not simply a matter of presenting a superior product/service but also knowing, in a different way in each country, how to behave, present oneself and the product, and negotiate and build relationships so that sensitivities are not aroused which could impair or even prevent a successful outcome. This text should meet the needs of both enterprises and individuals, as well as slotting into overall government imperatives for many Western countries who wish to advance economic and trade relations in the Asia-Pacific region.

Since culture is learned, it is possible, though difficult without being totally integrated into a community, to learn the culture of another group. This book will not enable you to learn and become part of that culture, but to understand some of the major elements that may impact on your professional activities there, and enable you to behave in ways that will not offend but facilitate the success of your enterprise. This text needs to be supplemented with other secondhand insights that can be obtained from magazine articles, former expatriates, members of other cultures, government departments that have dealings overseas, other country's diplomatic and trade services, and professional associations.

Structure of the text

The first chapter will discuss the general issues of the need for cultural awareness with examples of 'horror stories', blunders that wrecked some project. A definition of what 'culture' is, with an explanation of its major universal dimensions, along which the cultural practices of most countries can be delineated (e.g. universalism v. particularism; individualism v. collectivism; attitudes to time; power distance), will form the bulk of the chapter. The text will then adopt a country/culture by country/culture approach covering the major countries of Asia.

For each country the content will outline as appropriate the general cultural, historic, political, religious and economic background to provide general overview. This will be followed by detailed coverage of specific aspects of the culture that impact on doing business there, such as negotiation style and holding meetings; management/leadership style; work-related values and motivation; etiquette; dress; entertaining/ banquets; greetings; gifts; inter-personal communication styles; nonverbal communication; and gender and religious issues (e.g. the role of women in society/organisations) as appropriate.

The concluding chapter will deal with general matters, such as the problems faced by expatriates living and working overseas, and training in cultural awareness for overseas assignments.

This book was written by an Australian expatriate, who lives and works in Asia, in the hope that the odd snippet of knowledge will prevent Australian and other Western business people making cultural blunders that will damage their own chances of success and future endeavours.

The book is dedicated to my family who have all suffered the traumas of periodic moves around the world, but who have enjoyed the better moments and have become more enriched persons.

DR ROBERT BURNS
Canberra, January 1998

Prologue
The Asian economy:
Seize the opportunity

You may ask yourself why bother reading this book?

Daily news reports depict Southeast Asia beset by economic and financial problems, suggesting that potential lucrative markets and business possibilities no longer exist there any more. The warning is—keep out!

Nothing could be further from the truth!

While *Doing Business in Asia* does not focus on financial matters, these have become the current focus of attention in the news, and it is essential to have a general understanding of the situation in Southeast Asia in order to realise that out of the debacle is emerging a more secure, controlled and opportunity laden context in which Australians can conduct overseas business.

In fact, the paradox is that the context will be far more secure than that which existed before the crisis, when the business world there was replete with loose financial controls, nepotism, and undisciplined borrowings into which Australians were only too keen to get enmeshed.

The aetiology of the crisis

A four letter word sums up the root and continuing bane of the crisis:

DEBT—Too much of it

Unsecured loans strangled banks while foreign borrowings, multiplied by local currency falls, bankrupted banks and companies. Loose monetary policy throughout Asia bankrolled a bubble economy that burst in 1997-98 leaving a residue of bad loans, sick banks and credit-starved companies. In a sense it is not an economic crisis but a financial one; specifically a debt crisis that has affected banks, businesses and people.

What caused the debt crisis?

There is a tapestry of reasons, including overvalued currencies, speculation, cronyism, excessive investment in property and stocks, and lack of financial safeguards. In the under-regulated context there was little accountability for financial institutions which had no qualms about overlending or lending to high risk borrowers. This excessive investment fuelled asset inflation. Over-inflation increased debt. When over-optimistic returns on assets failed to eventualise, the bubble burst. This led to the collapse of the financial system, as bank bailouts and liquidity injections became too expensive for other banks and governments to honour. Asset deflation then occurred, undermining banks and finance firms who had lent on the basis of higher returns. A loss of confidence followed as investors divested themselves of assets and local currency. The currency falls were more a symptom than a cause. The whole root of the problem then was implicit government guarantees to financial bodies, and the absence of adequate supervision.

The Asian boom originally started after the G7 Plaza Accord in 1985. At the time the yen strengthened and investors salivated. But regulation was rudimentary and cronyism and monopolies continued to distort many economies in the region. Imports outpaced receipts from exports, as people and economies sought improved standards. Easy money funded showcase infrastructure projects and property speculation. By the end of 1996 currency speculators smelled blood, and foreign creditors started to call in loans. The skirmishes started when a major Korean *chaebol*, Hanbo Steel, collapsed in early 1997, and in July 1997 the Thais gave up the struggle to protect their currency.

Other Asian currencies succumbed later that month as the Philippine peso, the Indonesian rupiah and Malaysian ringgit hit all-time lows. These events eventually led to Thailand, Indonesia and South Korea signing up for IMF loans and programs, while others adopted similar tight money and austerity policies. With devaluation, high interest rates and a spending crunch, domestic banks and companies in most Southeast Asian countries wilted, further undermining the financial health of the already crisis-beset economies. This led to the deadening hand of recession, with consequent rapid increases in unemployment, while exports, earnings and investment declined, and consumer spending was slashed. All Southeast Asian countries have trimmed growth·targets, while only China and Taiwan appear likely to avoid recession. Governments are therefore now straining at the leash to rev up their economies as people sink into destitution levels. Unfortunately, the worst hit country, Indonesia, is having to grapple with a complete reorganisation of its political as well as its business life, in order to remove crony capitalism. This has to happen before the economy can start lifting and the estimated 100 million people who live at subsistence levels (with inflation approaching 80 per cent) can be given any hope.

Table A Some indicators of the Southeast Asian problem

	Currency fall v $US	% decline in stock market	Unemployment 1997 June 98		Vacant office rate 1997 March 98	
	%	%	%	%	%	%
Indonesia	-83.2	-88	14.2	16.8	12.4	13.6
Thailand	-40.2	-66	3.0	8.8	21.9	26.7
Malaysia	-39.4	-76	2.7	5.0	2.9	10.6
Philippines	-36.1	-58	10.4	13.3	2.0	3.5
S Korea	-34.1	-71	2.6	6.9	N/A	
Singapore	-16.5	-53	1.7	2.2	6.1	8.7

Source: Asiaweek, July 1998, p. 41.

The preferred IMF policy is for countries to restructure and recapitalise their financial institutions in order to revive domestic lending on a sound footing. Currently there is an excess of bad debt and lack of adequate capital. Restructuring will bring inevitable pain as defaulting businesses are foreclosed and insolvent lenders are shut down. Thailand, South Korea and Malaysia have led the way in this with a resulting sign of recovery in their economies. In Korea for example, fifty-five firms have been classified as non-viable, which means they will not receive new credit and will be subject to mandatory closure. For recession-hit economies some governments are attempting to stimulate new growth by increasing public spending (e.g. Singapore, Hong Kong, Malaysia, Thailand and Japan) and by reducing personal taxation.

Thailand and Korea have indicated that their current high interest rates are likely to come down in the second half of 1998 to increase credit and relieve borrowers in a cautious way. Malaysia has indirectly increased money supply by reducing the amount of reserves that banks need to keep with the central bank. Most countries are restructuring their financial institutions to make them more responsible and secure. This has often been at the expense of weaker banks and finance houses, which have been closed or amalgamated with more stable entities. This is starting to bring more confidence back to the economies.

The phoenix will rise

From the ashes of the corporate rubble a new Asian economy will rise—more efficient, innovative, transparent and dynamic, moving on to the next Asian miracle with the 1997-98 crisis perceived as a necessary and salutary blip on the road forward.

The lessons learned from the Asian crisis will improve the standard of financial accountability and security of business dealings in the future.

What are the main lessons Asia has learned?

1 **Debt equals risk.** Prior to the crunch Asian borrowers seemed to believe that debt equalled cheap funds. Even banks had no hesitation in lending to doubtful creditors for dubious schemes.
2 **Get the basics right.** The benefits of international capital mobility only accrue if there are appropriate macroeconomic policies, institutional frameworks, regulation, supervision, transparency and information disclosure. Everyone must play by and obey the rules; the rules must be fair and they must exist.
3 **Transparency is essential.** Hidden problems, government favours and unprofitable friendly deals must no longer happen. The more doubt that is generated, the more the integrity and viability of the system is harmed.

The cosy nexus of government and business of family and friends that created an apparent economic miracle based on 'Asian values' placed the state before the individual and stability before freedom. The new leaders will assist in the maturing of democracy in those Asian countries where the mighty have fallen. Prime Minister Chavalit of Thailand, who was regarded as beholden to vested interests, has been replaced by Chuan Leekpai. The election of President Kim of South Korea will facilitate the rebuilding of the economy as old acquaintances lose out.

The new Japanese leadership of Prime Minister Obuchi aims to revamp the Japanese economy after the previous period of Hashimoto vacillation. The Philippines, under recently elected President Estrada, shows evidence that the authoritarian road to prosperity is not the only way to go. Suharto has been toppled, but the intricate economic-financial-political debacle there will take longer than elsewhere to clear up—perhaps another five years. However, a start has been made by President Habibie towards more financial responsibility, removal of cronyism and tentative steps towards democracy, despite his associations with the previous government and some doubts over his legitimacy. Even the PRC under Jiang Zemin is restructuring state-owned industries and attempting to soften the economic and social effects of such change by the occasional soft touch on the pedal to more openness. Of elected leaders, only Prime Minister Mahathir of Malaysia has maintained his position, and he faces a dilemma. To move forward in a context of financial discipline means he has to disavow the methods of the past with its overambition and cronyism.

The benefits to Australian businesses of getting involved in Southeast Asia

Buy-outs, joint ventures, and stock acquisition

As part of this restructuring, foreign buy-outs, takeovers, and increasing shareholding will be required. Most of the Asian economies are now relaxing their foreign investment and ownership rules to permit these changes to happen (e.g. Malaysia; South Korea) . The injection of overseas money and involvement will also improve the standards of management and accounting in financial institutions and businesses. In particular, more foreign involvement will increase the independence of institutions from government and political influence, and help remove one of the major causes of the financial debacle—that of providing loans to 'friends' without ascertaining proper collateral or credit-worthiness, or close investigation of the viability of the project. Financial sector reform will change the way of doing business, with institutions becoming profit-seeking bodies rather than instruments of policy or mutual funding agencies for 'top people'.

Now that stocks appear to be at rock bottom (see Table A), and although cheap isn't necessarily attractive, a shrewd investigation of the companies which are likely to show growth and earnings, as the economies pick up, will repay handsomely. The same goes for partial or full buy-outs and joint ventures. Provided the necessary homework is done, and the proper financial controls exist nationally, and in the particular businesses that permit confident assessment of financial liabilities, and real asset values etc., then some valuable ingresses can be made into the internal business life of some Southeast Asian countries. Singapore, Taiwan and Hong Kong still lead the pack in this as their banking systems are stable and liquid. Generally, Asia is under-owned and even in Thailand, as it rebounds, many overseas companies are sniffing around and buying their way into local ventures. After months of adapting to harsh austerity and tight monetary prescriptions from the IMF, Asian economies now need capital to start flowing back. There are strong fundamentals to support continued growth of the Asian economies into the twenty-first century, given political stability and a will to rectify the known problems of financial indiscipline and cronyism—a will that is strengthened by the presence of more Western business involvement with its demand for accountability.

The market is huge

It may be less well-off but it is the *largest* market in the world. Imported goods are still needed; products are still being made to sell overseas (how else will they survive?); many small but viable businesses need investment cash to come good again. This is the time to get in at the ground level, after intensive and sensible evaluation, while stocks and buying in are relatively cheap. Governments are expanding public works projects and programs which require overseas assistance (consultants, project management etc.) to stimulate the economy and provide some local employment.

High savings ethic

The savings habit is entrenched among East Asians as few of the countries have strong welfare schemes. Out of necessity, people try to save for the proverbial rainy day as they must fend for themselves. Compared to the Western average of 15 per cent GDP spent on welfare and social security, most Asian countries spend around 1 per cent. The savings habit is further enhanced by compulsory savings schemes in Singapore and Malaysia. There is an entire new middle class developing with savings to invest, just as the world is getting hungry for such funds in South America, Africa and former Communist bloc countries, as well as elsewhere in Asia.

There is usually no tax on savings, no capital gains tax, nor inheritance tax. Corporate rates are usually much lower too than in the West. These low tax regimes are an incentive for people to work hard and save more. Instead of the Western preoccupation with income redistribution, East Asia focuses on income generation, a bigger economic pie for all. Overseas businesses can now be part of that pie.

Ambition to catch up with the West

Up to two decades ago many parts of Southeast Asia were backward, or in ruins, or going through reconstruction after the Second World War. Having now emerged from poverty and having tasted the fruits of success, the powerful combination of fear of poverty and ambition to overtake the West will propel Asia forward, particularly in the high tech fields. This motivation could be harnessed into parts of many Australian operations.

Strong and stable government

Most of Southeast Asia has been characterised by strong and stable if rather autocratic government (e.g. Malaysia, Brunei, Singapore, Taiwan, Korea).

This still remains, but it is now moving into the hands of leaders who espouse more responsible financial policies. Thus, hard medicine can be dished up to end the crisis more quickly without too much unpopular unrest. Apart from Indonesia, where the political situation is unstable, it is unlikely that political instability will mar other major Southeast Asian countries, with their combination of democracy and strong central control.

Current account deficits for valid reasons

While Southeast Asian countries have current account deficits, these are due to the import of investment rather than consumer goods. These investment imports are a necessary evil in upgrading infrastructure, manufacturing capacity and providing for future economic growth.

Investment in education and research and development

There has been a deliberate policy to ensure the provision of an educated and trained workforce. Both Singapore and Malaysia are boosting their technological capabilities. Singapore has also allocated S$1 billion to promote innovative thinking and problem-solving in its schools. Many well-trained overseas students return to their Southeast Asian homes after graduation, and foreign universities are being allowed to establish offshore campuses within several Southeast Asian countries as these countries plan to increase the number of local graduates—up to fourfold in some cases. Given the increasing importance of computers, the Internet and other communication technologies, the use of English is also being promoted in many Southeast Asian countries. There is a well-educated professional level, and increasingly a well-educated workforce developing in most Southeast Asian countries. A clear and deliberate shift to high technology was already established in the region, and the number of Asian students studying engineering and applied sciences exceed those in the USA.

An outward orientation to the market

Southeast Asians have always been traders, growing, making and selling to the outside world. This outward orientation still exists and xenophobic nationalism is unlikely to develop. But trade requires two parties. Are you or your international competitors going to be the other half?

Many vacant office premises (see Table A) can now be rented quite cheaply. One consequence of the crisis has been to lower office rental prices, as firms have collapsed and excess office space has remained empty. It is currently possible to obtain a good foothold in acceptable business districts at a minimum cost.

Co-operation

Initiatives like the ASEAN Free Trade Area and APEC are enabling economies to work together for the common good. These are supplemented by smaller groupings such as SIJORI (the Singapore, Malaysia and Indonesia triangle), the Mekong Basin co-operative effort and BIMP-EAGA (Brunei, Indonesia, Malaysia and Philippines economic grouping).

In summary, the current crisis will allow the economies of the area to consolidate, and reassess their competitive and strategic positions. The application of painful policies will bring back stable currencies, investor confidence and in two years' time, the current events will be but a memory of a necessary correction that will have led to a far more robust system of regulation and supervision and laid the foundation for continued but more secure growth. Only Indonesia is likely to lag behind as its solves its overarching associated political issues. Australian businesses must consider their policies in relation to the new context in Asia and respond positively and sensitively after full and thorough evaluation.

Given the fact that business persons from all over the world will be trying to gain a competitive advantage from their early involvement in the rebuilding of Asia, your ability to compete will also depend on your understanding of the cultural factors far more than it did before when there was a 'free for all'. You must present yourself as the acceptable face of business, acceptable in your personal relationships and in your demeanour and sensitivity to local norms.

A study of this text will therefore prime you for taking part in the resurgence of the Southeast Asian economic growth for their benefit and for yours.

Cultural understanding and international business

'I came, I saw, I blundered...'

International business is like Topsy—it just keeps on growing

Next to the innovation of the information super highway, the most important and dramatic modern change has been the development of global business through international and supra-national organisations. The economies of most countries are bound up with business conducted beyond their territorial confines. Large organisations cross borders in search of resources, labour and markets. Free trade areas are being promoted, tying large groupings of countries up into single economic units. However, when organisations and individuals start to operate in countries with a different culture from their own many problems surface. There may be global economies, but there are no global cultures.

Today the Asian economies comprise a significant global force. By the end of the century Asia alone, with enormous potential markets, is expected to account for half of the annual growth in world trade. For global companies this means that if they want to participate in the expansion of trade, they must do business with Asian countries. The Asian countries covered in this book account for well over two billion people and many of their national economies have experienced extra-ordinary rates of growth.

Business blunders: Errors we don't want you to make

In order to conduct business with people from other cultures, the greatest challenge is learning not to apply your own value system. There is no right and wrong when dealing with other people, simply differences. All cultures and countries have their own social, religious and political values and ideologies; their organisations possess different structures; their managers and employees manifest different attitudes, expectations, motivational characteristics and behaviours. Some of these differences are overt, patently direct and observable; other aspects are far more covert and difficult to detect until stumbled over. Appropriate interpersonal behaviour can cement a relationship; but if inappropriate, it can function as a fire wall.

Western business styles are often too pressurising, confrontational and demanding for many Asians. Conversely, Westerners perceive Asians as secretive, holding back information, suspicious about the purpose of foreigner interest, or selectively controlling the flow of information to maintain control of negotiations. Westerners have therefore reported difficulty penetrating the Asian market and business world. However, these difficulties disappear if the smart Western business person attempts to understand the Asian way of doing business and adapts their own approach.

The success of business overseas, whether marketing, negotiating, advertising, setting up joint ventures or an overseas project funded by government, depends on how well the staff can deploy their job-related skills and personal sensitivity and responsiveness to the different cultural environment in a new location. Failures in overseas business ventures most frequently result from an inability to understand and adapt to foreign ways of thinking and acting, rather than from technical or professional incompetence. At home, businesses equip themselves with a plethora of information about employees, customers, suppliers and business partners; they commission costly market research and develop skills in negotiating with unions. Yet in the international arena most businesses and staff attempt to operate and deal with overseas partners, customers and employees with inadequate information. Conducting a cultural analysis must also become part of that accepted practice. There are numerous instances where deals, which would have been successfully completed if finalising them had been based solely on business factors, were lost due to cultural blunders. A slogan, advertisement, motivational tool, argument or negotiating ploy that may go down well at home is unlikely to be equally effective in other parts of the world, and in fact may be counterproductive.

There are three major questions any overseas business person or potential overseas business person hoping for success overseas must ask themselves—and answer:

1   What do I know about the social and business customs in country X?
2   What personal skills do I need to be effective in country X?
3   What prejudices and stereotypes do I have about people and their culture in country X?

Some very embarrassing examples litter the international path of failure and provide valuable lessons. For example:

- President Clinton made a terrible gaffe when he addressed President Kim's wife as Mrs Kim in a public speech during a visit to Korea. Korean women do not take their husband's name on marriage, but retain their own.
- An advertising campaign in green colouring did not work in Malaysia where green is associated with disease and death.
- A Chinese translation of 'come alive with Pepsi' appeared as 'Pepsi brings your ancestors back from the grave'.
- An overseas airline operating out of a South American country once advertised that it had plush 'rendez-vous' lounges in its business and first class pre-flight areas, little realising that 'rendez-vous' lounge implied a brothel there.
- One top oil executive working out of Bahrain, where liquor was permitted to expatriates, went to nearby Qatar to sign a contract that had taken many months to finalise. He took two miniature brandies into his case for celebration with his junior colleagues who had handled the negotiation. He was deported immediately on arrival as Qatar is a strict Moslem country for trying to smuggle alcohol; the company was deemed unsuitable and barred from ever returning; and of course the contract was never signed.
- ESSO had difficulties with market share in Japan until it realised its name phonetically meant 'stalled car'.
- One major hotel compared itself to the Taj Mahal—'service and appointments fit for royalty'. The Taj Mahal is actually a mausoleum.
- One firm issued promotional photos with an executive on the phone with his feet propped up on the desk. This document was regarded as insensitive by potential Southeast Asian customers where the display of the sole of the foot is insulting.
- The toothpaste ad 'I wonder where the yellow went' was seen as a racial slur in Asian countries.
- 'Finger lickin' good' came out in Mandarin as 'eat your fingers off'.
- The Swedish Industrial Development Association (SIDA) used its acronym in a huge billboard advertisement in Vietnam to advertise itself. It did not know that SIDA is the acronym for AIDS in Vietnam.

All cultures have problems in adapting to foreign markets. Have you tried these products???

Libido – a Chinese soda	**Last climax** – Japanese tissues
My Fanny – Japanese toilet paper	**Ban Cock** – Indian cockroach repellent
Hornyphon – Austrian video recorder	**Shitto** – Ghanaian pepper sauce
Ass Glue – Chinese glue	

Should any reader wish to 'enjoy' a compendium of international business blunders, a collection by Ricks (1983) is well worth thumbing through. Not only is it amusing (although obviously disastrous for those involved), it may provide a few more little hints and insights into the nuances and subtleties that make the difference between success and embarrassing failure.

The fallacy of universal business practice

Managers and business students learn all about TQM, MBO, JIT delivery, flat structures and matrix management, but do they learn about the problems of applying such management solutions in other cultures? To what extent are these universal management solutions? Modern management books such as those by Drucker, or Tom Peters appear to promote the fallacy that there is one best way. However, the ten management commandments of Western business are not necessarily appropriate tenets of faith in the Islamic, Shinto, Confucian or Buddhist cultures.

Business, management and marketing are no longer parochial. Even though some staff may never leave their own country to conduct business, they may do so by global communications networks. Mergers, acquisitions, joint ventures, expatriate assignments, all lead to contact and relationships with colleagues from other cultures. Management styles, motivational techniques, even the nature of the organisation, may need to be completely rethought.

- The well-established (Western) dichotomy between task orientation and relationship orientation does not hold in Asian countries, where relationship formation is seen as an essential part of doing business.
- MBO and performance rewards fail in Asian cultures where the focus is on group solidarity/membership and where there are unspoken rules about the awarding of rewards and promotions, since individual rewards may imply loss of face and the shortcomings of those not receiving rewards.
- Job enrichment or rotation are not motivational tools when the cultural need for the avoidance of uncertainty is high, or where there is great power/status differences and group coherence is strong (e.g. Confucian cultures). An individual may feel they are being banished from their group to a job of lesser importance which they are uncertain how to do.
- The matrix organisation is disliked in Asia as it is perceived as creating disloyalty to the functional boss.
- Many Asian countries take offence at the 'quick buck' slick presentation sales pitch; they prefer to build up relationships carefully before entering into negotiation. There can be no quick visit, slapping the counterpart on the back with an insincere 'Good-day

mate—I've got a great product here you won't be able to resist. Oh, before we start, can you book me a taxi back to the airport , I'm off to Manila tonight'. Business in Asia requires time—lots of it.

- Can established business ethics (Western) be maintained when there is requirement to provide a 'gift' to a government official or potential customers?
- Is the notion of human resource management feasible in countries where beliefs in unlimited personal development/potential are not held?

These and many other issues face the international manager and expatriate staff member in promoting the activities of their enterprise. The high failure rate of expatriate assignments bears testimony to the inadequate preparation of organisations and individuals for such cross-cultural interactions, both in the business aspects and in simply just living abroad. The successful manager in one country may not be able to adjust behaviour patterns sufficiently to be successful in another.

Superficially there does appear to be a common global culture. As we travel the world there is always a McDonald's or KFC to grab a snack in, a Coke or Pepsi to drink, a Walkman to listen to and the Internet to communicate through. There are many products and services that are global, but what is important is not what they are and where they are physically, **but what they mean to the people in each culture.** The Internet is perceived as a freeing up of information by Western democracies; some Southeast Asian countries perceive it is a threat to stability and security, advocating a degree of censorship. Dining at McDonald's in the West is a fast cheap meal for people in a hurry; in India it would be perceived by some as anti-Hindu, and a show of status in Moscow and Beijing.

There also appears to be a superficial similarity in organisations across the world as judged by such criteria as span of command, levels of hierarchy etc. This means little more than technologies have their own imperatives, and the leading practices may have been carefully imitated. A four-level hierarchy in similar small companies in Australia and Singapore may mean a chain of command in the former with consultation between levels, but a 'family' in the other with strictly allocated functions at each level and unquestioning obedience to the 'head'.

What is culture?

'Culture' is often narrowly used to refer to the finer things in life, so that a cultured person prefers Handel to Rap, can distinguish between a 1992 and 1996 Cabernet Sauvignon, understands the skills of the potter rather than those of the wrestler etc. However, culture has a much broader meaning than personal refinements. The only requirement for being cultured is being human—all individuals live in and have a culture. In the jungles of Kalimantan the blow pipe, spear, the skull hung outside the wooden hut, are as much a cultural element as the oil painting, the Ford car, garden gnome and surfboard in Manley or Santa Monica. Culture refers to the shared ideals, values, formation and uses of categories, assumptions about life, and goal-directed activities that consciously or unconsciously are accepted as right and correct by a people who identify themselves as members of that particular society.

Hofstede (1984) defines culture as 'the collective programming of the mind that distinguishes the members of one category of people from another'. Its main features are:

- Culture is based on a system of values about how things ought to be;
- Culture is learned and not innate;
- Culture influences the behaviour of group members to act in predictable and uniform ways;
- Culture is particular to a group;
- Culture is both explicit and implicit.

In short, it is a shared system of meanings that is coherent, orderly and makes sense; the mental map that guides our relationship to our surroundings and other people. The shared meanings are learned through interaction with the environment. A person from a different culture will learn a different set of shared meanings. An oil refinery is always an oil refinery in a physical and technological sense. From a cultural perspective it can range from being an imperialist plot to exploit resources that really belong to the indigenous people, to being the basis of the economic take-off after the Second World War, a financial prop for a feudal potentate, or an economic weapon to be used against the West. We can be repulsed by spitting in the street, seen so frequently in China and Malaysia; however, they are equally repulsed by Westerners carrying around a germ-filled handkerchief in their pockets for several days. The bone through the nose or the ring through the ear are simply alternate forms of adornment.

Some cultural aspects are so explicit that we easily recognise them. We recognise that Chinese cultures use chopsticks, that Islamic persons in Malaysia will fast during Ramadan, that Thais use the *wai* (placing the palms of the hands together at eye level) as their form of greeting, and that Hindus do not eat meat. More difficult to discern, until stumbled over, is implicit culture—the assumptions, values and beliefs people use on a day-to-day basis without them even thinking that their behaviour is 'culturally' prescribed. It is not unnatural for people to assume that their own ways of thinking and behaving are un-questionably 'natural', logical' or 'human'. The 'programming'

Hofstede referred to in his definition of culture is the conditioning that goes on inexorably and unquestioningly from birth. We assume quite blandly that shaking the head from side to side indicates 'negation' and that this is so obvious it would be universal. Not so! This same gesture in parts of India communicates the very opposite, which the people there also regard as equally 'rational' and 'normal'. A man and woman in a close relationship will hold hands in public in Australia, but in India it would not be normal for even a married couple to do this, despite the fact that male couples will regularly do so, this having no relevance to sexual preference there as it might in Australia. In what circumstances should a Thai, realising that a *wai* is not appropriate as a greeting, either shake hands, slap someone on the back, or simply say 'Good-day mate'? Each culture constructs a theory of how life should be conducted based on their assumptions of reality to which they are strongly conditioned.

Culture enables a society to continue its existence. Societies all over the world 'teach' their cultural ways through a combination of informal conditioning and formal education. Culture is not synonymous with country, although there are attempts to make it so in such places as Afghanistan or Iraq where there are deliberate attempts to impose a uniform way of life. Most countries usually contain a dominant culture and several subcultures which are often limited segments such as the middle class (status culture), adolescents (generational culture), street kids (social culture), or even a minority ethnic or religious group within a large country (for example, Islamic peoples in the Southwest of the mainly Christian Philippines). Countries that have been the recipients of emigrants and refugees, like the USA and Australia, may have within their borders a fair representation of many of the world's national and religious cultures, although each is small in number. Other countries like Malaysia and the Philippines possess only a few, but quite strong, minority cultures. Therefore, for example, it is difficult to argue that Malaysia is a Malaysian culture — the dominant culture would certainly be Malay Islamic, but there is a large Chinese and Indian Hindu culture too. Cultural variations are so subtle that it is fallacious to assume that even what is defined as a culture is in fact homogeneous. Arabs are not all Muslim and Muslims belong to many different antagonistic sects. European integration is seriously hampered by strong cultural differences. Is it even possible to talk of an Australian or American culture, given the variety of cultures within each?

The fact that cultures differ leads unfortunately not only to attempting to understand things from the other's point of view (empathy), but also to stereotyping. Stereotyping is based on generalisation about what people in a specific group are like. We all hold some stereotypic views; these are usually less than complimentary, e.g.

- English people are all class conscious pompous prats;
- Italian men are amorous;
- People who wear earrings in places other than their ears are drop-outs;
- People of the Islamic faith are narrow-minded intolerant reactionaries;
- Immigrant Vietnamese are all involved in the drug trade;
- Australian men think of nothing else but a beer and a barbie.

Stereotypes are generalisations based on a single or a few specific examples that fit the case, ignoring the massive majority of people who don't fit the stereotype. Stereotypes create a simplified map of our social world where identity is described in terms of group memberships. Unfortunately, it is normal to stereotype when faced with a new reality, as it provides a clue as to how we should behave and how the other person will behave. This of course can lead to some gross misjudgments of the other person and erroneous forms of interaction and behaviour. Stereotyping is also a way of upholding our own group and attributing positive characteristics to it. Even after considerable experience with a particular group it is difficult to break the old stereotypic mould and perceive individuals in a more flexible way. You will still tend to disregard evidence that contradicts the fixed image or else distort it to fit. For example, when 'everyone knows' people in culture A are 'inherently unintelligent', a high achiever is explained as an exception, 'he had the benefit of living in the UK for six years', or given the benefit of being distinguished separately—'you are not like the rest'. A responsible cross-cultural manager would certainly use generalisation, but in a more creative way. Behaviour that was unusual or unexpected would be set within a hypothesis to explain the behaviour. The hypothesis would be tested and refined in the light of experience. In this way a flexible and updated conceptual map of the other's culture is formed.

There is a common misconception that all Asian countries share the same Asian values, attitudes, and mind-set. This is even promoted on occasions by some Asian politicians who emphasise pan-Asian values when arguing against the incursion of Western influences into their countries. Lee Kuan Yew, the father of Singapore, and Dr Mahathir of Malaysia, have both railed vociferously against Western values and developed strong economic states based on an Asian neo-Confucian soft authoritarian orientation in which order, respect, and harmony permeate behaviour. The East—West tension is also focussed on whether 'democracy' promotes social stability or destroys it; whether free speech is worth the cultural trash it produces; whether the health of the ingroup matters more than the unfettered freedom of the individual. As a result, effective participatory democracy is absent or subdued in Asia. It could be argued that the emphasis on Asian values such as collectivity (family and ingroup), authority/hierarchical status, and respect/patriarchy have been a major cause of economic collapse in Asia, as such values have led to such financial distortions as croney capitalism, favoured treatment in bank loans, and family nepotism. However, in detail, the cultures of China, Thailand, Japan and the Philippines differ in a substantial variety of respects, just as the more open Western cultures of Britain, France, Greece and Spain do.

The dimensions of cultural differences

Using the work of Hofstede (1983; 1990; 1991), Hall (1987), Ting-Toomey (1992) and Trompenaars (1993), it is possible to identify some of the major dimensions along which cultures differ that have particular and significant impact on business activities. The three major dimensions are:

- the bases of relationships with others;
- attitudes to time; and
- the relationship to nature.

1   The bases of relationships with others—or how people deal with each other

There are a variety of significant orientations for relationship bases that differentiate cultures:

a) High power distance versus low power distance

Power distance is the extent to which less powerful members of government and work organisations, and of institutions like families, accept and expect that power is distributed unequally. This dimension indicates how far the culture tolerates and fosters pecking orders.

Most Southeast Asian countries are high power distance cultures (see Figure 1.1), reflected in rigid hierarchy, ascribed status, strong formal structure of social relations, and great social distance between those who wield power and those who are affected by that power. Children are educated to be obedient; teacher-centred education instils order, and learning is the transmission of standardised acceptably sanitised knowledge.

When extended to the workplace it implies that workers expect to be told what to do, that the owner/senior manager is a benevolent autocrat and that the organisation is hierarchically structured. Coercive status and referent power is stressed over reward, expert and charismatic power. Lower level managers and supervisors avoid decision-making, are reluctant to take on responsibility, and prefer to follow instructions of superiors closely. Security is assured in exchange for compliance.

MBO (management by objectives) does not function well in high power distance cultures where issues are settled by reference to established rules rather than personal negotiation. The status value of a product (such as a gigantic screen size on the household TV and a top of the range Mercedes used for the 10 km crawl in the traffic jam everyday), rather than utility, is the selling point in high power distance cultures. Names, titles and other honorifics are strongly emphasised and are used in all contexts. For example, Vice Chairman Guo or Yang Berhormat Haji Ali are always addressed as such. In the West, a title is a specific label for a specific situation, so that Company Chairman Richard Smith is Mr Chairman at a formal meeting, Mr Smith to his secretary, Richard at a business function and Dick as the host at a New Year's Eve dinner for some golf club friends.

In high power distance cultures the seller is subservient to the buyer, therefore the hard sell is out and considerable respect is shown to the prospective buyer. There is less inclination to trust unknown foreigners because they are seen as a potential threat to those in power. Business can therefore only be developed after trust has been established.

Low power distance cultures like Australia, New Zealand and the USA, play down status distinctions and power differences and have less formal forms of communication. Children are encouraged to learn how to make decisions, education is more student-centred, involving understanding and a willingness to tolerate other points of view rather than there being one truth. Translated to the workplace, subordinates expect to be consulted, and the manager is a resourceful democrat. Inequality of roles is instrumental, purely for getting the work done, and acceptable when based on expertise, experience, and knowledge. Management is practical and systematic with subordinates not under close supervision. Rarely does a Thai, Korean or Japanese go to a meeting alone, whereas the lone Australian representative is perceived to lack status and power if there is no support group to take notes or carry the briefcase.

b) Individualism versus collectivism

This dimension contrasts whether people see themselves as individuals or part of a group, and which they regard as more important. Individualistic cultures emphasise the 'I' identity, while collectivistic cultures emphasise the 'we' identity, providing a fundamental difference between Western and Eastern cultures (see Figure 1.1). Collectivism has no political connotation as it refers in this context to group bonds and not to the state.

Individualism prevails in Western society, with a stress on individual achievement and rights, and personal responsibility for actions. Conflict and competition is expected as individuals test their individual rights.

Ties between individuals are loose and the individual is expected to look after themself and their immediate family. Extended family ties are not too important, although the family remains the primary group to which loyalty is given.

Within the Western culture a major contemporary approach in psychology and child development is to encourage the person to become an autonomous fully functioning individual (e.g. self-actualisation—Rogers 1959), while motivation theory (e.g. Maslow 1943; McClelland 1975; Adams' equity theory 1965; Deci 1985; Vroom's expectancy theory 1964) emphasises how individuals work at satisfying individual external and internal needs, culminating in personal achievement, self-esteem, autonomy and actualisation. Schooling encourages self-reliance, personal opinion forming and individual problem-solving. We encourage children to 'look it up for yourself' rather than relying on adult authority. Self-help books fill bookstores to enable the individual to improve in some way.

In the workplace this translates to tasks prevailing over relationships, others seen as resources and/or competitors, with the same standards and expectations applied to all. Management lacks emotional attachment to the organisation and employee involvement in the organisation is primarily instrumental and self-interested. The employer–employee relationship is calculative. Individualism is correlated strongly with low power distance and mobility between classes.

Collectivism and group loyalty is deep-rooted within many Asian societies where the primacy of the group, particularly the extended family and the work group, is fundamental to the working of society and the social context in which the individual gains identity. However the focal ingroup may differ between cultures, for example in Japan loyalty is towards the organisation, whereas in China it is to the family. This loyalty, co-operation and support is not altruistic; it does not extend to outgroup members to whom—depending on circumstance—animosity, distrust, exclusion and even unethical conduct can be displayed. From birth onwards people are integrated into strong cohesive ingroups which protect them in exchange for loyalty. People feel more comfortable working as a team member. Thus using individual motivation techniques or Western performance appraisal systems in Asian businesses often deteriorates performance, makes the rewarded person feel ashamed and leaves others in the group feeling uncomfortable. To claim an individual reward denies the importance of relationships, including feelings of affection, support and respect for peers with whom you have shared 'space' and life. There are strong obligations to the group, particularly in regard to shame, harmony and respect for opinions predetermined by the group. At work, relationship prevails over task. The employer–employee relationship is a moral one.

The growth and prosperity of collectivistic businesses are not seen as bonanzas for shareholders or gravy trains for managers, but valuable ends in themselves.

So while personal recognition, skill level development and achieving success are focal elements of gaining self-esteem in an individualistic culture, mutual interests, group rewards and advancing the interests of the group are the basis of work relations in collective societies in Asia. Collectivist decision-making can take a long time, as efforts focus around gaining consensus. The aim is not the quick deal, but the building up of a relationship. Voting, with its possibility of dissenters being revealed, is rarely allowed to occur in the workplace, as this could cause loss of face for those who lose. The final result takes longer to achieve but it is more stable than the 'one minute management' decision which others can conspire to defeat by implementation manipulation. Detailed consultation and pressure to achieve consensus ensures that consensus occurs.

Patronage is common in collectivist societies, as power distance is usually high. Patronage reflects the needs for vertical dependency and a tendency to distinguish insiders from outsiders. Patronage is a reward for loyalty to the more powerful person who controls resources, and demonstrates feelings of mutual dependency, obligation, loyalty and trust. The 'gift' made by the patron may be of little value to the recipient, remains unstated and is not necessarily immediately reciprocated. For example, the official who signs a letter to gain a job for one's relative does so at no cost to themselves and does not expect immediate recompense. The unspoken reciprocation may be required at a later date. A patronage relationship can last a lifetime and cannot be bought out of without feelings of betrayal by the other. Personal connections are vital in order to get things done.

In individualistic cultures, patronage is much weaker as public officials abuse their power more rarely, social and economic mobility is strong, and there is low power distance. People enter business relationships because it is in their individual interests to do so and are bound into it with abstract and legal ties. In a patronage society, expatriates developing a business will find the patronage network will never guarantee employees of good quality (a major customer or government official always has a relative who needs a job), and patrons must be found who can suitably grease with 'tea money' provided by the expatriate business, the government and trade officials, who can so easily block an essential permit, as in Thailand or the Philippines.

The combination of high power distance, collectivism and respect for authority leads to the criticism that many Asian countries are run in an authoritarian way, and their claim to be democratic is hollow, with the sacrificing of personal freedom for the greater good. Awareness of major Asian cultural dimensions provides understanding of why the Western form of democracy is modified or difficult to sustain when the culture respects status, power and age, and people are conditioned from birth to be a good group member and not rock the boat.

c) Uncertainty avoidance versus uncertainty tolerance

This dimension focuses on the extent to which a culture socialises members into tolerating uncertainty and ambiguity, and the extent to which members of the culture feel comfortable in unstructured, novel or different situations. Most Asian cultures have difficulty tolerating uncertainty and minimise the possibility by strict laws/rules, and at a religious/philosophical level by a belief in absolute truth and acceptance of divine or political authority since what is different is dangerous.

Considerable energy is put into 'beating the future' and minimising the effects of change, so education is structured with precise objectives and teachers providing accepted answers. At work there is emphasis on formal structure, standardisation and obedience, with initiative shackled. Job security (even lifetime employment), career patterning, and work benefits are emphasised. In developing a business connection in these countries, uncertainty reducing elements must be emphasised, such as an established brand name, money back guarantees, superior warranty. Such cultures, often conservative and traditional, are exemplified by Japan, Korea, Taiwan and Thailand. Interestingly, Hofstede's research showed Singapore to be the most tolerant country for uncertainty of those he studied, illustrating the point that all Asian cultures are not alike! Strong uncertainty avoidance cultures are not congruent with strategic management processes.

In Western uncertainty tolerant cultures, there is acceptability of different opinions, rules are as few as possible, there is a higher level of risk-taking and less emotional resistance to change, with different beliefs flowing side by side. Students are comfortable with unstructured learning contexts, teachers who admit they don't know, choice in assignments and the acceptability of alternative viewpoints and arguments. In the workplace there is a less formal and standardised environment. Strategic management techniques work well as deviant ideas are encouraged but there is a higher level of intra-organisational conflict, which is considered perfectly natural and acceptable unlike cultures with a low tolerance for uncertainty. Formal rules can be broken if contingencies should arise and compromise is the route to reconciliation.

d) Universalism vs particularism

Universalism is based on abstract rules of law that always apply. Right and wrong can be defined clearly and behaviours allocated to one or the other. In particularism, more attention is paid to the obligations of relationships and unique circumstances. For example, friendship demands special obligations and therefore must be placed before obligations to non-friends, even if this means bias. This dimension is often seen as a subset of individualism–collectivism in that collective societies in Southeast Asia often apply particularism, whereby the standards for a way a person is treated depend on the group to which the person belongs. Positive discrimination within the ingroup is matched by negative discrimination to outgroup members.

Particularism and collectivism together help explain why Western eyes detect social, religious and ethnic discrimination in some Asian countries. These cultures are simply responding to the cultural values and traditions which state that some people are 'us' while other people are not 'us'; the former are to be treated like 'family', the others are quite legitimately not to receive what is restricted to 'family'.

Individualistic societies in the Western world tend to apply universalism, in that the standards for the way in which a person is treated should be the same for all. This focus on rules leads to universalist cultures using litigation far more than particularistic countries. Australia has many more lawyers in Sydney than exist in the whole of Japan, where disputes would be settled between the parties based on extant trusting and supportive relationships. The legal contract of universalistic countries setting out conditions and penalty clauses have an implied message in Asian eyes of lack of trust in personal relationships between the negotiating parties. To them, the request for a contract implies that the foreigner believes the Asian would cheat if legally not restrained from doing so. Moreover, good customer relations may involve doing more than the contract states. In doing business with particularistic cultures, Western business persons should not interpret the 'get to know you' chit chat in early meetings as trivial. It is part of the evolution of a relationship and trust building, the bonds of which can be as tight, supportive and binding as any legal contract.

e) Face negotiation

Face protection is very critical when learning to negotiate business deals and relate to people from Asian cultures. Face is symbolic and is a claimed sense of self-respect in a relational situation. Face is a universal phenomenon because everyone would like to be respected; everyone needs a sense of self-respect. However, in the West it is valued at an individual level (self-esteem); the importance of face is far greater in Asian cultures where behaviour and relationships focus on maintaining, saving, or honouring face for the group.

Figure 1.1 depicts the location of various Western and Southeast Asian cultures on the three dimensions already discussed. Major groupings have been boxed to highlight the grouping.

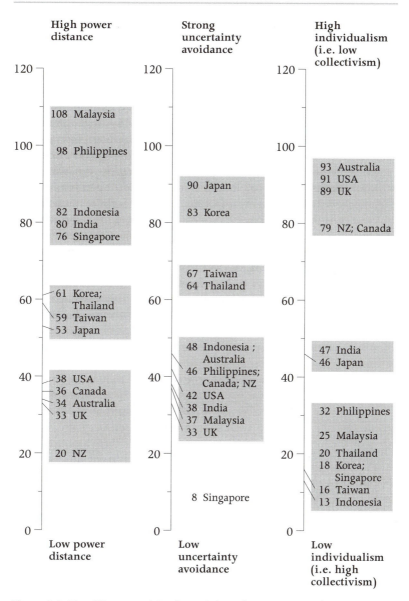

Figure 1.1 How Western and Southeast Asian cultures rate according to power distance, uncertainty avoidance and individualism.

Western self-esteem is essentially a self-indulgent desire, as it equates the concept of face with saving one's own face, i.e. pride, reputation, credibility and self-respect. It is a dichotomous concept: we either lose or gain it as part of our individualistic culture. Asians, on the other hand, understand the concept of face to be related to honour, claimed self-image, and the family/organisation. For them there is more awareness of relational dynamics in the concept of face saving. For Japanese and Koreans, loss of face means disrupting group harmony, bringing shame to their family, classmates, or company. Some political and business leaders in Korea have recently appeared in public with downcast eyes to apologise for misdeeds committed by relatives.

Western society has no real concept of face giving. To Asians face is a mutual concept, for giving face means allowing room for the other person to recover their face—room to manoeuvre, to negotiate, i.e. when I lose face, you also may be seen to lose face; or when you gain face, I can sometimes gain face. It is a mutual, interdependent group phenomenon. Face is always inseparable from the 'webs of relationship' in Asian cultures. In a sense everyone is interlocked in the group face.

Conflict is face-related, in that face appears to be a predictor of what conflict strategies are being used. Westerners tend to adopt self-face preservation and maintenance, focus on self-face issues, use control-focussed conflict strategies and confrontational strategies, and display stronger win–lose orientations. Humour is also a strategy used to recover from face loss in the West. Asian cultures, on the other hand, focus more on maintaining the image of a win–win process using face-smoothing strategies, mutual face preservation strategies, and conflict avoidance (compromise) strategies.

Most Asian people understand how much face they have; to have a greater face implies they are more powerful in organisations or know more people in the system. They learn how to deal with higher level people (greater face); and with subordinates (lesser face) who handle many of the job details and are influential. Lesser face does not mean that that person has no power, simply that there is a strong link between the concept of power and the concept of face.

Asians tend to use many intermediaries for the critical function of preserving face. Negative responses, 'cap in hand' requests, and some contentious elements of negotiations will be passed on indirectly by intermediaries to save a very senior person from losing face and simultaneously making you lose face by being refused or having to refuse. Westerners like to be more direct, get to the point, and avoid using intermediaries, but this increases the greater danger of someone losing face. That is why in Asia it is important to have someone recommend/refer you, rather than 'cold calling'. If they get rebuffed, then neither you nor the rebuffer have lost face directly.

e) Objectivity versus emotion
Cultures differ on the extent to which business relationships should be detached and objective, or part of our emotional lives. In the Anglo-Western cultures an instrumental approach to business relationships

dominates, as the focus is on achieving objectives. In Asian cultures business is a more human affair and functions best between persons who have built an emotional bond particularly based on trust, acceptance and respect. However, even in these Asian countries, where business is a human affair, the actual expression of emotion such as anger, complaint, or laughter is not appropriate for the business setting. To them, expression of emotion destroys the human relationship. The lack of emotional gesturing, strong facial expressions, and statements read out in monotone do not mean disinterest, only that they do not like to show their hand. Warm expressive, enthusiastic behaviours should be controlled as these may be interpreted as an inability to control feelings and are certainly inconsistent with high status and demand of respect.

f) Ascription versus achievement: Status and age versus merit

These terms explain different ways of gaining status. Ascribed status is attributed at birth by kinship, by the caste/social class your family belong to, by gender, by age, by who you know. In a society that ascribes status there is often little a person can do to improve their rank in society. In a society that focuses on achievement, the person is judged on what they have accomplished, usually in terms of their educational, financial or business success. The difference between ascription and achievement is that between being and doing. The Protestant ethic is one of the West's major values, placing a strong emphasis on work and achievement. Personal identity and self-esteem is related to occupation. In many Asian societies it is the older, wise, contemplative person who is held in high esteem.

Since statuses are allocated in ascriptive societies, anything that happens to the highest status person will cause waves down the scale. In one example a British general manager arriving in Thailand refused to take his predecessor's Mercedes. He requested a small runabout to cope with the Bangkok traffic. Repeated requests failed to produce the small car. Finally, his deputy tactfully informed him that if the small car was provided, all those beneath the general manager would have to cycle to work since car size declined through the organisational structure. If the general manager had the smallest car then . . .

It can be quite galling for managers from achieving Western cultures to deal with a team of ascriptive negotiators who have some 'eminence gris' looming in the background to whom all proposals have to be deferentially submitted. Alternatively, ascriptive negotiators find it upsetting when an achieving team of young aggressive go-getters of no known authority or status form the opposition. Can a 30-year-old Australian be as wise, know as much, or be held in as much respect as a 55-year-old Japanese?

In achievement cultures the individual has delegated authority to use personal judgment and pledge the company to decisions made. In ascriptive cultures the individual rarely has such power, hence agreements are tentative and subject to ratification by an older and wiser authority.

The West tends to emphasise and extol the virtues of youth, while devaluing the old, not only in terms of people, whom we retire early along with their experience, but also with things. Last year's model is passé, and a disposable mentality leads to a throwaway culture to make room for next year's new improved version. Youth are seen as the repository of characteristics such as energy, enthusiasm and the creativity needed to promote an achieving competitive society.

In most non-Western societies, age brings respect and honour. The opinions of older people are valued because of their experience. Asian cultures respect status, usually age and maleness, and that is why sending younger promising managers overseas on challenging assignments without realising that the local culture will not accept them, is dooming the person to failure. You will not be taken seriously as a clever but younger person. How can you deliver your company's agreement if you carry no status at home, is the implied message. Respect for the senior members of the hierarchy is seen as a measure of your company's commitment, so expatriates must use or devise the most senior title they can get away with for themselves. Most older people do not try to hide their age but use it to enhance their authority and status. If you are white haired and older you too can use this to your advantage in Asia.

g) Nonverbal communication

Seventy-five per cent of all communication is nonverbal. Body language and the packaging of information must be treated with sensitivity. People may not understand your words, but they will certainly interpret your body language according to their accepted norms. It is their perceptions that will count when you are trying to do business with them. Touching others, the space maintained between people, and privacy are major nonverbal forms of communication that exhibit considerable differences between cultures.

General forbidden body interactions throughout Asia include social kissing, although Western-exposed Asians may attempt to engage in this; and never use the left hand alone to greet someone or to pass food or other items as it is considered the hand used when at the toilet. Asians generally consider it rude to point at someone. It is usual to beckon by using the whole hand, palm facing down and fingers pointing away from you, but moving towards you in a scratching motion.

Handshakes are gentle in Asia. Women may barely touch an offered hand. Asians view the handshake as a courtesy made to Westerners, and are often unaware of the importance placed by Westerners on a firm grip. In all Asian countries, never place your feet upon a table or chair, regardless of how informal you think the setting is. To avoid cultural misunderstandings, refrain from all physical contact such as back-slapping. In Western countries eye contact is crucial to confirm interest. However, in many Asian countries eye contact between those who are essentially strangers is minimal, as it is disrespectful to maintain eye contact. Western cultures like more personal space and privacy than Asian cultures. In Asia, people will stand against you as you phone, queue and converse.

h) High versus low context

Low versus high context parallels individualism and collectivism to a large extent, and focuses on the communication process itself. Context level refers to how much you have to know before effective communication can occur, i.e. how much shared knowledge can be taken for granted. High context cultures like Japan and China are subtle and rich cultures with much implicit meaning in what is said, using a shared code, centring on group orientations and stressing nonverbal communication. For example, the statement, 'If you can see your way to kindly troubling yourself in this minor matter I would be in your debt for ever' really means 'you had better do this or else our future business relationship will never take off'. Early business discussions will be tactful yet circuitous, opaque and ambiguous. The situation and environment in which the behaviour is manifested gives clues as to what meaning is being communicated. So the Chinese and Japanese will talk round the point assuming that intelligent people will understand it from the context, as all ingroup members should.

Low context Western cultures centre on individualistic values, logic and a direct blunt explicit communication style requiring little inference from the receiver. The West values communication openness, self-disclosure, clarity, and straightforwardness; all of which contribute to a positive management climate. Western cultures also tend to value personal involvement less and have shorter less deep relationships in business with greater job and social mobility, while high context collectivistic group-oriented cultures in Asia utilise indirect communication because the image of group harmony is essential.

'Don't mix business with pleasure' and 'don't talk shop' all point to the desire in low context countries to separate specific parts of life. Arguably this can be valuable in Western individual achievement cultures as we don't have 'all our eggs in one basket'; compartmental-isation permits maintenance of self-esteem even if one aspect produces a lack of success. But doing business in high context countries is time consuming, as business is not seen as something apart from the rest of life. Everything is connected to everything. Business discussions will include art, literature, politics, music, food, holidays, family etc, as such interests and preferences reveal who you are, what you are like, and become the basis of business trust and friendship. Business only proceeds when the high context side has built up trust in you and feels comfortable to do business with you. Don't be impatient, let it all flow, giving the occasional nudge, and remember that many roads lead to Rome. In low context cultures you can get right to the point of the meeting at the outset, as a degree of interest by the other is directly obvious through their conversation soon after the start, so that negotiations can be broken off early without wasting too much of everyone's time. Personal involvement with the negotiating partner is not necessary or even desired; it is only each person's identity as a representative of a specific organisation that is central to the proceedings. In contrast, in the high context approach you don't get locked into a six-year deal with an unsavoury partner as you detect the problems early, through exploration of the person in the relationship building stage.

MBO does not function well in high context countries. In the West we wonder what could be fairer or more logical than agreeing with others on specific objectives to be met over a particular time period with some measurable criterion used to establish whether the objective has been met. High context cultures approach the issue from the opposite direction. It is the relationship between A and B that increases or reduces the output, not the other way round, since the objectives may be out of date by the time evaluation is performed, or even though B has not performed as originally agreed, other more valuable things may have come out of the relationship. The legal status of contracts in such circumstances are not as they are in Western countries. Even after signing, many Asian cultures believe that if circumstances alter, so should the contractual terms.

2 Attitudes to time

Since businesses across the world need to co-ordinate their activities, they require some sort of shared expectation about time. Cultures differ in whether they have a long-term or short-term time orientation, and whether they perceive time as sequential, i.e. a series of passing events, or synchronic, with past, present and future interrelated, shaping present action.

Many Western cultures are caught up in a sequential short time span, with their peoples living for today and immediacy. In most Western societies, what matters is present performance and short-term planning to see you through—the Henry Ford 'history is bunk' approach that things past are best forgotten and cannot be changed. Time is a straight line; you cannot go back, only forward through a series of successive events. To most Western business people time is money, so we schedule it, set deadlines, establish timetables, devise critical paths, produce products that have a life cycle etc. To be kept waiting is irresponsible or an insult and lateness demands an apology. We save, spend and waste time; it is not something to savour.

While Western business people always seem short of time because they are chasing it, in the East time has less importance and will come to you with its opportunities. The Western thinking in straight lines has a flaw to the Asians; it is blind to the effectiveness of shared activities and cross connections. The synchronic approach on the other hand allows people to track activities in parallel, using interchangeable stepping stones to reach a goal rather than a 'critical path' delineated in advance which unanticipated events can negate. If the environment changes, everything has to be replanned. Asian counterparts, well aware of the Western preoccupation with time, may make their bid for some concessions as soon as they know you have just made your confirmation of the flight home and ordered the taxi. Rather than upset your schedule you are more than likely to concede.

Our preoccupation with time is seen by Asian cultures as an affront to personal relationships; rushing through a meeting to get to the next appointment is undignified and dehumanises human relationships. As a result there is lack of promptness in many Asian cultures. Meeting times will be approximate. You will often be kept waiting even if you have an appointment. It is not that time is unimportant, but that other values are more so. Actions are prompted by social events such as kinship obligations, relationships and natural occurrences such as sunset and the new moon, rather than manmade schedules. In the West if it is noon, it is time for lunch; in the East eating is a social event, one eats because there is someone to share the meal with. If you have not time to greet the friend or relative who arrives unexpectedly they will be offended.

The Western sales pitch often seems impatient and aggressive, using customers as stepping stones to its advantage. If a business relationship is to last what is the hurry? Negotiations do not end with a final 'yes'. For synchronous cultures there is no end, the partnership continues. Given the deluge of information that must be assimilated, linked to past information and used for future activity, the synchronous approach relating past, present and future may be more effective. This difference in attitude to time showed up in a study of managerial goals of business (Chung et al. 1989). The US managers rated 'return on investment' and 'stock holder gains' as the two most important goals—short-term ones. Korea and Japan both rated 'market share' as their top goal—a long-term one, while 'stock holder gains' was rated last by both.

Cultures that think synchronously are 'we' oriented (collectivist). People prominent in the hierarchy must be given time (ascription). Cultures more concerned with sequential time tend to see relationships as instrumental; present activity is a means to realise the short-term future. Rather than 'making it', the time circle requires that your actions and plans are in harmony with the culture. These views make a difference in the way that planning, investment and strategy are considered.

Some Asian cultures even seek a return to, or retainment of, the golden age of their society, living in a nostalgic past which controls present events, values and behaviour. Islamic societies seem to try to do this with laws and customs that date back to the 600 AD period. In fact their current year of 1419 (1998), would in many eyes represent in *anno domini* years exactly the dating of their culture. They resist innovation. Synchronic cultures will be doubtful about change unless convinced their heritage is safe.

3   Attitudes to the environment/nature

Human development has been a process of improving skills to keep nature at bay. Cultures differ in their beliefs as to whether they can or even should try to control nature. Western cultures tend to aim for control for the convenience of people. So we dam the river, tunnel through the mountain, drain the swamp and in humans, give organ transplants, control the natural birth processes etc. Asian cultures tend to see people more as a part of nature who must go along with those forces and live in harmony with it. In many eastern sports the opponent's force is harnessed to your own, using each other's powers in a more effective way to gain the advantage or better balance (as in Judo). In Western sports, it is a clash, one on one.

In Japanese culture for example, there is an emphasis on the integration of people with the natural world; in Hindu and Islamic cultures a fatalistic philosophy implies that people are dominated by nature—'it is the will of God'. So the West's desire to transform the natural environment is not the desire of other cultures. Nature is to be respected and revered. Whichever God is worshipped in Asia, the common theme is that nature is the dwelling place of God, natural events and phenomena are God's creation and symbols of God's presence and therefore must not be interfered with.

But it is not just in major depredations on natural forests by loggers, or disturbances to the natural feeding chains upset by commercial hunting and farming, that we must conceive of our relationships with the environment, but in the smaller and more subtle ways. For example, the chairman of Sony conceived of the Walkman as a way of enabling individuals to enjoy their music without imposing on the environment, i.e. bothering other people. Most Westerners would conceive of the Walkman as a device for listening to music without being disturbed by other people. In Japan many people wear face masks in winter—the reason, so the wearer will not infect others by breathing on them. In the West face masks are worn to prevent the wearer being polluted by the environment or others.

Cultures also differ in the relative importance they place on environment or heredity in the determination of behaviour and action. If morality, intelligence and personality are innate (coming from within), then there is little others can do to alter a person. Many Asian cultures have this fatalistic approach. If however, environment is the moulder of the individual, then people can be changed with the appropriate training, education, experiences or conditioning. This is the dominant thinking in the West, and lies behind human resource development endeavours, life-long learning and self-development.

Overview

It is vital to realise that the dimensions discussed above provide only a rough guide to the general ways in which cultures vary. Individuals within cultures will display differing degrees of adherence to the values and behaviours of their culture, reflecting such things as their own experience in living overseas, and their personality. The dimensions reflect a model indicative of trends only and it is easy to point to exceptions and contradictions within any culture. Even in Australia, with its low context, low power distance and individualism, there are associations with restricted membership, hierarchical structures, formal behaviour and strict rules that influence power structures within society, such as the Masons, Rotary, political parties, the church, and even the trade union movement. It could be argued that government departments in most countries operate in very similar bureaucratic ways. Even the same term may not mean the same thing in different cultures. The USA rates high on individualism, reflecting a competitive concept; in Thailand individualism is seen in terms of needs of independence from authority. The loyalty in collectivist cultures can be towards very different groups depending on culture, with the Japanese focussing on the organisation, the Chinese on the family, the North Korean on the party and the Bruneian on Islam. Yet using these dimensions it becomes understandable why the Japanese travel in groups, insist on careful preparation of meeting protocols, slow down their decision-making and foster loyalty to customers, while Western managers can be expected to take responsibility on their own, be individually confident and trust in their own ability to improvise and problem-solve.

What is apparent from consideration of these various dimensions is that it is essential to realise that organisational and national cultures cannot be turned around to suit the needs, structures and planning of the overseas company or expatriate manager. It is the other way round. The dimensions elaborated above are useful as a starting point to guide you in identifying major cultural elements that could impact on your activities. The dimensions provide a framework and starting point to help understand how a culture operates which can be modified and refined in the light of particular experiences.

Table 1.1 A summary of Asian and Western values

Asian values	Western values
collectivism	individualism
harmonious relationships	self-actualisation
hierarchies and power distance	democratic
low tolerance of uncertainty/risk	tolerance of uncertainty/risk
respect for elders	respect for merit
respect for status	respect for achievement
face, sensitivity and feelings	objective facts and data
indirect; third party assistance	direct to the point; one to one
shame culture—external control	guilt culture—internal control
modesty and humility	winning, assertive, active and outspoken
guarded; limited disclosure	more disclosure
consensus seeking	consultative; debate
collaboration	competitiveness
personal and group face	personal pride and self-esteem
relationship focussed	task focussed
family spirit; unity	role and boundary definition
time is life	time is money
being	doing
humanistic and spiritual fulfilment	mechanistic and materialistic

Some general issues

i) Language

This is a secondary, but still important factor to gaining acceptance, but don't lose sleep over your language skills. It is certainly regarded as courteous and showing an interest in the host country if you can say a few general phrases such as greetings. But be careful; some Asian languages (Mandarin and Vietnamese for example) are tonal languages, so the same word spoken with a different tone means very different things. If you are involved in several countries it is better to stick to English if you are unsure, than offer a Japanese greeting in Korea. However, it would be a significant advantage to get a basic grasp of the language if you were going to be based in one country for a length of time.

ii) A few day-to-day problems (from my own experience)

1   As power cuts can occur quite frequently during electric storms in the early evening in the less well-developed Asian countries, carry a small battery torch.

2   You will need an adaptor in most countries for your personal appliances, particularly your laptop computer.

3   If you believe you can use your golf prowess to host a potential customer on the golf course, take your own golf shoes. Golf clubs can be rented, but Asian feet tend to be smaller than Western ones and most males would have difficulty finding a big enough size. The same shoe problem occurs in the popular ten pin bowling.

4   Use an international telephone company or call back system. The call will usually be much cheaper. Better still, use e-mail. Fax transmission and reception tends to be variable.

5   Carry some tissues or toilet roll sheets. There is a marked absence of toilet rolls in most Asian toilets.

6   Don't rent a self-drive hire car in major Asian cities. You will never find your way around and the traffic can be horrendous (including hordes of bicycles which have no lights at night). Use taxis, or have your counterpart pick you up, or hold the meetings at your hotel. Some Asian countries drive on the left and others on the right (or even straight down the middle!) so depending on your country of origin this could add further difficulties.

7   You will frequently have to slip off your shoes in Asian countries to enter homes, some restaurants or religious buildings. Make sure there are no embarrassing holes in your socks or pantyhose!

iii) Bribery

One issue that can face Australian organisations conducting business in Asia is that of bribery. While we acknowledge the unethical and criminal nature of bribery to gain business favours, it unfortunately can be a part of the corporate and public service culture in many Asian countries, and it is very difficult to obtain necessary consents, permissions and signatures on application forms or contracts etc., if the Australian company does not play the game by their rules. However, Australian businesses already, or planning, to undertake business in Asia should be aware that the Australian government at the time of writing is proposing to introduce a law which would make bribery of public officials overseas a criminal offence, carrying penalties of up to ten years jail and a fine of A$750 000. All members of the OECD are introducing similar laws. Unfortunately, this may place Australian business on an uneven playing field as they compete in tight Asian markets with competitors from non-OECD countries. While each company must make its own decisions on their policy towards bribery, constantly reiterated in this text is the advice that where such activity is implicitly indicated by the other party, negotiations on such 'commissions' should be at arm's length and dealt with by your local representative, joint venture partner, etc.

Activity

1   At this point it might be useful if you have had some overseas experience or contact with overseas business visitors to identify if any of the above dimensions were apparent in behaviour you experienced and whether any difficulties you encountered now become more understandable.

References

Adams, J.S. (1965), 'Inequity in social exchange', in *Advances in Experimental Social Psychology,* ed. L. Berkowitz, Academic Press, New York.

Caudron, S. (1991), 'Training ensures success overseas', *Personnel Journal,* December 27–30.

Chung, K. et al. (1989) *Korean Management Dynamics,* Praeger, New York.

Deci, E.L (1985), *Intrinsic Motivation,* Plenum, New York.

Hall, E.T. (1987), *Hidden Differences,* Doubleday, New York.

Hofstede, G. (1983), 'The cultural relativity of organisational practices and theories', *Journal of International Business Studies,* vol. 14, pp. 75–89.

Hofstede, G. (1984), *Culture's Consequences,* Sage, Beverly Hills.

Hofstede, G. (1991), *Cultures and Organisations,* McGraw Hill, London.

Hofstede, G. et al. (1990), 'Measuring organisational cultures: A qualitative and quantitative study across twenty cases', *Administrative Science Quarterly,* vol. 35, pp. 286–316.

Kupfer, A. (1988), 'How to be global manager', *Fortune,* 14 March, pp. 52–8.

Maslow, A.H. (1970), *Motivation and Personality,* Harper, New York.

McClelland, D.C. (1975), *The Achieving Society,* Van Nostrand, Princetown.

Ricks, D.A. (1983), *Big Business Blunders,* Dow Jones-Irwin, Homewood.

Ting-Toomey, S. (1992), Cross Cultural Face Negotiation. Paper presented to Pacific Region Forum on Business and Management Communication, Simon Fraser University, 15 April.

Trompenaars, F. (1993), *Riding the Waves of Culture*, Blackwell, London.

Vroom, V.H. (1964), *Work and Motivation*, Wiley, Chichester.

Two general books that give further insight into cultures and customs around the world are:

Axtell, Roger (ed.) (1990), *Do's and Taboos Around the World,* John Wiley and Sons, New York. ISBN 0471-52119-1. A humorous and insightful bestseller compiled by the Parker Pen Company on different customs around the world that contains information on Taiwan, China, and Hong Kong.

Axtell, Roger (ed.) (1991), *Gestures: The Do's and Taboos of Body Language Around the World,* John Wiley and Sons, New York. ISBN 0471-53672-5. A follow-up to the preceding book focussing on body languages of different cultures.

China

'It is harmony that is prized'

Confucian saying

THIS CHAPTER will focus on the Peoples' Republic of China (PRC) which now includes Hong Kong. Taiwan will be covered in Chapter 3. Never confuse mainland China (PRC) with Taiwan (The Republic of China or ROC). As far as the PRC is concerned the old Republic ceased to exist in 1949 when the communists came to power, and Taiwan has no national status or right to call itself a republic. The PRC considers ROC to be a renegade province that it will bring back into the fold of the Chinese nation sooner or later. Chinese culture can also be found in many Asian countries, and often has a major share in the economic activity of those countries. In Singapore they form about 80 per cent of the population, in Malaysia 30 per cent, in Thailand 7 per cent, in Indonesia 5 per cent and in Brunei about 10 per cent. When dealing with Chinese in these countries it would be wise to bear in mind the general flavour of what is conveyed in this chapter since the Chinese maintain their culture and ways of doing things to a considerable degree wherever they go.

General background

Economy

Since the late 1980s the centrally planned communist economy has been in a slow transition towards a more market-driven one, characterised by the development of special economic zones. This has produced a rapidly developing market sector and a weakening of central control. Over the last two decades industrial output has increased more than 600 per cent, due mainly to overseas manufacturers and investors who have set up operations in the PRC.

China however remains essentially an agricultural society with 80 per cent of the country's population still living subsistence economy lives in rural areas. Urban dwellers, employed in factories and workshops, have benefited most from the economic reforms. Per capita income, purchasing power and living standards in major cities have increased dramatically. According to one estimate (*Ming Pao Daily,* 17 February 1995), the average income in Guangdong is eighty times that of the poorest regions in the country. With the return of Hong Kong, the PRC has assimilated one of the world's ten richest countries, with a population of 6 million.

Only in the freer market environment of the special economic zones and Hong Kong is the work ethic strong, where highly competitive, entrepreneurial and commercial instincts exist. Until recently every Chinese was guaranteed a job for life. This is changing quickly, especially in the special economic zones. Labour quality is low with around 70 per cent having an educational level below secondary level. Two-thirds of Chinese managers have no qualification beyond middle school. Women are still discriminated against, although there are increasing numbers in positions of responsibility.

Due to the vastness of China, different Chinese have varying business styles. In particular, the Cantonese in the south tend to be more Westernised due to the influences of Hong Kong and constant contact with Western traders for the past four hundred years. Throughout the country, there is still very little accountability, as incentives to perform well are not common.

Society and culture

Ethnicity

China is the most populous country in the world with approximately 1.2 billion people. Over 90 per cent of the population are Han Chinese with the remainder scattered around fifty-five minority groups, 'the National Minorities'. Even among the Han Chinese there are wide differences in physical features, languages and dialects, social customs, and attitudes; so much so that it is very difficult to generalise about the Chinese.

Religion

Four main religions dominate Chinese life and values: Confucianism, Buddhism, Taoism, and ancestor worship. The beliefs and practices of these religions are interwoven, but it is Confucianism, more a system of ethics than a religion, emphasising obligation as a function of relationships, especially family relationships, that has had the major influence on Chinese life. Respect for elders, deference to authority, rank consciousness, modesty, ancestor worship, and harmony (avoidance of direct confrontation) are focal elements in Confucianism. In fact the collectivist, high power distance culture and hierarchical bureaucracies of the PRC are modelled on Confucianism (Confucius extols the 'superior man'), rather than communism. Rank and privilege are defined clearly, with decision-making a top-down process as expected in a collectivist and high power distance culture. Personal and family loyalty leads to nepotism and cronyism. Innovation and equality are unwelcome. Thus there is a cultural focus on team effort and enhancing ingroup harmony. A major Confucian saying is 'It is harmony that is prized'. Chinese society collectivism is exemplified by the work organisation or *danwei,* not only an economic, but a socio-political collectivity inheriting features of the older kinship group process as worker mobility to the new economic zones reduces the kinship ties. China is also a seniority-based society with older persons in both family and business revered and obeyed out of respect for their wisdom that comes with experience.

Confucianism proposes a practical view of life, promoting a value system to maintain social order and an emphasis on personal character. Those who behave in accordance with family ethics will not only manage their family well, but can be trusted to manage competently in other activities such as business and government. If you can't handle a marriage relationship how can you handle relationships in a *danwei?* Harmony as the primary value in Confucianism spills over into the business context and must be evident in the way each person operates in all daily life activities. Competency is a lesser priority than creating a harmonious working group and being a benevolent autocrat. Harmony in a company obtains employee loyalty and develops strong relationships. Employees are seen as children and their performance affects the employer's 'face'.

A pseudo-religious concept that affects Chinese behaviour is faith in *feng shui,* (wind and water). *Feng shui* (pronounced 'foong schwee') is a set of environmental and cultural doctrines encapsulating the idea that humans and nature must exist in harmony. A *feng shui* expert will be consulted before building anything new to ensure a propitious site or in laying out the furnishings in a building. So be prepared to bring a *feng shui* exponent in to bless, approve or advise on new ventures, constructions or redecoration/refurbishment of premises, or else employees will not work there. Bad spirits must be placated, while good spirits must be encouraged. While Hong Kong Chinese are less religious and more focussed on material wealth, they too still perform rituals to keep the spirits happy.

Attitudes to foreigners

Chinese collectivism spills over into the narrow perspectives of ethnocentrism and xenophobia. There remains a lurking suspicion of outsiders, or *gwailo* (foreign devils). The Chinese regard themselves as culturally superior—even the name 'China' means the centre of the universe. Non-Chinese are despised because they were not lucky enough to be born Chinese. The tendency to adopt Western ideas and technologies slowly is an attempt to maintain the Chinese cultural identity. Hong Kong, with its greater exposure to Western ideas, is far less xenophobic. Even in simple things the Chinese will rarely go out of their way to help someone they do not know. They will say *mei-you* (pronounced 'may yoa'), meaning 'Don't bother me', 'I don't want to deal with you (it),' 'It's too much trouble'. Around Beijing, business people can be quite brusque, and shopkeepers will throw your change across the counter in a manner quite unlike the politeness and deference generally shown by Chinese in other parts of Asia.

It is a paradox that collectivist cultures like China, which emphasises personal relationships and harmony, actually exhibit far more aggression and confrontational behaviours with culturally different persons than do individualistic cultures (Khoo 1994). Bias towards outgroup members is a corollary of tight ingroup feeling and high uncertainty avoidance. Therefore, how a culture behaves towards its own people cannot simply be generalised to how they will act with culturally different others. Even Chinese from Hong Kong, Singapore and Taiwan are resented, so it is better to hire local Chinese who are acceptable and have established relationship networks.

Most Chinese exhibit modesty and humility. They are unlikely to acknowledge a compliment with a 'thank you' and will reject or minimise the importance of their presence or what they have done. For example, you will be invited to a 'simple meal', even though it patently isn't.

Overall, China is a traditional homogenous society with little tolerance for deviance. There are proper and improper ways to behave towards people depending on their in or outgroup membership, with no grey areas in between.

Collectivism or group centredness

The Chinese are a collectivist, particularist, high context, high power distance culture and this is reflected in the fundamental difference in the role played by the individual in society between Western cultures and China. For the Chinese, your importance as an individual is no-where as great as your role in the larger group where you submit unquestioningly and willingly to authority. The work group and the delegation are two such cohesive groups in the business world. The group process is not just based on authority; it is also strongly focussed on consensus. Matters will be debated at great length, but once a decision is agreed, all are expected to embrace it. The Chinese negotiating team will have done just this prior to meeting you and the negotiations with you will aim for the same end. This social compact has its positive side, in that obedience and loyalty are repaid by support and protection, with the welfare of individuals being the responsibility of the group. Thus the work group extends its tentacles far beyond employment matters into the personal lives of members, over where you live and whether you can marry. Individualism is perceived as personal selfishness. Only in joint venture units will a more Western approach to hiring and firing be operated.

The importance of family and friends

For the collectivist Chinese, their family, including extended family and friends, is the prime group towards which allegiance is owed and paid. Confucian values continue to influence family member relationships. Senior family members are obeyed, for they acquire dignity and status as they age. The Chinese take care of each other and the part of the world in which they live. Everything else is irrelevant because it does not affect their family or themselves. Their own homes are kept very clean, but streets and public areas will be untidy with litter.

The importance of family and friends has increased lately. The country, party and work unit used to be seen as the organisations that would take care of a person for life. Economic changes have reduced their saliency and the only stable elements in the environment to count on are family and friends. Yet with more job mobility and the urban migration the extended family is under pressure too.

Many people expect their employers to provide housing, health care, take care of older parents and even schooling for children. These benefits offered by the employers are often as important as salary and career advancement opportunities for the Chinese. In order to attract, motivate and maintain high quality local Chinese, foreign employers have to offer competitive benefit packages that address concerns in these areas. Foreign organisations that show sensitivity towards the Chinese values of family and friends can gain from doing so, *'After we used the company car to take the employee's sick mother to hospital, which is not allowed by company policy, the overall employee morale was boosted'*, said one Western joint venture manager. *'The employees saw us as caring for their families, not just in it for the profit. They worked harder and became more motivated.'*

Nepotism in Chinese businesses occurs because as group members relatives are seen as more trustworthy than unknown people. There is little delegation of authority either as this is synonymous with giving away control and influence to someone from outside—a totally unthinkable event to the Chinese. As a result, in smaller family firms, the head of the family is the autocratic head of the company and each family member will have a senior position in the company; outsiders will never be more than workers. A foreigner in China who eventually becomes part of a Chinese person's circle of family and friends also takes on the traditional Chinese obligations of being a friend by being reliable and dependable at all times, not just a fairweather friend. Thus maintaining friendships, given the Chinese high expectations from friendship, can be burdensome with its needs to reciprocate support. Friendships are expected to be lifelong, each providing help to the other as required.

Communication guidelines

Nonverbal communication hints

The Chinese are not a 'touching' society, particularly with someone of the opposite sex in public, so avoid any prolonged body contact. However, it is acceptable for persons of the same sex to hold hands or touch each other without any sexual preference overtones should it happen to you. Never pat another person on the back. Hong Kong is more Westernised, but be circumspect over being physically demonstrative, particularly to those who are older or higher in rank, as they may hold to traditional views.

- To beckon someone, use your palm facing down, fingers pointing away from you with a waving motion toward you.
- Always yield to your Chinese counterpart when choosing seats, passing through doors, and entering cars.
- Personal space is a little greater than in Western society; during conversation the Chinese will stand further away than you are used to.
- Direct eye contact used by Westerners to show interest and attention may be taken as an intimidation tactic by the Chinese who will not look you in the eye as you are talking since to them it is rude. They are still attending to you. Not looking at a superior directly in the eye indicates subservience and obedience.
- A negative response may be indicated by waving the hand in front of the face in a fan-like motion. Other signs of disinterest, anger, or discomfort with what you are saying are the cessation of question asking, looking at watches, an inquiry by a lower level person as to how long your presentation will last, or an impatient smile/nod.
- The Chinese love to applaud, so don't be surprised if you are greeted at meetings by a round of applause. If this happens be respectful, stand and applaud back.

- Chinese people will generally not smile when introduced as they are socialised to keep feelings internal.
- The sucking of air in between the teeth often follows a request that a Chinese finds difficult to satisfy. It buys time for reflection. If it occurs, modify or retract the matter to avoid putting the Chinese person in a difficult position.
- Don't slump in a chair when conversing, hold an upright posture and when taking or giving something use both hands. These are all signs of respect for the other person.

Low context Westerners vs. high context Chinese

Some Chinese have complained about difficulties communicating with foreigners and that their recommendations and suggestions are often ignored. This reflects the different communication patterns used. While the Chinese often use high context patterns, Westerners are more inclined to use low context patterns. The Chinese know the underlying assumptions of the conversation but low context people do not possess this store of contextual information and require explicit discussion to transmit the needed information. Thus many Western negotiators feel that the Chinese are withholding information. A typical Chinese way of making a suggestion is through less formal conversations. What appears to be a suggestion from the Chinese side *'I think it is going to be better if we do it this way',* is actually meant as a definite statement ('that is the way it is going to be').

From the point of view of a low-context person the recommendation made by a high context person may not register as a recommendation. It might be barely a comment because it is not backed up by supporting evidence. Therefore, to communicate effectively with a high context person, the high context Chinese has to be encouraged to elaborate their idea further and provide the reasons behind the thinking. The Chinese may be annoyed by such questioning because it could be interpreted as distrust. *'It is frustrating when we see opportunities and make suggestions to our overseas friends and they decide to ignore them so that the opportunity is lost',* a Chinese manager in a Sino–US joint venture in Beijing said.

The Chinese are very comfortable with silence during a discussion. For them it signifies reflection and assessment. The use of silence can be quite subtle among the high context Chinese, for what is left unsaid can be as important as what is said directly. Silence at a well chosen moment can speak volumes. If a Chinese has the floor it is their silence; it is not your duty to break in. Occasionally the Chinese will laugh at mishaps. This is an uncertain reaction to an uncomfortable situation and does not imply amusement at another's expense.

Being modest versus being aggressive

One traditional Chinese value is to be humble: a good mannered and well-cultured person is not supposed to boast about his/her achievement and capabilities. If one is talented and capable, one will shine without boasting. Many Chinese find this traditional value incompatible with the modern competitive world where advertising, promotion and marketing play important roles. Even when one is confident about something, the Chinese will say 'I think I could do that', which in a Western context could mean 'I am not sure, but I think . . .' instead of the firm 'yes, I can'. The implication here is that in recruiting local Chinese employees, the latter are probably more capable and qualified than they are comfortable in expressing directly and openly.

Making contacts

You should obtain an introduction through some intermediary before you arrive. Only through connections and relationships can you ensure an attentive audience for your proposal and subsequent interactions. Your ability to get things done will depend largely on the amount of influence and connections your host organisation has, as well as your ability to cultivate personal friends. Using an intermediary with the right connections who can vouch for you is useful if you are not known to the organisation or individual you wish to meet. Someone introduced through a trusted friend is also deemed worthy of trust.

Don't worry too much about meeting the right person, as no individuals can make business decisions which lie within the authority of the collective leadership or unit. Any invitation to visit China will usually come from an organisation, not an individual, and likewise you will be seen as your organisation and not as an individual.

Provide as much background material as you can in the initial overture with more crucial parts translated into Chinese. Make sure there is sufficient interest on the other end before you translate everything. Give the Chinese time to study this advance material. Knowing up front what you want or have to offer enables them to gather all the collective wisdom and forge their own position prior to meeting you. The Chinese don't like being suddenly ambushed with proposals. If you do that they will politely listen and defer the matter. No Chinese manager/negotiator ever makes an off-the-cuff decision. Knowing why you are coming also helps the Chinese tee up the correct persons on their side.

In providing preliminary material don't reveal your 'best possible offer'. This will be viewed by the Chinese as the starting position and they will start bargaining from there. The company will then find itself in an impossible bargaining position. It is appropriate to make the first move, as the Chinese do not feel comfortable actively pursuing foreign companies to convince them to do business in China. Their view is that if a foreign company is interested in doing business with us, we would expect them to visit, show interest and actively promote themselves.

Either you, your counterpart, or local representatives should schedule meetings before your arrival. Give clear instructions about accommodation and transport to your business contact/intermediary or else your host organisation will make arrangements without consulting you, leaving you overwhelmed with both hospitality and costs. You will arrive to the ritual of an airport meeting to offer respectful greetings (and also on departure). A Chinese business contact/host will make an effort to fulfil anticipated needs and ensure comfort, care, and protection. Politely decline any service that you do not want, and if you wish to spend some time alone, indicate so, perhaps by indicating a time when your counterpart should meet you later.

As a collectivist culture the Chinese are more comfortable dealing with the visit of a well-organised group, rather than a single individual. Even a group of loosely affiliated industry representatives will be seen as a delegation, and delegations to the Chinese have a culture all of their own. The delegation is expected to act as a group, not as a collection of individuals expressing different opinions. It is expected to be structured with a leader who has status back home, who speaks for the group, and some sort of protocol ranking of members. If they do not know statuses and rank order, the Chinese have considerable difficulty deciding what rank the leader of their own hosting group should be, the order of presentation or dining seat position. If these matters are not clear the Chinese are likely to assume the leader is the top name on what is often an alphabetical list of the delegation, and send a person to lead their delegation of too high or low a rank which would cause considerable embarrassment to them and loss of face. A liaison person must be nominated as well to deal with controversial issues at a lower level. Another senior person should lead for you in the negotiations. In this way leader to leader discussions are always cordial and replete with compliments and accolades with neither leader exposed to potential disputes and loss of face likely in negotiations. Obviously with very small company groups or individuals, all members will be present at all negotiations since these are likely to be carried out with lower status officials. The real Chinese decision-makers will never be seen.

Relationships first—business later

Some Western business people have found the Chinese difficult to deal with at the outset. Only when the Chinese get to know and feel comfortable about you, will they gradually ease off their guard. To most

Western companies, relationships are secondary; in China, like the rest of Asia, relationships come first. Relationship building is the essence of the strategy, not a by-product from it. A personal relationship helps foreigners to get past the hard and distant surface of the Chinese to the easy-going person inside. One senior Canadian expatriate described the Chinese as coconuts—hard on the surface, but very soft inside. The Chinese see us like peaches: soft on the surface but very hard at the core. Chinese do find it hard to develop deeper personal relationships with foreigners after some lower level of personal relationship has been formed because foreigners become less approachable after that point. From a business point of view, there is no short-term oriented 'disposable relationship' mentality in China; an organisation that casts off its counterpart when a purpose has been served will not find it easy to do business in China again.

Greeting people

The Chinese may not smile on first meeting you as they tend to hide their feelings. A handshake is common at greeting and departure times. The Chinese are very traditional in all interactions. One common greeting is *Ni hao,* which means 'Hello.' Another is *Ni hao ma,* which means 'How do you do?'. You should try to use these greetings too. Remember that most Chinese speak Mandarin, but in Hong Kong and the south, Cantonese is more frequent, although since the takeover Mandarin is being encouraged in Hong Kong.

There are not many widely used family names and the most common surnames are *Chang (Chan* in Cantonese), *Wang, Li, Chao, and Liu.* The family name comes first, followed by the second name and often a third name. For example, *Lim Chee Ming* would be called *Mr Lim; Chee* would be his generational name and *Ming* would be his given name. Where there are only two names the second name is the given name. Thus the sequence is the reverse of the Western naming system. In China it is rare to use the given name even when you know the person very well. Some Chinese, particularly from Hong Kong, adopt Western names early in their life, which are then listed first with the surname last as in the West. Thus *Danny Chang* is a Westernised Chinese name with the surname in the second spot. If you are unsure about which is the family and which is the given name, ask, as the Chinese are happy to explain their family lineage to you. A given name is no indication of a person's gender.

Address your counterparts with the appropriate 'Mr', 'Mrs' or 'Miss', along with their family name. Official and occupation-related titles, such as 'Dr', 'Director', 'Ambassador', are used wherever appropriate but follow the family name, e.g. Zhao Jingli is Manager Zhao. Married women usually keep their own family name. So do not refer to Mr Tan's wife as Mrs Tan.

The presentation of the business card (*ming pian*) is the entree to all future relationships and should be presented when everyone first meets. Always give and receive them *with both hands*. When you receive someone else's card, spend a few seconds reading it, not only to try and remember the name but signalling respect for the other person. It is demeaning to pop the card straight into your pocket. Your business card should state your name, your functional responsibility, and your title, as well as your organisation's kind of business. Have the same information printed on the reverse side of the card in Mandarin and present this side upwards. Most hotels in China and Hong Kong can assist you in organising the printing of a bilingual card.

To conform to the Chinese respect for rank and seniority, senior members of an organisation should enter the room first and be introduced first, so don't wander into the room in any order as the Chinese will take the first person as leader even if it is the technical director's assistant. The overseas leader will be seated at the right hand side of the senior Chinese present. In formal meetings each delegation will sit facing each other with lowest ranking members furthest away from the principals. In less formal meetings such segregation will be less necessary. The Chinese focus on the senior representatives of foreign organisations. The organisation name is also important, as the Chinese believe that they are dealing primarily with the organisation rather than with you as its representative. It impresses the Chinese if you state you are the 'biggest' or the 'oldest'. Don't be surprised if the meeting room has spittoons and the Chinese use them!!

Try not to schedule meetings between noon and 2:30 or 3:00 pm. Many Chinese take a one-hour lunch sometimes followed by a *wushui*, an afternoon nap. Punctuality is viewed as a positive asset in others, even though the Chinese may be late. In fact, arriving early indicates respect for the host.

Tea and small talk will dominate the early part of the first meeting. Talk about bland issues like the weather and your journey, but avoid all sensitive political and human rights issues as these make you seem like a troublemaker. They also place your Chinese counterpart in an awkward position because criticism of the government is not permitted. This idle chatter is very important; it is the start of trying to establish a smooth business relationship and friendship in which trust and co-operation are the keys. The Chinese are trying to find out what sort of person you are by getting you to talk about yourself. Business comes later. Regardless of the circumstances, it is important to be patient. Your Chinese counterpart may eventually make a brief introduction, particularly if they work for a state-owned entity. The introduction will include the history and statistics of the local area as well as general information on the company. The ensuing discussion will be a structured dialogue between the principals; others participate by invitation. Any nods or affirmative grunts simply imply 'I understand' and *not* 'I agree'. It is considered rude to interrupt anyone who is speaking.

The Chinese tend to maintain a level of formality in the early stages of a relationship. This fosters respect for each side and ensures that contacts will proceed harmoniously. To become informal too quickly would upset the balance the Chinese require to develop a meaningful business and personal relationship. The Chinese often interpret Western informality—for example, the early use of first names and disclosure of too much information—as a means to bypass forging a close, durable relationship and simply do business without delay. Although this is not necessarily the Westerner's intent, misunderstandings damaging to business can occur. Gifts are not required or expected at initial meetings, although a small sample of your company's product or an item with a corporate logo might be appropriate.

Getting down to business

Corporate structure

One of the most frustrating aspects of doing business in China is determining who actually has authority for decision-making, particularly in the public sector. Your Chinese negotiating counterpart may have limited or no decision-making power, since approval of the project may rest with another authority. As authority becomes more decentralised in China, identifying the correct trade organisation and level of authority is crucial if you want to be efficient. Most traditional companies are state-run and have a hierarchy in which party officials parallel management people. All import–export companies are state-owned enterprises. There are also numerous companies owned and operated by the People's Liberation Army. Since the recent economic reforms, many commercial and industrial operations have been turned into semi-independent enterprises. In Hong Kong most businesses are family-owned and operated. The main decision-makers there are usually the senior male family members with whom strong relationships need to be built.

Guanxi—Business relationships and networking

The main business-related cross-cultural difference between the West and the Chinese lies in the importance of the business relationship—what it is based on, how it is built and how it functions in Chinese society. Having a good relationship (*guanxi*) network in China is the single most important factor for business success (Abramson & Ai, 1995), although this is not as important in Hong Kong. G*uanxi* is the intricate, pervasive network of personal relationships which every Chinese cultivates with energy and imagination. The *guanxi* is not just a relationship network but a relationship network *with obligations*. The Chinese business relationship is built on personal contacts and relationships which in turn are built on a mix of complex factors, including trust. Relationship and *guanxi* networks are the arteries of Chinese culture and affect the daily activities of everyone. People rely on *guanxi* networks with people of connection and influence to advance their goals, careers and to be protected. *Guanxi* also reduce or eliminate the negative impacts of the whimsical constantly changing government laws and regulations by providing contacts in bureaucracies who will do things for you, to bypass problems. Members of *guanxi* networks value reciprocity, trust, and implicit understanding between the two parties involved; nothing gets written down.

In extreme cases, these *guanxi* and connections put an individual above the law, as those with the connections will often try to profit from them. Some offspring of high ranking Chinese officials have been reportedly taking advantage of their family and *guanxi* connections to reap enormous economic gains (c.f. the Marcos family in the Philippines; the Suharto family in Indonesia).

But for foreigners, *guanxi* relationships often serve a practical purpose in smoothing out operations. Many foreign companies have either a full-time staff member or a division, often named *Guanxi* Administration (Public Relations Administration), the sole purpose of which is to ensure that the company is on good terms with the authorities, the banks and creditors, suppliers, customers and the tax authorities. This expedites decision-making and reduces the undesirable impact of government regulation.

Usually the company expects the *Guanxi* administration to do whatever it takes to facilitate business. *Guanxi* often becomes a quid pro quo—mutual backscratching—as it creates an interdependency between the two parties, because favours received must be reciprocated at some future time. The Chinese carry a ledger around in their heads—to whom they owe a debt and who owes them a debt. This includes business, so that sellers look after buyers' wishes and in return they receive loyalty from buyers. As indebtedness causes anxiety in the West, reciprocation is immediate with instant trade-offs. In China repayment is delayed and quick pay-backs are seen as an unwillingness to become involved with the other party, as balancing the debt ends the relationship.

Being flexible and willing to bend the rules

Coming from a society where social order and business practices are regulated by law, Westerners often find it difficult to adjust to the

Chinese business environment: the Chinese are willing to bend a rule in order to get things done. It is regarded as reasonable and acceptable to find ways to avoid the consequences of rules so that Chinese with *guanxi* connections can and do circumvent government regulations for their own benefits and for those to whom they owe an obligation. Whenever the Chinese help solve a foreigner's problem, they have likely bent a few rules and circumvented government regulations.

With increasing exposure to Western business practices and attempts to crack down on corruption and unethical conduct, businesses' reliance on *guanxi* may gradually reduce. It is almost certain, however, that *guanxi* relationships and networking will continue to play an important role in the forseeable future for individuals and organisations wanting to do business in China successfully.

Conducting negotiations

The crucial feature of any negotiation with the Chinese is to identify common interests and not just a mutually acceptable outcome. The Chinese are looking for a commitment to work together and the possibility of developing a relationship that will enable the inevitable unanticipated problems that arise later during the contract period to be solved. Only when you are regarded as a friend will there be an agreement, as one of the principal responsibilities of a friend is to help solve problems. Therefore negotiations are never over. There will be further discussions, and the relationship between friends constitutes the only way in which this can be done. Building effective relationships is therefore vital to the success of business negotiations and are often more important than the negotiated document. There is less concern with a neat package and no loose ends from the outset.

Your team leader should appear older, as grey hair obtains respect; implying experience and status. The person should not be one who's career advancement depends on successful negotiation in China, for not only can negotiations fail, but a younger go-getter who just has to succeed will be seen as too pushy or give away too much to gain any sort of respect or contract. Personality is very important—patience, unflappability and temper control are essential.

The Chinese do not always respond favourably to the direct approach. It is best to allow your counterparts to set the tone and level for frankness, and follow their lead. All negotiations and interactions should be conducted in low-key manner with little or no publicity. This will help to keep possible political pressures away from the negotiating table.

In the negotiation process, it might appear that the Chinese are deliberately attempting to slow down discussions to wear down your patience. In reality, Chinese decision-making is slower than the Western style because achieving consensus is very important and may require input from a range of national, provincial, and local sources as technical details or contract terms are passed from one agency to another for advice or approval. Don't reveal your frustration, for the Chinese will attempt to use your impatience to extract more concessions from you. In Hong Kong the Chinese are more business oriented, and more conscious of time. Decisions will be made more quickly.

Principles first, specifics later

The first stage of the negotiation will be an attempt to articulate general principles and mutual goals to establish common ground. The Chinese will be assessing your negotiating position, sincerity and trust-worthiness, to see if you and your organisation are likely to be reliable business partners, leaving concrete arrangements 'to later negotiations'. Therefore don't disregard this early discussion as unimportant. For the Chinese side, these declarations are an important step; they establish a framework for the negotiations and provide ammunition should the foreign negotiators go beyond the boundaries. In fact, this general tactic of focussing on general principles has several advantages. The very wording of such principles can often make it possible to extract movement from the other party later on. The Chinese will also quickly turn an agreement on principles into an agreement on goals and then insist that all discussion on concrete arrangements must foster those agreed-upon goals.

Only once this testing period is through will negotiations start in earnest. The Chinese start high and bargain; they expect to compromise. The negotiator will want to win concessions from the foreigners to win respect and face from colleagues. Any deal in China must result in prestige and privileges for someone to get approved. Individual or group gain is crucial in achieving closure of a deal. However, the Chinese will make concessions to you to give you some face. Accommodating to others is not perceived in China as self-sacrifice but a way of maintaining relationships, so that a favour offered today will be returned at some future time. Accommodation is then the second best option to satisfy one's own concerns in the long run. Chinese negotiators and business people therefore adopt long-term holistic approaches to business ventures.

The main negotiations may be divided into two phases depending on the particular nature of your venture: technical first, then commercial or business issues. The Chinese technical experts will focus on detailed technical matters until they are satisfied with basic issues of quality and usefulness. It is essential to include at least one strong technical expert in your negotiation team who can handle the detail confidently. Your team must establish beforehand how much technical information you are willing to disclose as the Chinese will push on technical details as far as you will permit. The commercial phase will usually proceed relatively quickly once they are satisfied with technical matters.

The Chinese negotiators may not have the authority to commit financial resources. Depending on the size of the deal, most transactions must be approved by senior officials—even small changes to existing agreements often cannot be made without their approval. This is one reason why relationships with both senior, and lower-level people are essential.

Negotiating team dynamics: Group identity vs. individual identity

Many negotiators discover that the Chinese have two distinctive 'faces' or dual roles. One is an individual face, and the other is a group face. When in a group the Chinese are inflexible, demanding and difficult to deal with. But when you are sitting down with an individual Chinese, they are more straight-forward, open and flexible. To understand this phenomenon, one has to look at the dynamics of Chinese groups.

Negotiations in China are generally conducted by teams rather than individuals. This runs counter to the core Western value of 'individualism' with its preference for individual decisions and independent, autonomous expression (discussed in Chapter 1).

In contrast, co-operation and collaboration in teams is a more natural form of behaviour in a collectivist culture. Chinese negotiating teams are almost often larger than Western teams. However, size is not the only difference. There is a paradoxical contrast in the character of typical Chinese and Western negotiating teams. In the preliminary stages it is the Chinese who stress personal interaction and friendship; when serious negotiating begins the Chinese side usually becomes highly bureaucratised, requiring co-ordination with layers of hierarchical committees and senior officials. Western negotiators at the early stages may use elaborate teams in making technical presentations, but when serious negotiating begins the instinct is to move towards a one-to-one relationship between the two high level status persons.

Most Chinese negotiation teams have a similar structure: a team leader (who could be a figurehead and/or non-active in the negotiation), and members from functional areas who usually have no decision power. Sometimes, the negotiation team is only permitted to collect information and get the best offer possible during the negotiation, with no decision-making authority. The Chinese may go through several rounds of this type of negotiation before they are willing to commit. The words used by their negotiators are carefully selected and the negotiators constantly check with the team leader to ensure unity among members and that

Table 2.1 Chinese negotiating team dynamics

Group leader	Group members
1. Usually high level official	1. From functional areas without decision-making powers
2. Serves as co-ordinator to direct /assign questions to team members	2. Members must use pre-agreed answers and cannot take personal initiative
3. Questions have to be directed at team leader	3. When unexpected questions are raised, members will discuss among themselves first then team leader will designate a speaker
4. More formal and less willing to share information with foreigners	4. Might be more willing to share information informally if get some information in return
5. Always tries to be friendly	5. May engage in manoeuvre and test the other side

'everybody is beating the same drum'. Table 2.1 summarises the aspects of the Chinese negotiation group dynamics.

During the process, the individual members are not encouraged to be creative, nor to take the lead. Spontaneity during interaction and negotiation is almost out of the question, and the course of the discussion is pre-determined. Westerners often get frustrated and wonder who they are negotiating with, who is the decision-maker behind the curtain. Questions have to be directed to the team leader first, who in turn will direct the question to specific team members. When a translator is talking, maintain eye contact with and smile at the person who made the statement.

When unexpected issues are raised, the Chinese often gather to discuss amongst themselves first, and if the issue calls for more discussions than is possible at the negotiating table, they may defer the answer to another session. They have to be very careful about what they say because they may have to explain to their superiors why they went beyond what they had internally agreed to beforehand. In fact, there is little or no reward for creativity during the process, but punishment for making mistakes or crossing pre-determined 'lines'. As a result, the individuals in the group are more likely to say what was previously agreed rather than responding flexibly to a changing situation. Remember the final decisions will be made by Chinese who are absent from the negotiations. Helping your Chinese counterparts devise language that are acceptable to the *'eminence gris'* behind the scenes will be a key to success.

Once a Chinese individual is out of the team environment and away from the watchful eyes of fellow members, they become quite different, often more willing to respond to questions and more inclined to speak their mind. This is the reason why it is valuable to get to know and socialise with individual Chinese negotiators beyond the formal business relationship. Foreign companies have been stuck in negotiations for months without making any progress because the Chinese will not speak their minds during the negotiation. But later at a function in a one-to-one chat over a drink, certain hints were dropped by a Chinese negotiator about the problems with the negotiation. Always make time allowance for some socialising with the Chinese—it will be to your advantage.

Bargaining ranges

Negotiation is the process of establishing agreement between a target point (objective) and a resistance point (bottom line or fall back position). Western negotiators tend to set these points close together, leaving little room for movement. As Chinese negotiators look for compromise they give themselves greater room for manoeuvre by setting initial higher demands, but being willing to compromise enables them to give you some face too. Western confrontational styles expect resolution closer to their own terms. But don't concede anything too quickly, even if it is unimportant, as it can be used to extract something you want. Don't reject a proposal out of hand; counter it with a more constructive approach.

Profit may be perceived as Western exploitation

Despite Chinese acknowledgement that they expect a foreign investor to make a profit, if the investor does make money it is a subject of scandal and rumour. The Chinese will cite previous foreign domination and their country's relative poverty to justify this view (the orphan strategy). Be cautious about including in initial MOU's a general statement about 'commitment to help China develop'. It will be thrown back in your face to extract concessions. During negotiations the Chinese will want to know the Western partner's actual cost of manufacturing or operation in order to reduce their share to the least possible amount. Upon achieving that goal they will feel that they've done a good job for their country morally and for their side of the enterprise. Unfortunately, this attitude jeopardises the success of joint venture investment.

Inexperience may lead to suspicion

The Chinese inexperience in international business and/or lack of knowledge of technology and business professionalism may lead to feelings of insecurity and vulnerability. They will try to compensate for those feelings of inadequacy by 'encircling and disarming' the Westerner in order to reduce a perceived unfair advantage. This is the 'CEO Syndrome' where the foreigner receives special treatment and is made to believe that they belong to the 'ingroup', receiving preferential treatment because they are a special friend of China. In the course of this 'treatment' the overseas business person is likely to agree to all sorts of schemes and concessions. Upon return to corporate headquarters it may be impossible to implement what the senior executive has promised.

Common ground and compromise

Many negotiation handbooks stress the need to focus more on what unites the parties than on what divides them. A study of Chinese negotiating behaviour reveals several ways in which this is done. Firstly, we have already referred to the Chinese habit of seeking agreement on general principles early in the negotiation, which can be seen as an attempt to establish a form of 'macro-level' common ground. Secondly, the natural Chinese preference for compromise as a conflict resolution mechanism points to a greater willingness to focus on areas of potential agreement.

However, you need to be aware of the precise meaning of compromise in relation to Chinese negotiation. In the West, compromise is generally seen as a process of horse-trading, trade-offs, give and take, and mutual concessions. It represents therefore, not a win-win solution (as in collaboration) but a half-win-half-win situation. However, the Chinese aim for ideals of mutual interests, of joint endeavours, and of commonality of purpose. They will set high opening positions and be willing to move to a compromise position (as with all negotiators), but when they reach the point of settlement they prefer to play down the fact of retreat by both sides and play up the idea that all along both sides have had mutual interests that have finally been recognised. Thus for Westerners, compromise is acknowledged as a necessary but suboptimal solution where concessions are articulated and justified by identifiable concessions from the other side. For the Chinese, compromise is acknowledged as the reconciliation of mutual interests through a commonality of purpose and thus an optimal solution.

Sequential vs holistic bargaining

There is a predetermined logic in Western negotiation—issues are settled one at a time. In China there is holistic approach, settling nothing till the end. Chinese people see things in wholes rather than in parts. This proclivity may be related back to traditional Chinese values of the spirit or principle of harmony in the realm of the intellect. Secondly, there is the relatively high intolerance for uncertainty in Asian countries noted by Hofstede (1990). Together these tendencies lead to a holistic approach to negotiation and bargaining.

Confrontation

There are a number of 'key' cultural values in Chinese society which re-inforce a less confrontational approach to conflict resolution. Confucian values lead to conformity being a central value in Chinese society. This conformity, together with its associated collectivist orientation, leads individuals to avoid confrontation for fear of disturbing relationships. Similarly, the Confucianist concept of 'Chung Yung' from the Doctrine of the Mean asks individuals to adapt themselves to their collectivity; to control their emotions; and to avoid conflict and competition. In such a culture the disturbance of these inter-personal relationships gives rise to powerful feelings of 'shame'. As a result of these cultural values the Chinese generally exhibit low levels of assertiveness and confrontation, engage in less extreme verbal posturing, less emotive language, and in general, lower levels of verbal interaction. In terms of negotiation this is represented by less open argument and debate.

Face and conflict resolution

The influence of face (*mianzi*) in social interactions is universal, but is particularly important to the Chinese. Having 'face' commands respect, trust and influence within the Chinese cultural environment. It is similar to the reputation and image one has in one's peer group or community. 'Having face' comes with one's position, ability, economic status and social ties with other influential people, and how much trust others put in that person. A group leader, for example, may have a lot of face, because they are respected and others rely on them for advice and help. The most important part of having face is that one has to be perceived as trustworthy. To preserve one's own face, one has to live up to the expectations of others and preserve the trustworthiness that others have bestowed on one.

Preserving the Chinese face

During negotiations, the following activities or gestures threaten a person's face and may provoke defensive reactions:

- Being openly challenged or disagreed with. If you ask a question that the counterpart is unable to answer, or challenge them on a point in public, they will be embarrassed and lose face in front of other colleagues. Discuss contentious issues in private or better still with a lower ranking Chinese who can act as intermediary.
- Being openly criticised. If the Chinese make a mistake, the expatriate is not supposed to point it out in front of others and should avoid

using the term 'mistake' altogether. Instead foreigners should subtly let the Chinese know that they are wrong by, for example, giving them some material to read about the right answer.

- Being openly denied. When communicating a 'no' to the Chinese, you should be less direct than is normal.

A little more sensitivity to the Chinese need for 'face' is often greatly appreciated by the Chinese, as one company learned. The Chinese, in this case, incorrectly calculated the number of products that needed to be imported and ordered too few. The mistake was discovered when the items arrived and the Chinese manager was quite embarrassed and concerned about losing face in front of peers. The company's export manager, aware of the cultural issues, admitted it was the company's fault and sent more, thereby saving the Chinese manager's face. This of course placed him under an obligation at some future time!

Preserving the visitor's face

To preserve face for foreigners, and to avoid embarrassment and losing face, the Chinese are often very subtle in their communication, to the extent that Westerners think the Chinese are not straightforward. The Chinese dislike saying 'no' directly to foreigners as it puts them into a position of causing you to lose face which in return loses them face. They have come up with high context implicit ways to say 'no' , such as:

- 'let us think about it';
- 'let us talk about that later';
- 'we need to discuss this with my supervisor';
- 'it is inconvenient just now';
- 'it is under consideration or being discussed'.

This gets the host out of a tight situation and if you are smart you don't press the point, for at the very least there is no way a 'yes' response will be given at this time. Remember all parties must maintain face. If you think the answer to an issue is really 'no,' verify your feeling by asking questions that can be answered positively. Some requests may be totally ignored in the hope you will read the handwriting on the wall. The Chinese will give a 'yes' response to almost everything. This often means 'I understand' and not 'I agree', so don't get your hopes up. Verify what has been said to you.

The adoption of face-giving or face-saving behaviour in conflict situations by overseas business people is valued and noted by the Chinese and will often evoke reciprocation at a later date. Harmony, face and relationship have to be preserved in interacting and dealing with each other, including doing business.

Recognising the need for compromise and concessions and the willingness to do so are often critical to resolving conflicts with the

Chinese. Without such willingness and determination, it is very unlikely that the two sides could work out any constructive resolution. The following observations summarise some helpful ways to deal with potential conflict situations in China.

- The Chinese prefer mediated discussions and negotiations rather than a direct confrontational approach to conflict resolution. Avoid formal legal mediation unless it is absolutely necessary because it may result in loss of face for the Chinese and damage the relationship permanently. Once the relationship is lost, or the Chinese feel humiliated, the situation becomes irreversible. Use a go-between, original introducer or your number two to mediate with the other side.
- The Chinese often work hard for a business opportunity, and will work equally hard to resolve a conflict instead of walking away from the opportunity.
- The Chinese may know they are wrong, but a foreigner must give them a way out to prevent loss of face. The Chinese do not like being cornered. If they lose face and come to regard the foreigner involved as an enemy they will hit right back as hard as possible and the conflict will become irreversible.
- Westerners should be willing to make concessions even when the Chinese are at fault. The Chinese are not blind and know when you give them face. The reward may be bigger than what you were hoping to get. Chinese do not do business with pushy and aggressive people. The right attitude is short-term pain and long-term gain.
- Do not finger point with the Chinese, though this is sometimes tempting and justified. It is better to admit there are problems or concerns and ask the Chinese to discuss them and find solutions
- Focus on common ground such as shared goals, visions and interests.
- Reinforce the commitment to each other even when it seems to be difficult, and make the Chinese know that they are on the same side. Signs of wavering confidence on the other side in difficult times threatens the willingness to commitment to solving the conflicts.
- Develop good relationships with the Chinese individuals beyond work. Showing a bit of compassion and the human side often helps Chinese individuals to loosen up, become friendlier and easier to deal with. Because the Chinese act differently as individuals than as a group member, personal relationships often become very critical to preventing and resolving conflicts.
- Encourage open discussion and communication as a way of problem-solving. The Chinese believe that they are reasonable people and open to reasoning and discussion, but usually do not budge when being forced or under pressure.
- Avoid losing your 'cool' no matter how much 'heat' there seems to be. Losing friendliness even in the toughest times can only cost the

foreign company: contracts do not get signed, relationships may be broken off. Suggest taking a break and send junior staff to ask the Chinese for input and feedback on solving the problem. This often helps the two sides from getting into the more destructive head-on confrontation with each other at managerial level.

- Never single out a Chinese for praise or encouragement; always focus on the group which is working for a particular goal. Conversely, avoid excessive use of self-centred conversation using 'I' as it looks like you are singling yourself out as superior or looking for special treatment.

Negotiation tactics to watch for

- The Chinese may change their negotiators and the terms of a deal even after a long period of discussion. In such situations, you should be slow to concede to these new demands in the hopes of expediency. Instead, detail the progress made so far and the status of the existing negotiation terms to your new counterparts and emphasise your commitment to finalising the negotiations regardless of the time required. They may even pull rank and send in a negotiator who demands that a more senior negotiator lead for your side. They are trying to humiliate you and implicitly indicate that your terms are not good enough and negotiation must start again with your CEO.
- The Chinese may wine and dine you excessively. Exotic and unusual specialities might be served to you. Only eat a little of whatever is served so that next day you are not negotiating under the effects of a tummy upset and/or headache.
- You may be asked on arrival the date and time of your departure flight. This information enables the Chinese to delay decision-making and possible concessions until you are about to leave, forcing you to accept a less favourable deal or go back empty handed. Simply say 'I will stay here as long as it takes to finish our business'. Chinese negotiators who sense that their counterpart is more concerned with deadlines than negotiations will manipulate that to their advantage.
- A Chinese negotiator will be a bit vague about their role, position and responsibilities. They will often seem manipulative, using conflicting feelings of friendship, withdrawal, guilt, obligation and dependence. 'If you cannot give us better terms you will be responsible for the failure of the discussions'; 'if you were really a friend you would help us on this point'. Don't feel shame or believe that your career is at stake if you return home empty handed. While being empathic and understanding about what is going on, develop an elephant's skin. They will also claim ignorance as a means of gaining technical information. Don't reveal more than you need to keep them baited.

- Frequently they let it be known that they are simultaneously negotiating with the competition—whether true or not.
- They will deliberately attend negotiations 'mob handed' leaving the overseas counterparts feeling outnumbered as well as outfoxed. Many of their delegation will not contribute but simply maintain a presence. You will never know who they are, why they are there or even which side they are watching.
- They will take detailed notes and throw back at you what you said. You must keep accurate notes too and nail the Chinese down politely with minimal face loss should the occasion warrant. This can often be done in private or via the liaison officer after asking for time out.
- The Chinese negotiator can play it both ways. They may claim not to have the authority to make decisions when they have. This enables them to claim that they must 'talk to their boss' so that later they can bring back a negative response.
- They will cite some nebulous 'law' which surfaces only when negotiations are getting difficult for them. They can dissuade you on a certain clause by claiming the law prohibits it. Who are you to know?
- They will seek out any weakness and use it to gain concessions, e.g. your price is higher than the competition, your technology is second best, you are unwilling to share your technology, you have a lack of office presence in China.

Be prepared for tough negotiations. Adhere to your principles and objectives. Maintain a quiet and dignified manner. If problems develop, you should be firm about your limits and your willingness to work with your counterparts to find a mutually agreeable solution. Fiery outbursts will not earn you any respect.

Contracts

Most Chinese believe that the primary purpose of a contract is to establish a positive relationship that focuses on shared interests. Accordingly, many contracts are drafted in terms of principles rather than specifics. They may appear to accept a mutually agreed contract, but will continue to renegotiate as external conditions change. The Chinese will interpret contracts strictly when it is to their advantage, particularly when they are purchasing products and the product specifications differ from those in the contract agreements. Problems for foreigners arise because the Chinese version of a contract governs in a dispute and because interpretations can differ due to the tonal quality of the language. Chinese officials have been known to disregard contracts signed by their predecessors. Attempts to document potential problems may be viewed as a lack of faith in the relationship. However, as a precaution, use your business sense and be as thorough as possible in drafting contracts, addressing all contingencies to the best of your ability without offending anyone. When disputes do occur the Chinese usually make attempts to resolve them amicably and outside of the legal system through negotiations.

A distillation of 'key injunctions' or rules for successful negotiation with the Chinese include:

- Always set explicit limits or ranges for the negotiation process.
- Always seek to establish general 'principles' early in the negotiation.
- Always focus on potential areas of agreement and seek to expand them.
- Avoid taking the negotiation issues in sequence.
- Avoid excessive hostility, confrontation and emotion.
- Always give the other party something to 'take home'.
- Always negotiate as a team.

The social context of business

Dining out—the banquet

Chinese will often hold informal business discussions over lunch or dinner. Entertaining, particularly the banquet, is an important element in conducting business in China. On arriving at the venue, you will be met and escorted to a sitting area where there will be polite conversation over tea (a delegation should arrive together). After tea, you will be taken to the dining table. The table furthest from the door is always the top table. Guests are not expected to bring gifts, however, if you are simply visiting China it is appropriate to present a gift to the host during the speeches. Gifts can be presented to all attendees, but they are not required. These lavish formal dinners signify the friendly nature of the relationship. Title and seniority control seating arrangements. The principal guest sits on the right hand side of the principal host. The host will begin by serving you. When you are host, serve your guests first too. Foreign spouses are welcome at banquets, but the Chinese will rarely bring their own.

Try to sample each dish out of politeness, even if you don't finish any of them. Push the food around on your plate so it looks as if you have sampled it. Try and master chopsticks before your visit as spoons and forks are unlikely to be provided. Never stick your chopsticks upright in your rice: this is only done at funerals and is synonymous with death. Knives are never placed on the dining table as it is impolite to brandish a weapon among friends. Leave a little food on your plate as this signals that your host has provided you with more than enough food. It is not polite to pour a drink for yourself; someone else should note your empty glass and take the initiative. Among the Cantonese, you rap your knuckles on the table to say thanks to someone who is filling your cup; when you stop the person knows to stop pouring.

Conversation should be cordial and face maintaining. The host is likely to make a short speech. You should return this to make a toast of general goodwill and friendship. Speak slowly, it might be being translated. Keep it simple, dignified and uncontroversial, full of well worn motherhood phrases about friendship between nations, hopes for a successful conclusion, pledges of co-operation and mutual benefit, and offers of reciprocal hospitality should the Chinese ever visit you. Banquets are meant to be warm, friendly, and filled with good humour. Other toasts may be made by individuals at your table. You can toast with a non-alcoholic beverage. Remember if you offer a toast it is to the People's Republic of China and not the Republic of China. Never refer to mainland China or Communist China as both imply there is more than one China.

If you host a dinner or banquet, arrive early because most Chinese guests will also arrive a few minutes early. The guests always leave before the hosts. The meal is near its end when fruit is served and hot towels are distributed. Sometimes the second-to-last course is plain boiled rice. There is no coffee or after-dinner cocktails. Banquets end abruptly with no lingering for after-dinner talk. It is polite to leave about ten to fifteen minutes after the hot towels are brought to the table and the last cups of tea have been served.

No formal thank you notes are required; appreciation is shown by returning the favour in kind. Your hotel can assist you in planning a banquet. Invitations to a banquet may be given verbally. However, the senior government official should receive a written as well as a verbal invitation. Be sure that the rank and status of the Chinese attendees is similar to those of your own party or they may feel awkward or make the other guests feel uncomfortable and constrained. Your seating plan must reflect the pecking order. Place the highest ranking guest on your right, and the second highest ranking guest on your left. If there are co-hosts, they should sit directly across from one another with the two highest ranking guests placed to the right of each co-host.

Heavy drinking of toasts is common at banquets, and can sometimes develop into a contest, so stick to soft drinks. Some of their liquors can be 106 per cent proof. All guests are expected to participate in the toasts by drinking some beverage. The proper toast when drinking *moa tais*, a traditional sorghum liquor served at special occasions and banquets, is *gan bei*, 'empty your glass'. It is a Chinese custom to provide food for the chauffeurs. After dinner karaoke is becoming very popular throughout China; your participation is expected and is more important than your skill, so just enjoy the experience!!

The home visit

Because they are embarrassed by their small homes, few Chinese will invite foreigners home unless they know them very well. For a home visit, suitable gifts include sweets, chocolates, or a small token from your home country. It is advisable to leave shortly after the meal, unless you know your hosts very well. If you have to decline an invitation, give a plausible reason or else it will be viewed as a rebuff, providing loss of face.

Giving gifts

Visiting business people are expected to give a gift to those who host them. However, providing a 'gift' or paying someone something 'to get permission' can be a cost of doing business, and little headway will be made without it. You may be asked to finance a 'working trip' via Port Douglas, the Gold Coast, Hawaii or 'Disney World', technically to visit the company, but more likely for leisure purposes. Your local partner or representative should manage such issues.

Gifts of reasonable value, exchanged to mark the conclusion of successful negotiations and the establishment of a relationship, are a normal part of business interactions and are not considered to be graft in China. Wrap your present in red paper, as red is a very auspicious colour in China and used on happy occasions such as weddings, and to welcome the New Year. Do not write in red ink as that implies severing a relationship. Give and receive gifts with both hands.

One large gift to the host organisation sidesteps the problem of providing personal gifts for everyone. However the practice of giving individual momentos is very common and acceptable, provided it is done in moderation with items of nominal value. The value of each gift should relate to the rank of the recipient. Place small personal gifts at the table settings, but present the large gift publicly at a suitable moment. Personal gifts include pens, books, cigarette lighters, leather writing cases, leather wallets, imported whisky, brandy, chocolates, and company logo gifts. For the large gift some object of art or handicraft from home (say Aboriginal) that can be displayed in the work unit area is sensible. For a very senior Chinese, a piece of Wedgwood, figurine or crystal is very acceptable. Hong Kong Chinese have far more discriminating taste than those in the PRC who may have no idea what Wedgwood is. Another option for a work unit that is in a specialised area would be a textbook, piece of equipment, or other similar materials that would advance their knowledge in that area.

If you are in China on a return visit, an expensive looking photo album of your counterparts' visit would be well received, particularly if inscribed by your organisation's top person. This is a signal that business with China receives attention at the highest level. For personal friends, liquor, cigarettes and T-shirts with English words on them (logos of English first division football teams or American baseball teams etc.) go down well. Chinese friends are always happy to receive personal care toiletries that are difficult to obtain in China, particularly perfume for the spouse. Custom dictates that your Chinese recipient declines the gift several times before accepting so insist several times until they take it. Similarly, you should do the same when offered a gift.

Never give money and avoid gifts of watches, clocks, handkerchiefs, white flowers, scissors, and knives—all these things have negative connotations or associations with death. Do not give gifts involving amounts of the number 4 as it has a negative connotation for the Chinese. Gifts are often given in groups of two; gifts in sets of two, six, and eight are appropriate, with 8 being the lucky number. Expensive gifts should not be accepted as it will create significant future obligations that you may not be able to fulfil.

At Chinese New Year, gifts of money (*ang pow*) in a new red envelope may be made to the children of Chinese friends. The Chinese do not open gifts in the presence of the giver. To them it is the thought that counts, not the gift, and a public opening overvalues the gift. In the PRC tipping is prohibited but it doesn't mean it does not go on, particularly if you want something extra doing in a rush. In Hong Kong tipping is expected.

Other useful information

What to wear

The dress code, while informal, is somewhat conservative in colour and style. Ties are not required, even in the best restaurants. Dress more formally for the first meeting. After the first meeting, it may be appropriate to dress less formally, particularly in warmer weather when an open neck shirt is sufficient. For women, nonflashy suits and dresses are acceptable with a minimum of jewellery. Follow the tone set by your counterparts. Many Chinese women wear trousers, but these are not advisable for first meetings. In Hong Kong, it is better to dress a little more formally for business meetings.

Holidays

Do not attempt to do business during the Chinese New Year/Spring Festival period. It would be akin to them trying to do business in the West over the Christmas/New Year break. As this holiday is based on the lunar calendar, the date changes annually. Currently it is in late January. Other days to avoid for business activity are:

	March 8	International Working Women's Day
	May 1	Labour Day
	May 4	Youth Day
	May/June	Hong Kong Dragon Boat Festival
	June 1	Children's Day
	July 1	Anniversary of the Founding of the Communist Party in China
	August 1	People's Liberation Army Day
	October 1-2	National Day

Language

Some Western executives believe that the ability to speak some Chinese (Mandarin, Cantonese or Fukanese) and some knowledge about Chinese history is necessary and helpful to dealing with Chinese. This is a very valid point because the Chinese often regard foreigners with such ability and knowledge as paying respect to the Chinese culture. Australian and US companies would seem well placed to take a Mandarin or Cantonese speaker with them, depending on the area of China visited, due to the large number of ethnic Chinese living in Australia and the USA. The extent to which companies will take advantage and tap into this resource is yet to be seen.

English is taught at school, but the level is fairly elementary; little reliance should be placed on your counterparts having much ability with the language unless they have been educated overseas.

In summary

- China is a collectivist, high power distance culture, more or less held together by relationships and *guanxi* connections.
- The Chinese prefer to do business with people they know. Therefore *guanxi* and rapport have to be established before doing business. Remember relationships first, business later.
- Westerners need to know when and how to give face to the Chinese and avoid making the Chinese feel that they have lost face (i.e. no honour and no respect from others). To preserve face for the Chinese negotiation must be resolved in a non-confrontational, more conciliatory way.
- Ranks and titles are important, clearly defined and respected among the Chinese.
- Patience, flexibility, respect and creativity are the keys to negotiating successfully in China.
- Extracting as many concessions from you as possible is a critical part of the Chinese negotiating strategy.

- Chinese tend to employ high context communication patterns. Western managers need to encourage the Chinese to engage in more open communication to avoid misunderstanding.
- Pressure is useless if the Chinese show discomfort. Leave room for them to report to a higher authority or consult together.
- Leave plenty of time at the end of your trip for unexpected delays.
- A bit of understanding of the Chinese language and culture is positively received by the Chinese.
- Chinese behave differently when in a group than as individuals. The group atmosphere usually makes the Chinese more cautious, less open and inflexible. Individually they behave almost the opposite way.

Activities

Try working out the solutions to these two problems, then check your responses with those in Appendix B.

1 Phil Kostas, a retired military attaché with considerable experience in Asia, was hired by a large computer software company to represent it in a number of Asian countries. Having received an introduction from a mutual acquaintance, Phil arranged to meet with Mr Chang Yew En, a rising and wealthy Chinese industrialist in Guangzhou, to discuss the prospects of a joint venture between their companies. Having spent many years in Asia, Phil was well aware that they would have to engage in considerable small talk before they would be able to get down to business. They talked about the weather, Phil's flight, and their golf games. Then Mr. Chang inquired about the health of Phil's parents. Without missing a beat Phil responded that his mother was dead, but that his elderly father was doing fine, although the last time he saw his father at the nursing home several months ago, he had lost a little weight. From that point on Mr. Chang's demeanour changed abruptly from warm and gracious to cool and aloof. Though the rest of the meeting was polite enough, the meeting only lasted another hour and Phil was never invited back for further discussions on the joint venture.

What went wrong?

a

2   Marina Dawe was a well-known architect and had designed many award winning buildings in a number of Western countries. She was excited when a large Hong Kong business organisation asked her to design their new corporate head-quarters. Several months later she travelled to Hong Kong and proudly displayed drawings and models that met the site, office space and amenities requirements, using computerised displays on a screen to make the static models and architects' plans come alive. She had even made the proposed building environmentally 'green' using new technical knowledge about insulation and temperature/humidity control.

She sat back and waited for positive responses. The elderly chairman looked pained and said that the main entrance, the orientation of the building and the internal layout of the offices would have to be drastically altered. If it stayed as it was, the company would have a very unsuccessful future and he would not be willing to use the capacious office allocated to him. He added that few of the employees would be happy working there either. The rest of the board nodded their agreement and Marina was requested to redesign the office block after taking advice. The effect of the changes were so monumental that the design would have to be commenced from scratch.

What was the problem? From whom should she take advice? What had Marina forgotten?

References and further reading

Abramson, N. & Ai, J. (1995), 'Slow boat to China', *Business Quarterly,* Winter.

Hofstede, G. (1991), *Cultures and Organisations,* McGraw Hill, London.

Khoo, G. (1994), The Role of Assumptions in Intercultural Research and Consulting. Paper presented at Pacific Forum on Business and Management Communication, Simon Fraser University, 10 November.

The preceding discussion of Chinese business culture and etiquette is by no means complete. The reading listed below can give the reader additional insight. Many of the customs discussed are equally applicable to Taiwan and Singapore.

De Menthe, B. (1989), *Chinese Etiquette and Ethics in Business,* Business Books, Lincolnwood, Ill. A broad cultural survey of Chinese morals and values related to business interaction, mostly in mainland China.

Kirkbride, P. et al (1991), 'Chinese conflict preferences and negotiating behaviour', *Organisational Studies,* 3 Dec. pp. 365–86.

Zhao, D. (1993) 'The path of pluralism', *Far East Economic Review,* 7 Jan. p. 13.

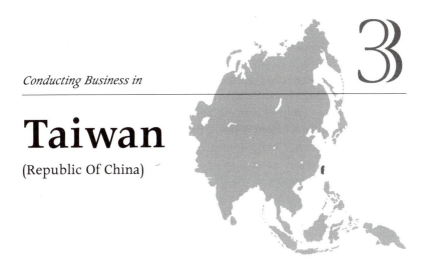

Conducting Business in

Taiwan

(Republic Of China)

THE ISLAND OF TAIWAN (formerly Formosa) lies about 160 km east of mainland China. Officially called the Republic of China (ROC), Taiwan is regarded by China (PRC) as a province of the PRC. Most of the people live in the Western third of the island in urban areas away from the mountain and forest of the east. It is making a transition to more democratic rule and open political system after years of authoritarian rule.

General background

Economy

Taiwan is one of the world's most dynamic economies. It has built a modern internationally-oriented economy almost from scratch over the forty-eight years since 2 million Chinese Nationalists fled from the mainland to continue their struggle against the communist overthrow of the mainland government by the forces of Mao. Taiwan's economy is heavily dependent on foreign trade exports of high tech, clean, high value-added, capital intensive finished goods because it lacks natural resources. Although Taiwan has a predominantly free enterprise economy, the government has invested in key strategic areas such as petroleum refining, electricity generation, steel, banking, fertilisers, shipbuilding, railroads, sugar, tobacco and alcohol. In recent years Taiwan's high-tech industries and service sector have grown. Taiwan's wealth has enabled it to become a major regional investor in labour-intensive industries in mainland China and Southeast Asia. Taiwan has a pool of well-educated and skilled labour.

Society and culture

Ethnicity

The population of Taiwan is about 21 million. There are four main ethnic groups: Taiwanese (70 per cent), Hakkas (14 per cent), recent mainland Chinese (14 per cent), and aborigines (2 per cent). Most of the older generation who came from mainland China identify with China, and would like to see a union with the mainland again, although not with a communist government. However, the younger generation identify themselves as Taiwanese and, aware of the social, economic, and political advances in Taiwan, have no wish to see Taiwan lose its independence. There is great fear among the younger generation about the intentions of China.

The younger generation generally want more democracy and are less willing to tolerate authoritative government as Taiwan becomes more materialistic and capitalistic. They have had a more comfortable life than their elders and are less concerned about basic survival needs.

Religion

Confucianism, Buddhism and Taoism, as well as ancestor worship, are the main religions. As in China, the social values and customs that impact on business have been shaped by Confucianism, which provides the ethical code for family life and family relationships, focusing on obedience, respect, duty, loyalty, humility and harmony. Family ties are still important, though less strong than previously. This paternalistic ideology leads to managers and business owners acting as benevolent despots who must be obeyed by their workforce, yet who care about their employees as though they were family. There are some Christians and adherents of Islam as well.

Social

Although a high power distance culture, the Taiwanese are less collectivist than the mainland Chinese. There is a general attitude that one can only get ahead by stepping on someone else. As a result, the Taiwanese do not work well in teams and tend to be very individualistic. This is believed to be one reason why the Taiwanese have demonstrated an entrepreneurial flair. The Taiwanese are not service-oriented and like the Chinese are not always helpful to outsiders using the common phrase *mei-you* (pronounced 'may yoa') which is the equivalent of 'I don't want to deal with this' or 'Don't bother me'.

Their collectivism forms round the family as the focal element in society and around which a lot of business and networks operate.

Taiwanese see themselves as a family member first and an individual second. Even between families the Taiwanese do not initially trust each other and tend to be vindictive and willing to do the other down. This is another example of the paradox of collectivist societies where strong ingroup bonds not only promote strong ties and support for members but at the same time evoke strong outgroup suspicion and hostility, particularly to fellow Taiwanese who are outside their own group. However, towards overseas persons who offer no threat, who are unlikely to disturb internal group harmony and who offer potential benefits, the Taiwanese can be quite courteous and welcoming.

Only if overseas persons appear to know the country, culture, or language too well, do the Taiwanese feel threatened. Their original coming to Taiwan and the pressures from China and international intriguing about recognition has made them wary of foreigners, in case they are let down or information about the country is passed to the 'enemy'. However, due to trade and political contacts they are beginning to trust and accept outsiders.

The Taiwanese are high context people, and like the Chinese on the mainland will not say 'no' and will not be direct in their communication. They dislike the Western directness which is regarded as disrespectful and hostile. Unlike the Chinese and Japanese, the Taiwanese are prone to emotional outbursts and allow their feelings to show.

Face

As a Confucian society, 'face' *(mianzi)* applies in all situations, including greetings, departures and general conversation; there is a prizing of dignity, mutual respect, courtesy, humility and deference. You must be on your guard all the time not to say anything that can be implied as criticism. You should alternatively ensure that you praise or thank your contacts/hosts/counterparts whenever appropriate and if possible in front of others but never so effusively that it appears deliberate or insincere.

Should an overseas business person do anything to cause a Taiwanese to lose face they will reciprocally have lost their business prospects with that Taiwanese and their partners. Losing face can be caused by criticism, insult, embarrassing a person, treating a person with lower status than is due to them or merely poking fun in a typical Western good humoured way. The aim must always be to show respect to the other person.

On the positive side, face can be given by praising in public, deferring to those of higher status, etc. However, an over-lavish supply of praise will equally be unwelcome as it bodes of disguised contempt and sarcasm. If you are invited to play golf or other sport, ensure your counterpart just about wins—not by too much of a margin or else it looks suspicious. If the Taiwanese is a poor exponent of the activity, you can still give some judicious praise and try not to win too well. Given that most businesses in Taiwan are small family affairs, the face you give to the senior person reflects on all the family and company. So your relationships with the owner/senior manager is vital to your business success with that company.

In attempts to prevent loss of face to either party, there is the tendency to avoid 'no' and provide communications that seem on first hearing to meet the overseas business person's expectations. There is no malicious intent in this; it is similar in most of Asia and for the same reason. The same phrases heard in Tokyo and Beijing will be heard here: 'it is inconvenient just now'; 'we will look into the possibility'; 'we will consider that' etc.

Young people are expected to obey their elders without question and this impacts on the workplace where the owner or manager is the boss. Thus older overseas business people will receive deference, respect and serious attention. A younger overseas person will have a harder time attempting to be received as a worthy counterpart.

Throughout Taiwan the work ethic is sound, with work placed on a pedestal as a virtue. It is not regarded by most as a means to wealth or an easy life. Most Taiwanese will quite happily work longer hours if required and self-employed persons will often work ten hours per day, six days a week.

Women are generally regarded as inferior in what is still a male-dominated society, occupying lowest level positions of 'office lady' or 'tea lady' to the other, mostly male, office employees, illustrating the influence of the Japanese. Nevertheless, women are gradually moving into positions of authority and have achieved success in some professions, such as medicine and academia. Women tend to run the household finances and, in some instances, even the finances of a family business.

Education is highly prized and is embraced by Taiwanese as the route to social and economic progress and mobility.

Who do you know? Relationships and guanxi

As in most other Asian countries it isn't what you know but who you know that impacts on business success. Having strong and relevant connections are the key element in Taiwan too where business and personal relationships are one and the same. Therefore to achieve your business goals, the cultivation of respect and trust through close personal ties is essential. Only in the export trade, where close ties are not required and where Taiwan has been operating impersonally with a multitude of different overseas businesses, does this not hold. But joint ventures and the marketing of overseas goods in Taiwan does require connections.

The Chinese *guanxi,* or network of personal connections, is the life blood of Taiwanese society, where individuals are parts of the collective whole, in particular the family, which even today provides the source of identity, protection and strength in Taiwanese small- to medium-size business organisations. In the last fifty years the Taiwanese family structure has been a bastion against the hostile outside world, where few can be trusted. Trust is retained for family members and extremely close friends, and through marriage or other means, connections can be established with others, thereby strengthening the support system. This has produced a 'clan' approach to ingroup and outgroup relationships. The overseas business person has to break into this extended closed clan system. Acceptance is an honour; it is the entreé for excellent business possibilities, yet it requires responsibility, integrity, sincerity and commitment to the other members of the network. Business can not just remain business in Taiwan, even for the overseas person. You get sucked into the system. But without that, little business is possible.

Taiwan business people work hard to maintain and extend their networks of connections. These *guanxi* are a means to an end; mutual personal financial profit through mutual personal relationships. A Taiwanese who does not already know a potential business associate will hesitate to do business until they can get acquainted and the associate's character and intentions can be sized up. This is quite an obstacle to the newcomer into the Taiwanese business scene.

Making contacts

The mutual friend

The major way to make contact with potential Taiwanese business associates is to have a mutual friend serve as an introducer and/or give you a referral. If the third party has close relationships with both sides, that alone may constitute solid grounds for the conduct of business. Finding an intermediary may be as simple as asking a Taiwanese person living in your country if they have any family members still in Taiwan who could be potential associates. Another key source is anyone who has worked in Taiwan or who has co-operated with Taiwanese successfully in the past. Chambers of Commerce, small business associations, and ROC international trade offices may also find contacts for you.

If finding a third party for introductions in your home country proves impossible, make a fact-finding trip to Taiwan. A trade show/trade fair in Taipei that would allow you to display your goods or services, gives you a good opportunity to meet potential third parties and even potential associates. Sending faxes to businesses or cold calling is unlikely to work; your attempts to contact will be ignored as they do not know you.

Your first two trips may accomplish nothing more than getting to know several possible candidates for business relationships. You must spend time deepening and strengthening relationships through visits, dinners, gift giving, and many small favours. As no favour goes unnoticed it will be repaid, as Taiwanese appreciate all sincere efforts in this area. You must keep an account of all favours done for you too, all small gifts received and the like, as you are likely to be called on to reciprocate in the future. So whenever someone offers you a favour, dinner, or gift, humbly offer some polite excuse declining the offer if you have no wish to be in that person's debt. As declining could be insulting to the Taiwanese, make certain beforehand that you have no need for a relationship with them.

As in most Asian countries decision-making is slow and successful endeavours will take time to achieve. Therefore, a local presence needs to be established either by hiring a local agent, consultant, or representative; by setting up a branch, representative, or liaison office; or by entering into a joint venture. When selecting an agent or representative, check references and financial conditions thoroughly, as many will claim to have the right contacts. Generally, friends of the ruling party tend to receive special treatment, as government work is usually awarded to political allies or in deference to long-standing relationships. Even the hiring of subcontractors and individual workers can be politically based. Foreigners based in Taiwan with strong relationships may be suitable local representatives.

The company face

A foreign business should designate a personable member of the company to represent them in Taiwan on a long-term basis. Taiwanese like to deal with the same individual, and they treat every interaction as a personal one. Over time, if the business relationship is a success, Taiwanese may come to regard the 'front' person as a close personal friend. Replacing that individual could jeopardise the business relationship, unless the current representative introduces the new representative and spends some time bringing them into relationship with the Taiwanese.

Meeting the Taiwanese

When meeting Taiwanese business people you should display sincerity and respect. Shaking hands is the accepted form of salutation, accompanied by a nod of the head. Business cards are then exchanged with the same ritual as in China. Take it with both hands and appear to spend some time reading it (even though it may be in Mandarin) to show respect to the person. Your business card should be bilingual, stating your title and department, as status is very important to the Taiwanese. Names can be transliterated into Chinese. Seek the advice of a knowledgeable person on the characters used for transliteration as some characters have better connotations than others. Hotels can help you find printers to produce these cards.

Presenting letters of introduction from well-known business leaders, overseas Taiwanese, or former government officials who have dealt with Taiwan is an excellent way of showing both that you are a person of high standing and that you mean business. Anything that you can do to enhance their regard for you is a plus, but be careful not to appear arrogant or haughty, as Confucian morality condemns such behaviour.

Punctuality is very important in Taiwan. You should take Taiwan's heavy traffic into account when planning your schedule. If you are going to be more than five minutes late, call your counterpart and explain your situation. Local Taiwanese usually meet in their office or over lunch or dinner. If you are hosting the meeting, a hotel room, coffee shop, or business centre is appropriate.

Conversation

Small talk is used to get to know you. Expect people whom you hardly know to question you about personal details, such as age, earnings and family. In the Western culture this may be none of their business, but over there this an occasion when you must self-disclose about yourself and your family; this is a sign of familiarity and trust, part of developing the relationship and getting to know you that is so vital for future business links.

Their questions focus on what they themselves consider to be important in life—essentially money and family. Family issues can be an important topic of conversation, because Taiwanese who want to find out who you are, are as interested in you as the member of a family as much as they are in you as an individual. You can ask Taiwanese about their families too, and they will love to tell you in rich detail about them. If you are divorced or unmarried, it is better not to be frank and tell a few white lies than jeopardise a potentially financially rewarding relationship. Some Taiwanese regard the West as morally loose and full of homosexuals, both of which they regard as unacceptable.

Avoid discussion of Chinese politics. While Taiwan is for all practical purposes an independent country, the official ROC government line is that Taiwan is part of China and that they are the legitimate government of all China. However, many Taiwanese would prefer total independence from China, and you can seldom be sure which side of the fence those with whom you are talking stand. In conversation some people refer to themselves as Taiwanese while others call themselves Chinese, a choice which may or may not have political implications. To avoid offence, simply call Taiwan what it is: Taiwan. The rest of China can be referred to as mainland China.

While English is a mandatory element of the school curriculum, few Taiwanese speak English well and this poses problems for meaningful dialogue between Taiwanese and foreigners. Some broken English is all you will find among family firms. The Taiwanese are most used to American-style English, so speakers of British or Australian English should try to use American equivalents of words like petrol (gas), pavement (sidewalk) and lift (elevator).

Having an interpreter of your own is a real advantage, although costly. In Taipei there are services that can provide you with an interpreter for the length of your stay. Look for an interpreter who is fluent in both Mandarin Chinese and Taiwanese. Although the official language of Taiwan is Mandarin, 85 per cent of the people speak Taiwanese as their mother tongue, and more than half of Taiwan's businesses use Taiwanese in the office.

Some nonverbal communication hints

Some elements of Taiwanese body language are very different from those of the West.

- Finger pointing at a person is considered accusatory, rude, or hostile. Moreover, a raised and slightly curved index finger implies death.
- While shaking hands is now the standard form of greeting, traditional etiquette calls for making a fist with the left hand, covering it with the right palm, and shaking the hands up and down. Some Taiwanese still do this, especially with close friends. It is also a formal way of saying thank you and a sign of reverence.
- When Taiwanese want someone to approach they place their palm facing down and fingers pointing away and wave toward you in a scratching motion.
- Holding one's hand up near the face and slightly waving means no, or it can be a mild rebuke.
- Taiwanese will often smile or laugh nervously when nervous or embarrassed by an inconvenient request or sensitive issue brought up in conversation. Another possible explanation is that the smiler or another person nearby has committed a *faux pas*.
- Taiwanese tell few jokes; their humour is associated with word play because in their language words that sound the same have many different meanings depending on the tone.

- It is considered impolite to wink or blink at someone.
- Do not touch someone's head, for the head is considered the spiritual part of a person.
- When Taiwanese are embarrassed, they cover their faces with their hands.
- Taiwanese sit upright in chairs with both feet on the floor. Women may cross their legs at the ankles. Do not slouch.
- It is impolite to point one's feet at another person. Do not touch or push anything with your feet because they are considered dirty.
- In public, Taiwanese rarely hug or display emotion through physical contact. Lightly touching another person's arm when speaking is a sign of close familiarity. Men and women rarely hold hands in public, but it is not uncommon for friends of the same sex to hold hands or to clasp each other by the shoulders. This is especially true of young people.
- Shoes are removed before entering a house. Check that your socks are clean and without holes!

Names and forms of address

As in China, a person's family name, almost always mono-syllabic, precedes their personal name. Due to the influence of Western business practices many Taiwanese business people place their surname last on a business card, but others continue to place it first. Ask a colleague or your host which is the appropriate surname and the suitable way to address the person since it is difficult to know whether a name has been inverted. As a general rule, assume that a name has not been inverted. Many Taiwanese choose Western names or words as names, some of which may seem odd to a Westerner.

Personal names are rarely used, even by people who are very close apart from those who use an English name. Use Mister, Miss, or Mrs (not Ms) when addressing Chinese. Although a woman does not take her husband's family name when she marries, it is acceptable for Westerners to use the Western form to address a married woman such as Mrs Wang if the woman's husband is Mr Wang. It is also acceptable to use a person's designated position or profession in society. For example, a director with the last name Chang can be referred to Director Chang. This form of address also applies to teachers, company managers, and higher-ranking officials etc.

When you are introduced, give a slight nod of the head, a smile, and a greeting. A common Chinese greeting is *Ni hao ma*, which means 'How are you?'. Out of respect for older people, you should greet them first and always stand when they enter or depart the room.

Getting down to business

The business world

Small businesses controlled by an extended family dominate the Taiwan economy. Usually a senior family member, most often a male, is the central decision-maker. Generally, promotions are based on a combination of both connections and ability, with the latter counting for more in private sector and the former counting more in the public sector. In general, Taiwanese business is more entrepreneurial, responsive and less rigidly hierarchical than other Southeast Asian countries, and the absence of large conglomerates, as in Japan and Korea, make it more accessible to overseas business.

The director title has become commonplace, so assess your counterpart's actual authority and responsibilities before you make any assumptions. Many Taiwanese enjoy displaying their power.

The typical Taiwanese business person is practical, down to earth and shrewd, as their business experience will have been moulded in a more poverty stricken context than exists now. Many older heads of family firms are self-made, after fleeing from the mainland with nothing. They cautiously guard their wealth, are apprehensive about the future, and often complain about the younger generation who have never experienced hardship and have everything on a plate. They have the 'put things away for a rainy day' attitude similar to those found in older British, European and American families who grew up in the Depression.

As a collectivist, high power distance society based on Confucian philosophy, each business has only one boss, who commands absolute respect and obedience from employees. In return they have benevolence bestowed on them, their personal and work wellbeing both a central concern of the employer. Consonant with the duty owed to family emphasised in Confucian ethics, the small business is a central part of the functioning of the family, with earnings often pooled. This locates the business within the concept of the traditional Confucian family—status, deference and paternalism dominate.

However, this is beginning to break down as Western values start to filter through and younger people seek more independence and control of their lives. Company loyalty is becoming more fragile since, with small businesses the norm, it is easy for a skilled, resourceful younger person to set up their own entrepreneurial activity. A common saying in Taiwan sums this mood up: 'it is better to be the head of a chicken than the tail of an ox'. This small-scale capitalism is a benefit for any overseas business person looking for a partner or distributor. Not only can a small but well-run business be located, but it is quite likely a mid-level skilled experienced employee would be willing to leave their existing job and develop an overseas branch of a company or set up a new company in competition with their former employer. Business rivalries are common in Taiwan and turn into very personal vendettas. Small scale is also the norm for service activities, so that shops tend to be neighbourhood ones rather than huge supermarkets. This makes distribution difficult for an overseas supplier.

Most business is done on a cash basis with transactions concluded with a handshake. There is thus little in the way of documentation, accounting standards are lax and income goes unreported. The bureaucracy is open to corruption and because the regulations are so complex and erratically enforced most small to medium businesses take the unofficial route on the basis that paying a fine is preferable and more acceptable than delaying business.

Trade delegations

Like the mainland Chinese, the Taiwanese are more comfortable with groups than with individuals and find it confusing if visiting group members utter individual opinions and policies. A consistent group view is needed and should be expressed by its designated speaker, who is also its most senior member. The Taiwanese will look to that member for all major communication and accept their words as the words of the delegation.

The status that an individual holds in a company or organisation is important to the Taiwanese, who evaluate the importance of the delegation by the rank of its members. No delegation will achieve anything if the Taiwanese believe that its leader does not carry clout back home. Make sure the Taiwanese have all necessary details about the purpose of the delegation and its products, along with details of all delegation members who will be present. Place the team leader's name first, with members listed in order of seniority or importance for the deal. The Taiwanese will try to match your team with executives of similar status from their own organisation. The number of negotiation members can vary from two to ten.

If the Taiwanese company is represented by someone who is obviously of lower rank, it can be an indication that it is not particularly interested in you or that they are unaware of the status of the members of your delegation.

A trade delegation should be led by older members of the company who have at least middle-level executive rank (as age is respected), and who are patient, genial, yet persistent. They have enough rank to make decisions on the spot without fear of repercussions from the home office. In contrast to many other Asian cultures, foreign business women are quite acceptable.

First day protocol

Limited serious business will be accomplished on the first day of a delegation's visit to Taiwan. This is a time for getting to know one another and for feeling out the personalities who will be involved in later negotiations. While they are 'sussing you out', you should do the same. Try to determine the status of all the members and their likely relations with one other. Always begin a meeting with pleasant general conversation. Avoid political topics, particularly mainland China and communism. It is appropriate to talk about your country, your travels, or the weather, or to offer general praise for Taiwan. The Taiwanese are more direct and businesslike than the mainland Chinese, although slower than people from Hong Kong. The subject of business usually comes up naturally after the participants feel comfortable enough to begin.

Because most Taiwanese companies are small, the person who heads the Taiwanese delegation may be the company's owner or senior executive. They will be the only spokesperson for the group on substantive issues, but other members will probably have some say in decision-making behind the scenes. Taiwanese place great emphasis on consensus, but they will never debate their position in front of the foreign delegation.

The Taiwanese are good hosts and will have created an itinerary that involves a variety of activities as well as business discussion. These can include a tour of the company you are dealing with, visits to cultural places, an evening traditional Chinese banquet, and likely a sing song at the local karaoke club.

Business negotiations

After banqueting and singing in karaoke bars, you may begin to believe that you have earned the relationship and deserve to get their business. Not so. The Taiwanese can be tough negotiators. In fact, the lavish entertainment is an attempt to soften you up psychologically and physically to gain maximum advantage in the negotiation process.

These will start in earnest on day two, usually in meeting rooms at the Taiwanese place of business, where the Taiwanese team will be waiting. The head of the visiting delegation must lead in the group. The Taiwanese will be confused as to who is the leader if this is not done. The interpreter should enter close behind the leader and remain by the leader's side throughout the negotiations.

Teams usually sit opposite each other across at a rectangular table with the heads of delegations facing each other. Other team members sit around the heads, often in descending order of importance. The guest delegation will be seated usually facing the door. Do not expect to jump into substantive negotiations right away. The usual small talk will dominate early conversation until the time is thought right to start discussing business.

Then the head of the host delegation usually gives a short welcoming speech. The head of the visiting group will then be expected to speak first in the negotiations. Team members should speak only when they are asked to do so. The discussion should always be directed at the head of the Taiwanese team, not at the interpreter. Only speak a couple of sentences at a time before allowing the interpreter to speak. Look at the host while the interpreter is translating. Interpreters need to rest at least every two hours. If negotiations are to be lengthy, you may need two interpreters. Using an interpreter also increases the length of a meeting by three times what would be normally expected, so the negotiation proceeds very slowly.

Ensure you have provided the Taiwanese with all necessary information prior to the negotiations It can also be useful to distribute sheets stating your main points in Chinese. A typical opening statement highlighting the major topics that need to be discussed can last between five and ten minutes. Taiwanese appreciate directness. Anything that you can do to clarify their understanding of your position is fine, as the Taiwanese will expect a very serious in-depth discussion on all issues as the negotiations proceed, covering all the major details and answering all foreseeable questions as each is dealt with.

After the overseas team has outlined their position, the Taiwanese team leader responds. Then the negotiation proceeds as a controlled conversation, not an open-ended chat. The Taiwanese approach is first to gain an overall view of the proposal, then to deal with specific chunks, focussing on concrete issues and problems.

Types of negotiations

A purchasing agreement to buy Taiwanese goods, exporting them for sale in another country can usually be completed quickly without major hassles. Price is the one area where disagreements occur. The Taiwanese are increasingly seen to be trying to squeeze unreasonable profit out of deals because of increasing labour costs. The change over to higher quality goods also means that 'Made in Taiwan' is no longer a symbol of low price and inferior quality.

If you want to conduct business with the ROC government good personal connections are essential, as well as the 'know how' that your side can bring into a project. The government expects the very best when contracting for foreign expertise. The presentation must be excellent and your team, especially the technical or other experts, must be able to answer questions thoroughly and impress with their expertise. In other negotiations, such as those for co-operative efforts between companies or for marketing, relationships remain the primary avenue.

Generally the Taiwanese are risk-averse and prefer calculated, limited, or no-risk situations.

They are tough negotiators. Having grown up bargaining for everything, they are comfortable and patient in their bargaining. The Taiwanese will try to get every concession possible from you. Outwardly, they value maintaining a pleasant, friendly, and yet slightly reserved atmosphere throughout the negotiations. The Taiwanese do not react well to a hard-sell approach.

Do not assume that a Western-educated or a Western-dressed Taiwanese is Western in attitudes. Taiwanese do not always say 'no' directly, for they do not like to give negative news. Further, they hope that if they avoid or ignore an issue it will simply go away. A Taiwanese will rarely admit that they have made a mistake and will avoid accepting responsibility for a mistake at all costs. Further, they will rarely tell you if there is a problem, regardless of how bad it is. Forcing a Taiwanese to take responsibility for a mistake will only result in a loss of face. Ask questions, but never cause your counterpart to lose face and never get angry.

Efficiency and initiative are not widespread and the Taiwanese are not consistent in meeting deadlines. Account for such lapses when you set your schedules and incorporate mini-deadlines. Often if a Taiwanese does not want to do something, they won't, even if they have already agreed to do it. Keep in close contact with the local office or representative and outline clearly each person's responsibilities. Taiwanese tend to procrastinate; be persistent.

Taiwanese negotiating tactics
Taiwanese negotiators are shrewd and may perpetrate some of the following on you.

- *Controlling the schedule and location.* As negotiations are usually held in Taiwan, they are aware that there is cost to you in time and money to come to Taiwan, and that you do not want to go away empty-handed. The Taiwanese may appear seemingly indifferent to the success or failure of the meeting, and then make excessive demands.
- *Threatening to do business elsewhere.* Taiwanese may tell you that they can easily do business with others.
- *Using friendship as a way of gaining concessions.* Taiwanese who have established relations with foreigners may remind them that if you are really a true friend you would put in 100 per cent effort to forge an agreement of maximum mutual benefit—creating the guilt complex.
- *Showing anger.* Although the display of anger is not acceptable under Confucian morality, Taiwanese may show calculated anger to put pressure on the opposite side, which may be afraid of losing the contract.

- *Sensing the foreigner's fear of failure.* If the Taiwanese know that you are committed 100 per cent to procuring a contract with pressure back home to succeed they will increase their demands for concessions.
- *Flattery.* Taiwanese are not above heaping praise on foreigners either for personal attributes or business acumen. Don't let their ego stroking skills give them an advantage.
- *Knowing when you need to leave.* Don't reveal the date of your departure, as they may delay substantive negotiations until the day before you plan to leave in order to pressure you into a hasty agreement. If possible, leave your departure open, and indicate that you are willing to stay longer than anticipated if there is a real chance for success.
- *Attrition.* Taiwanese negotiators are patient and can stretch out the negotiations in order to wear you down. Excessive entertaining in the evening can also take the edge off your performance.
- *Throwing your words back at you.* Taiwanese take careful notes at discussions and they have been known to quote a foreigner's own words in order to refute his or her current position.
- *Playing off competitors.* Taiwanese may invite several competing companies to negotiate at the same time, and they will brazenly let you know this to apply pressure.
- *Inflating prices and hiding the real bottom line.* Taiwanese may appear to give in to your demand for lower prices, but their original stated price may have been abnormally high.

Tips for negotiators
- *Be well prepared.* At least one member of your negotiating team should have an in-depth technical knowledge of your product and be able to display it to the Taiwanese. Be prepared to give a lengthy and detailed presentation on your side of the deal.
- *Play off competitors.* If the going gets tough, let the Taiwanese know that they are not the only ones in town. Competition is cut-throat and you can probably find other sources in the country for what your counterpart has to offer. If price is the problem you may be able to strike a cheaper deal in China or Southeast Asia. If quality is the concern, Japanese companies may be able to outdo the Taiwanese. Be willing to cut your losses and go home. Let the Taiwanese know that failure to agree is quite an acceptable alternative to you, rather than getting hooked into a bad deal.
- *Cover every detail of the contract before you sign it.* Talk over the entire contract with the Taiwanese side. Be sure that your interpretations are consistent and that everyone understands their duties and obligations. Take copious and careful notes. Review what the Taiwanese side has said, and ask for clarification on any possible ambiguities.

- *Pad your price.* Do as the Taiwanese do. Start out high, and be willing to give a little.
- *Remain calm and impersonal during negotiations.* Don't show your agitation, lest the Taiwanese know your sensitive areas. Even if you were good buddies the night before, an impersonal business-like approach in negotiations lets the Taiwanese know that your first priority is good business.
- *Be patient.* Taiwanese believe that Westerners are always in a hurry, and they may try to get you to sign an agreement before you have adequate time to review the details.
- *State your commitment to work towards a final but fair deal.* Tell them that your relationship can only be strengthened by a mutually beneficial arrangement. Be willing to compromise, but don't give anything away easily.

The Taiwanese approach to contracts

A few years ago many Taiwanese viewed written contracts as virtually meaningless compared to personal commitments between associates. However, Taiwan is rapidly evolving into a full democracy based on the rule of law, and most Taiwanese now accept that a contract is a legally binding document. Such a view is especially prevalent among people who have had experience with the West. But some Taiwanese still consider a contract to be a loose commitment to do business, not a document outlining every aspect of the business relationship. Some head executives would rather sign a short agreement on the principle of doing business and allow subordinates to work out the details at a later time. Avoid this situation if you can, because it increases the chance of misunderstanding on both sides and necessitates further negotiations, which can be costly.

While negotiating a detailed contract is important, the Taiwanese often view any deal with foreigners as only one component of a larger, ongoing relationship. The Taiwanese see the immediate issue as a sort of building block that allows them to measure and strengthen reliability and co-operation. This is a practical and realistic philosophy that any Westerner who wants to do business in Taiwan over the long term should appreciate and adopt for their own ventures.

Contracts are therefore viewed as a guide for developing a relationship. The problem with most contracts is that the Chinese version usually governs and interpretations of that version can differ due to the tonal quality of the language. If you have a legal dispute and the contract does not specify how and where to resolve problems, consider using third-party arbitration. It is rare for a Taiwanese to agree to foreign arbitration when signing a contract, but it is worth asking for it.

The social context of business

Banqueting: A national pastime

For details of the Chinese banquet please read the section in the previous chapter on China as the event is essentially the same in both countries.

The Taiwanese love eating. So if you like Chinese food, an invitation to a traditional banquet may be the high point of your visit. Although you will not be expected to know everything about proper banquet behaviour, some display of knowledge will please them because it shows that you have respect for Taiwanese culture and traditions.

Remember it is impolite to drink liquor alone and polite, but certainly not mandatory, to try a taste of each dish. Taiwanese banquets may include between ten and twelve courses, so go slow on eating, and only sample each dish. To stop eating in the middle of a banquet is considered rude, and your host may incorrectly think that something has been done to offend you. If you don't leave some food on your plate at the end it will be assumed that your host has not provided enough to eat. The host will also think they have offended you if you switch from alcohol to a soft drink in the middle of the banquet. It is impolite to fill your own glass without first filling the glasses of everyone else. If your glass becomes empty and your host is observant, it is likely that they will fill it for you immediately. When filling another's glass it is polite to fill it as full as you can without letting the liquid spill over the rim. This symbolises full respect and friendship.

Table manners in Taiwan are very relaxed. Elbows on the table, reaching across the table for food, or making loud noises when eating are quite acceptable. Usually it is impolite to touch one's food with anything except eating utensils, but when eating chicken, shrimp, or other hard-to-handle food, Taiwanese use their hands.

As in China, drinking and toasting punctuate the banquet. The head of the visiting group will be expected to toast the wellbeing of the hosts in return for their initial toast.

It is an expectation that the host will try to get their guests drunk. If you have a meeting the next day, make it known at the very beginning of the meal you do not drink alcohol to prevent embarrassment. One way to eliminate the pressure to drink is to inform your host that you are allergic to alcohol or teetotal. A number of the Taiwanese may become fairly inebriated, and may if you prompt them subtly unwittingly reveal aspects of the negotiation which can help your side.

Banquets just end; there is no after dinner talk. The host will rise, bid good evening to everyone at the door and stay behind to settle the bill with the restaurateur. Other hosts are likely to accompany guests to their vehicles.

Reciprocity

Unless time or other constraints make it impossible, it is very acceptable to provide a return banquet particularly when negotiations have been concluded or on the evening before your departure. Have an intermediary deliver your invitations to the Taiwanese in case they have to refuse. They will not lose face telling the third party than speaking directly to you.

Use a Chinese restaurant rather than a Western one as the Taiwanese prefer their own fare. Banquets are priced per person and cover all expenses except alcohol. Good restaurants and hotels know how to prepare a memorable banquet. It is acceptable for foreign business-women to entertain local counterparts.

Karaoke

The Taiwanese also love karaoke as they have always enjoyed singing with close friends. It will be difficult for you to avoid a session, perhaps after the banquet. Expect to sing at least once; you are not expected to be proficient, but simply to enter into the fun. Your contribution will be much appreciated and greeted with praise and applause.

Karaoke has become popular in most collectivist cultures of Asia because singing in front of peers is one of the very few socially acceptable ways in which a person can display skill and receive individual praise without accusations of arrogance or self-centredness. Your attendance might be under sufferance but it can pay dividends in firming up those necessary relationships. However, don't deliberately ask to go to a karaoke lounge as some Taiwanese view it as a bit low-class due to its association with hidden prostitution. Wait to be invited.

Other activities

Golf is high-status game to which Taiwanese businessmen devote much time. Being able to accept an invitation to join a golfing session again helps to bolster relationships. It is a definite asset if you are beyond the 'rabbit' stage and have access to equipment. The Taiwanese set great store by being able to do things such as golf well and you should enable the host to maintain face by either losing (not too badly), or if you are good winning only by a narrow margin.

Company outings are common, for example, picnics and hiking. It is important to participate in these activities if asked to do so. Organise similar outings for your staff and business acquaintances if you have an office in Taiwan. Your local counterpart should be able to provide suitable guidance in planning appropriate gatherings.

Visiting someone's home

As most business entertaining is done in restaurants it will be rare that you will be invited to a person's home. However, if you are, remove your shoes before entering and take a gift. Suitable presents include fruit, tea, flowers, or any memento from your home country that they can associate with you. Picture books of your home area make good presents. Presenting a wife with perfume or children with toys is likely to be appreciated. Such presents show that you are concerned about the welfare of the entire family, not just the business relationship. Foreign liquor e.g. French brandy, is another gift that is much appreciated.

At the Chinese New Year take a red envelope with about NT$100 for each child. Never give money to adults except for weddings, funerals, and sometimes birthdays.

Giving and receiving gifts

⌈Gift giving is a cultural must. Simply saying thank you is perceived as a conventional glib response to a Taiwanese. Gifts show friendship, or appreciation for a favour done; they can symbolise hopes for good future business, the successful conclusion of an endeavour, or place the recipient in a position requiring a return favour. Favours should be rewarded materially; gifts have more symbolic than monetary value. Avoid very expensive gifts unless the recipient is an old associate who has proved to be particularly important in business dealings. Gifts are not expected on the first visit, but they can be given if you feel that the beginnings of a relationship have been established.

Suitable gifts for a first meeting are inexpensive items with a company logo, nice pens, calendars, golf balls, and baseball caps. In an office or business environment it is best to present business-related gifts such as pens or paperweights with your company logo. If only one expensive gift is to be given, it should be presented to the head of the Taiwanese group at a banquet or on the conclusion of a successful meeting. If gifts are to be given to several individuals, be sure that everyone receives a gift of roughly equal value with the chief executive receiving the one with greatest value. Omit no one with whom you have a relationship when giving gifts to several people at the same time.

There are some gift giving issues to note. Do not give caps that have any green on them, for this implies that the wearer's wife or girlfriend has been unfaithful. Do not present any cutting gifts like knives and scissors, for they symbolise the cutting of a relationship. Handkerchiefs are unacceptable too, for they signify permanent departure. Clocks and watches are also not appropriate: they symbolise termination of time or death. Expensive, foreign-brand liquor is one of the best gift choices for senior people. Make sure that your foreign gift was not made in Taiwan!! Wrap gifts you give in the auspicious and traditional colours of gold or red. The usual gift for weddings (and sometimes for birthdays) is money. Money should be placed in red envelopes (*hung bao*), which are available at stores. Be sure to use new or clean, crisp bills. Although the amount you give will differ based on your relationship with the recipient, never give less than NT$600. Usually NT$2000 to NT$3000 is appropriate. Part of the intention of the wedding gift is to help defray the cost of the meal, so take the location of the reception into account. For wedding money gifts, do not give odd-numbered amounts. Odd versus even amounts are based solely on the digit before the zeros. For example, NT$680, or NT$1200 would be appropriate, but NT$670 or NT$1000 would not be appropriate. Avoid the number 4 in all circumstances, as it sounds like the word for 'death.' If your recipient is Taiwanese, it is also best to avoid 5, as it sounds like the word for 'mistake'. Never wear black to a wedding.

For funerals, money is given as well, but in smaller amounts. White and black are considered colours of mourning so use white envelopes for funerals. Send the envelope to the home of the deceased. Use amounts in odd numbers (the opposite of weddings). For example, appropriate sums would be about NT$1000 or NT$1100. Never wear red to a funeral.

For the Chinese New Year, suitable gifts include sweets and cookies. At New Year it is customary (and very important) to give bonuses to factory and blue-collar workers, secretaries, and household help. A bonus equal to one or two months' salary is appropriate for those who have worked for you or the company for more than one year. A bonus of half a month's to one month's salary is fine for employees who have worked for you less than a year. Check with you local counterpart to find out who else should receive gifts.

Present and receive gifts with both hands outstretched. Politeness requires the recipient to refuse a gift several times before finally accepting it. This can be tricky to interpret because there may on occasions be a real rejection involved. Usually after a few ritualistic protestations and your expressions that your gift is only a small token and to add that you would be honoured if it were accepted, the Taiwanese will accept the present graciously. If your attempts to give a present are rejected strongly with evident serious intent not to accept, don't press it. They may refuse your gift because they do not want to be in your debt or because they have no intentions of having a relationship with you.

When a gift is offered to you, you do not need to go through the initial refusal ritual, but do make your acceptance humble. The gift is an acknowledgment that a relationship with you exists. It can also be an overture before a favour is asked. In accepting a gift you are putting yourself into an obligation to reciprocate in kind or through a favour. It is not regarded as polite to open a gift in front of the giver unless they encourage you to. Don't tear off the wrappings; it is a sign of greediness.

If you have a local representative, they will invariably have to engage in some form of gift giving or commissions in order to keep business moving forward, particularly if you are bidding for government contracts. It is advisable to let your local counterpart manage this aspect of doing business in Taiwan.

Other useful information

What to wear

Except for formal situations, Taiwanese business people don't put a lot of emphasis on dress. Therefore you can't go wrong by following normal business dress codes in Western countries for both men and women. Conservative suits and ties are best. In the humid summer months more informal attire, such as a short-sleeve shirt and tie, are acceptable after your first meeting. Women should avoid trousers because they can appear too casual. For banquets more formal attire should be worn, such as suits for men or dresses for women. Don't wear black clothes unless you plan to attend a funeral. While at work in the factory, both managers and workers often wear company shirts with the company logo. Similar to short-sleeved pullover golf shirts, they are practical in Taiwan's hot, humid summer weather. Raincoats and umbrellas are a necessity all year round.

Major holidays

January 1	National Founding Day of the Republic of China
January/February*	Chinese New Year
February 6	Lantern Festival
Early March*	Spring Festival
March 29	Youth Day
April 4	Children's and Women's Day
April 5	Tomb Sweeping Day and Chiang Kai-shek's Memorial Day
May 1	Labour Day
June*	Dragon Boat Festival
September*	Mid-Autumn (Moon) Festival
September 28	Confucius's Birthday/Teachers' Day
October 10	Double Tenth National Day
October 25	Taiwan Restoration Day
October 31	Birthday of President Chiang Kai-shek
November 12	Birthday of Dr. Sun Yat-sen
December 25	Constitution Day

*These holidays are based on the lunar calendar and change yearly.

Language

The official language is Mandarin, called *gwoyu* (national language) locally, although Taiwanese, a southern Fujian dialect, is also widely spoken. A strong emphasis on learning English has just started with the language now introduced in elementary school. However, Taiwanese are often reluctant to speak English as they are self-conscious about their abilities. Many older people, especially those educated before the Second World War, also speak some Japanese.

Dates

The official way of stating the date is based on the number of years since the establishment of the Chinese republic in 1911. This translates into an official difference of 1911 years from the Western calendar. The official way to write the date is by year, month, and day. For example, August 21, 1997, in the Western calendar would be written as 97/8/21 on official documents in Taiwan. However, in international business most Taiwanese would use the Western calendar.

Transportation

Traffic congestion can be extensive, making a rental car an inadvisable option. Taxis are the most convenient method of transportation. Most taxi drivers do not speak English so carry a hotel card with the hotel's name in Chinese in case you get lost. Taxi fares are based on a combination of time and distance, so fares can increase dramatically during rush hours. Further, taxis add a surcharge when travelling to the airport. Hotels can arrange for a private driver and car, which is the best option if your hosts do not provide transport (they often will).

In summary

- The Taiwanese are a high power distance, collectivist society.
- Confucianism provides the basis for the culture.
- Most companies are small to medium in size and run as family enterprises with the head of the family in full control.
- Connections (*guanxi*), as in mainland China, and political ties are very important.
- Have a business card written in both languages and take your own interpreter if possible.
- Be prepared for tough negotiations, banqueting and karaoke.
- Gift giving is endemic and expected.
- The dress code is generally Western.

a

Activities

Try working out the solutions to these two problems, then check your responses with those in Appendix B.

1   After completing an MBA in international business and working for an international bank for several years, Colin Schofield was assigned for several weeks as a troubleshooter in the Taiwan office. To facilitate his adjustment to the Taiwan banking system and to assist with translation, Colin was assigned a bilingual female assistant accountant of the bank, Yong Kim Fa. She, like Colin, was single and in her early 30s, and she lived with her widowed mother. In response to a comment Colin had made about the joys of Chinese cuisine, she invited Colin to her mother's home for dinner. The dinner went well and Colin felt fortunate to have had a chance to be entertained in a Taiwanese home. Several days later Colin felt somewhat embarrassed because he had forgotten to take the mother a gift the evening he had gone to dinner. So before returning home at the end of his assignment he made a special trip back to the house to deliver personally a large bouquet of white chrysanthemums to the mother as a token of his appreciation for her hospitality. Kim Fa answered the door, greeted Colin, and took the flowers into the kitchen. But when she took Colin into the living room to say goodbye to her mother, no mention was made of the flowers.

What went wrong?

2   For the past three years Frank Hendrickson has served quite successfully as the manager of an American-owned manufacturing company in Taiwan. Shortly after arrival in Taipei he instituted a number of changes in the plant operation that increased both production and worker satisfaction. However, within the last several months a series of what seemed to Frank to be unrelated incidents had occurred. First, a local foreman was crushed by some falling crates, then a week later a fire burned down one of the warehouses. Later that month the young child of one of the other ex-pats working there was drowned in a swimming accident, and within the past several weeks there had been a rash of minor accidents on the assembly line, quite uncharacteristic given the plant's excellent past safety record. Rumours started to spread about

the plant being cursed by evil spirits, and absenteeism increased dramatically. To try to deal with these problems Frank called together his chief supervisors. His expatriate staff recommended that some experts from the insurance company come in to review the safety procedures, which, they argued, would show the workers that the company was taking their safety needs seriously. But the Taiwanese supervisors were adamant that the only helpful procedure would be to invite a local religious priest be come during company time and pray for the workers and ward off any evil forces. The Western managers saw this as simply pandering to superstition. They therefore rejected the suggestion and the meeting ended without any substantial agreement on what could be done to allay the fears of the workers.

How would you explain this basic cultural conflict?

3 Chris Giannopolous, a young, but bright and entrepreneurial executive for a global electronics company, was sent to Taiwan to work out the details of a joint venture with a Taiwanese electronics firm. During the first few weeks he felt that the negotiations were proceeding better than he had expected. Chris found that he had very cordial working relationships with the team of Taiwanese executives, and in fact, they had agreed on the major policies and strategies governing the new joint venture. During the third week of negotiations he was present at a meeting held to review their progress. The meeting was chaired by the president of the Taiwanese firm, Mr Liang, a man in his mid-50s, who had recently taken over the presidency from his 82-year-old father. The new president, who had been involved in most of the negotiations during the preceding weeks, seemed to Chris to be one of the strongest advocates of the plan that had been developed to date. Also attending the meeting was Liang's father, the recently retired president. After the plans had been discussed in some detail, the octogenarian past-president proceeded to give a long soliloquy about how some of the features of this plan violated the traditional practices on which the company had been founded. Much to Chris's amazement, Mr. Liang did nothing to explain or defend the policies and strategies that they had taken weeks to develop. Feeling extremely frustrated, Chris gave a strongly argued and eloquent defence of the plan. To his amazement, no one else

spoke up to support despite what had seemed as unanimity at earlier meetings. Tension in the air was heavy and the meeting adjourned shortly after. Later that week the Taiwanese firm terminated negotiations on the joint venture.

How could you help Chris understand this situation.

Malaysia and Brunei

Hidup di dunia biar beradat,
budi bahasa bukan dijual beli

(When living in the world be disciplined;
manners or politeness cannot be bought and sold.)

Malaysia

General background

Malaysia is split into two parts: Peninsular Malaysia, a long peninsula extending south below the tip of Thailand, with Singapore at the southern extremity, and East Malaysia, formed from the states of Sabah and Sarawak, separated by the Sultanate of Brunei on the northern coast of the island of Borneo.

Politics

Malaysia is a federal parliamentary democracy of thirteen states with its capital at Kuala Lumpur. A king (sultan) chosen for a five-year term, from among the hereditary state rulers, is head of the federal state, but has mainly ceremonial powers.

UMNO, the Malay political party, has dominated politics for over forty years. There tends to be an authoritarian tendency in the government, mainly to ensure that religious and communal tension is well under control, given the needs to balance the interests and demands of fundamental Malay Muslims against the moderate Malay Muslims, and the sizeable Chinese and Indian minorities. Memories of the 1969 race riots still haunt Malaysians. However, the current economic downturn caused by the currency problems of 1997/98 is unlikely to result in ethnic tension as all groups have gained over the past decade (unlike Indonesia), and there is no wish to rock the boat and destroy the benefits.

Economy

After independence in 1957 the general policy was to encourage businesses owned by *bumiputras*, or indigenous Malays, in order to develop the country and counter the entrepreneurial activities of the indigenous Chines and Indians who were dominating the economy. The current economic crisis has now forced the government to suspend the twenty-eight year old affirmative action program favouring Malays. This change now permits other races to buy into Malay firms to stop them going bankrupt.

Malaysia has access to willing cheap immigrant labour (mainly Indonesian, Thai and Bangladeshi), but is relatively short of indigenous skilled workers and managers with technical training and higher education due to extremely rapid growth, particularly in the computer/electronics areas.

Free trade zones have been established throughout the country to encourage the establishment of manufacturing enterprises with special concessions granted to export-oriented industries. A new Multi Media Corridor complete with a hightech city and new airport is currently being built to the west of Kuala Lumpur to become the Silicon valley of Southeast Asia. The island of Labuan has been designated a duty free financial and investment zone. While Malaysia has not been hit as hard as Korea, Thailand and Indonesia by the economic melt-down, due to lower levels of cronyism and more circumspect bank lending policies, a number of major developments are being slowed or not started.

Society and culture

Ethnicity

Malaysia, with a population exceeding 19 million and a labour force of over 7 million, has often been described as a 'minefield of multicultural sensitivities', due to its diverse racial and ethnic composition. There are three main ethnic groups: Malays (60 per cent), Chinese (30 per cent), and Indian (9 per cent). There are also several dozen small groups of indigenous peoples, fiercely proud of their ethnic identity and language, particularly in Sarawak and Sabah, which adds to the ethnic complications. As a result, *Bahasa Melayu* or English have to be used when dealing with another ethnic group.

The Indian community consists of a few middle class persons and a plethora of labourers. The positive discrimination towards Malays for jobs, contracts etc. has had negative effects on the development of the Indian community.

The Chinese community, like their counterparts all over the world, has been extremely successful commercially, and, demonstrating a stronger work ethic than the other ethnic groups, has focussed myopically on its business interests, particularly within the context of advancing the family firm.

Like its population composition, each workplace is culturally diverse. While Japan and Korea are mono-ethnic, homogenous, high power distance cultures, and the multicultural West is driven by values of individualism and achievement, Malaysia is a mixture of both, being multi-ethnic and achievement-oriented, yet also extolling high power distance and a national collectivism. Hence, in undertaking business ventures there an overseas business person or expatriate manager must be quite sensitive to the cultural diversity and base plans on harnessing a synergistic blend of the best from all the groups in the country.

Malaysia is a transitional society where traditional ways co-exist with a booming technological communications world. There remain very strong tradition-bound values such as filial piety and respect for hierarchy. An overseas business person therefore has to demonstrate a genuine attempt to understand these complexities and use the diversity as a strength rather than a weakness.

Religion

Religious practices play a significant role in the daily life of Malaysians. These practices must not be interfered with, nor attempts made to put your business needs ahead of your counterparts' religious requirements. Most of the Malay population follows the state religion of Islam. Consequently Friday tends either to have a very long lunch break to permit attendance at obligatory Friday prayers, or is a totally non-working day, depending on which state you are in. It is therefore not a good idea to plan meetings for Fridays. Moslems are also required to pray five times each day. One of these prayer times falls in the middle of the afternoon working session and it is imperative that those with whom you are conducting business, and employees of any locally-based Malaysian office, are permitted to absent themselves from work for a short time. Many larger companies provide prayer rooms (two—one for men, and one for women) so that staff can retire there at the appropriate time without having to leave the building.

During Ramadan, the fasting month when Moslems may not eat or drink during daylight hours, work effort and motivation declines since they try to preserve their energy. Often the working day is cut short for them during this month. During this period also, government departments are often undermanned and it is difficult to obtain permits, documents etc.

Most of the Indian community practice Hinduism. They believe in pre-destination or karma, and that their reincarnation will depend very much on their conduct in the present life. Most Hindus begin their day's activities with prayers to deities. Small Indian businesses often display pictures of deities in their work locations. The Chinese typically display a mixture of Buddhist and ancestor worship with Confucian values of obedience and family loyalty underpinning their value system. There are large pockets of Christians in Sarawak and Sabah among the Iban and Dyak peoples. With this heterogeneity of beliefs, the constitution guarantees freedom of religion.

The holiday period associated with each religious celebration also bites into the working year. The Moslems have a good week of feasting and house visiting at *Hari Raya* to mark the end of the Ramadan fast; the Chinese celebrate their New Year with gusto and the Hindus enjoy their *Deepavali*. These, added to the global shutdown over Christmas and New Year add up to an interrupted business year.

Some common cultural values

Each ethnic group in Malaysia has a rich and distinct culture based on age-old beliefs, traditions and practices that are mainly rooted in the Asian heritage. Yet in this diversity, Malaysians work in apparent harmony and unity brought about by a few unifying factors, the most important of which are common values discussed below.

Respect for age, seniority and social hierarchy (high power distance)

Respect for elders is common across all ethnic groups. Leaders are often considered as 'wise elders' and their authority is usually unquestioned and unchallenged. Subordinates often show their respect by allowing the most senior and experienced staff to speak first and set the tone for a meeting.

Leadership is accepted as a norm of Malay society—the *Sultan* is head of state, the *penghulu* is kampong headman, father (*bapa*) is head of the family.

In social conversation there are specific honorific terms used for each family member depending on their age and rank within the family. For example, there are a variety of words and phrases for 'you' when speaking to persons of different status and age. Malays will often affectionately use these terms with friends and workers. Malays rarely refer to family members by just their first name, unless the family member is a child.

Closely related to respect for elders, Malaysians are also conscious of the social hierarchy in their society. Honorifics are used to denote social status, levels of authority and wealth. It is always valuable to ask a Malaysian how to address any particular very senior Malaysian at a meeting since using the correct form of salutation indicates good manners and an understanding of the cultural prerogatives. Doing it right will enhance your social standing, acceptability and personal contacts whilst doing it wrong may cause the other person to be slighted, affecting a potentially useful relationship with a person of importance.

Like Chinese elsewhere, Malaysian Chinese hold the status of family as of utmost importance. The head of the family is considered the leader. A local idiom states: 'In a family of a thousand, only one is the Master'. The hierarchical reference is clearly evident where reverence is shown by hanging portraits of deceased elders at the praying altars among the traditional Chinese and in the customary ancestor worship. Besides respect for elders, the Chinese also place in high esteem the educated and wealthy businessmen who support and help their clans through associations and guilds.

Collectivism ('we' orientation) and co-operation

Malaysians, regardless of ethnicity, are highly group-oriented. This translates into a willingness to prioritise group interests over individual concerns. Real identity comes from belonging to a collectivity or group. Hence, fulfilling obligations to family members, close relatives, friends and the work team is very important.

The need to be part of a group is often expressed in a desire for a strong support system in the form of a 'big brother' or 'big sister' mentor from whom advice and support can be sought. If you are an ex-pat manager or even in a visiting capacity you will find yourself being sought after by counterparts and your staff, not only in a deferential way, but in an honest attempt to gain your advice/expertise/support and know that you are there for them. This mentor role can also serve as an emotional valve for staff who are not comfortable in communicating their worries/frustrations/need for help on the job to their local supervisors directly. It also assists newcomers assimilate into the workplace. They feel happy in their work and secure if others in the organisation—especially their superiors—are aware of them, understand their situation, treat them fairly and assess them accurately.

You will find that Malays will work far better in a team environment/ spirit which gives them a sense of belonging, opportunities to receive respect from fellow colleagues and harmonious, predictable and enjoyable friendships with subordinates and peers. They do not find it easy to separate professional affairs from personal life. A relationship is a total relationship, whether at work or in a social situation.

Loyalty

This value links with the acceptable authoritarian style of management and paternalism. Employees are loyal and tend to act deferentially and obediently towards their elders/superiors. The overseas business person is perceived generally as a superior/expert and will find that counterparts as well as lower level staff will show respect and deference. However, this apparent status comes at a cost. If you are involved in a joint venture or other long-term business arrangement you will have thrust on you, without choice, a moral obligation for colleagues' and employees' general welfare, in return for loyalty and commitment during your period of operation in Malaysia. In many businesses, employees are considered as members of an extended family and the employer a good parent who will protect them. Malaysians live in a complicated web of kinship ties based on the concept of mutual and traditional obligations within relationships in family, kampong, state or social group. It is likely that an employee who has a good relationship with their manager/ supervisor will also be loyal to the organisation.

Harmony, non-assertion and non-aggressiveness

The Asian virtues of humility, reserve, modesty and consensus result in Malaysians of all ethnic groups being perceived by Westerner business persons as subservient and timid. They prefer compromise to confrontation, seeking consensus and harmony in business dealings to avoid damaging self-esteem or face. Open public criticism and outspokenness are rare as are overt displays of anger and aggressive behaviour. An aggressive, 'go-getting' and 'take charge' kind of overseas person may be perceived as brash, rough and insensitive, clearly threatening preferred social harmony, and can cause employees/counterparts to be withdrawn and non-contributory. Malaysians consider frankness and directness as inconsistent with respect. Tolerance and understanding count more than legalistic and rationalistic arguments based on objectivity.

Malaysians tend to respect those who come across as nurturing, caring and supportive elders in their tone of voice, the expressions they use and the postures they take when communicating with subordinates. Shouting or raising one's voice is usually frowned upon and considered rude or improper (*tidak manis*). In the Malay social milieu a person who comes across as too direct, even to the point of being terse, is often thought of as lacking proper breeding.

Malaysians are extremely dedicated to doing a good job. They are eager to please and find it difficult to say 'no' or insist on their rights. The values of humility, modesty and politeness prevent the projection of self-confidence. Thus they are less articulate and assertive than overseas peers in Singapore or the West, and less forthcoming, even uncomfortable in expressing opinions, when it involves evaluating peers and subordinates. Communicating feelings and ideas to others, and giving and receiving praise makes them feel ill at ease. As direct criticism is rare, it is taken over-seriously when it is given.

However, this behaviour may be perceived differently by an overseas business person whose culture stresses informality, directness (low context) and verbal expression of emotional feeling in language. Being used to subordinates or trainees speaking up and even challenging their ideas, they may interpret the Malaysian value of respect for rank, age and expertise as a sign of lack of confidence or disinterest.

Malaysians are often indirect in responding to difficult questions. They may make a point, elaborate on it and then go off at a tangent. Westerners who are used to direct and linear communication may find Malaysians rather 'circuitous' in their ways. In actual fact, Malaysians are aware of what they are doing, but prefer to take time to establish relationships with those they interact with.

Malaysians tend to mask their emotions with a smile, giggle, or laugh when they are shy, nervous, confused or embarrassed. Some may not even establish eye contact with the person with whom they are communicating, because doing so may be construed as rude or disrespectful.

Preserving face

Preserving face (*jaga maruah* in Malay or *lien mentzu* in Chinese) has considerable significance in the various cultures of Malaysia and by extension into the business world and workplace. As relationships are personalised, face is important and needs to be preserved because of the overriding aim of maintaining social harmony and cordial relationships.

Face therefore prevails as a form of an ongoing sensitivity. Preserving another's face is part of good manners and proper civilities. Putting on a face means concealing or at least 'prettying' up how one really feels. You must learn to save the face of another by delaying a negative reply, not communicating negative feedback or embarrassing the other in any way. This means thinking about what you are going to say or do all the time in terms of its effect on the face of others, for if face is preserved, interpersonal relations will be smooth, and harmony and respect will be maintained. However, once a person loses face they may totally withdraw from the interaction or business activity altogether. If you are running into contentious issues, employ the services of a third party as a go-between to handle the problems. Your approach will be respected as an attempt to maintain good relations, and will usually lead to a resolution acceptable to both, for of course your Malaysian counterparts will be trying just as hard not to make you lose face. As the individual is part of a family and a group (work team for example), embarrassing them would also embarrass family, group and community.

Generally subordinates will not argue with the boss, in case the latter loses face. For the same reason, a subordinate will pretend to understand instructions given by the superior for fear of being thought stupid and will usually not ask for help if they do not understand or refer back when problems arise.

Good manners and courtesy

All Malaysians engage in and tolerate elaborate forms of courtesy and standardised rituals which are calibrated according to the rank of the recipient, and the formality of the occasion. They tend to be very cordial and polite in making their requests and conveying disappointment when dealing with authority or those from overseas who are deemed to carry authority by virtue of their obvious expertise and qualities. Why else would they have been sent or decided to come!

A person who does not demonstrate proper and refined behaviour, but persists in coarse (*kasar*) and impolite behaviour, is therefore insensitive to the dignity of others and often described as poorly educated (*kurang ajar*) and behaving like an animal—which is very insulting to Malays. Calling seniors or elderly people by their first names is considered ill-mannered, especially if they have been conferred titles, as many successful business and political personages have. It is not uncommon for young Malaysians to address elders and overseas visitors as 'Uncle', 'Auntie', 'brother' or 'sister', rather than 'sir' or '*tuan*'.

Trust and relationship building

There is a strong preference for a relationship-oriented approach rather than a task-oriented approach. Developing trust and partnership understanding are more important than the contractual obligation of getting the job done. There is a tendency to deal with problems, difficulties and uncertainties by using the indirect approach of a third party. Bad news becomes more palatable to the recipient when communicated through a respected party, and the relationship can be maintained. Truth may often come off second best in the drive to preserve harmony. Avoidance is the preferred mode of solving conflicts. As a result, an intermediary is also useful to make first contact with a prospective client, for established goodwill and trust count a lot.

Underlying religious values

Most Malaysians (Islamic, Hindu and Buddhist) identify with a Supreme Being. They believe that happiness comes through self discipline and from suppressing self-interests for the good of others or discovering it from within oneself through prayers and meditation. Contentment is obtained through religious and spiritual pursuits, with a strong belief in fate rather than proaction. It is difficult for Malaysians to relate to self-actualisation needs without taking into consideration the needs of others, especially their loved ones. A person who is individualistic may even be ostracised by the family. Because of this, Malaysians tend to take a stance which is likely to be considered as reactive rather than proactive, although the notion that hard work brings success is rapidly gaining ground, as the work ethic becomes more widespread along with materialism.

Communication guidelines

There are a number of guidelines which will help you in your interactions with the multi-ethnic Malaysian business world and workforce.

Speak interculturally

If you will be working there for some time or making regular visits, learn to speak interculturally by code-switching and code-mixing. Being able to mix a bit of local language with the English language as locals do in the urban areas of Malaysia, is one way of building rapport, relationships and facilitating intercultural understanding. Communication in several ethnic languages (or dialects) all at once is common in a multiracial business organisations. For example 'Let's go for *makan*' (Let's go and eat), '*Boleh datang* do overtime *tak*?' (Can you do overtime?), or 'meeting time *hari ini fix tak*?' (Have you fixed the time for today's meeting?) . This language mix is a strategy to establish rapport and a sense of shared identity with the recipient in a multi-ethnic context.

Share common grounds

Engage in social pleasantries before getting down to business to facilitate the flow of conversation and enable both parties to assess one another. In business, Malaysians like to know who they are working with, as trust is an important consideration—so details related to the business do not often take first priority. Conversations about the family, company or current events are often used to warm up relationships and establish familiarity.

Speak respectfully

Use a person's title in both written and oral communication, especially when relating with individuals of higher social status. Respect is shown by the marked emphasis on politeness and decorum, especially towards elders.

When making written requests to elders, junior employees will often ask them to 'consider' doing certain things and superiors should 'request' them to complete a task. Forceful imperatives (e.g. 'You must', or 'You are required') are considered impolite. The more subtle passive voice shows respect and to a Malaysian provides exactly the meaning conveyed by more brutal direct English. For example, 'May we suggest', or 'It would be appreciated . . .' are not inferred in Malaysia as a sarcastic barb but show respect. It may be advisable to precede any requests with phrases like: 'May I ask you a question?', 'Please don't be angry with me if I were to comment . . .', 'May I say something?'

Malaysians generally prefer to associate and do business with those who are accommodating and easy to get along with, not argumentative. Those who use a gentle tone of voice together with appropriate body postures, with a sincere desire to promote harmonious relationships, will normally gain considerable respect.

Indirect communication

There is a tendency for Malaysians to be indirect when solving a difficult issue relating to team members. In the attempt to use an indirect mode of communication the intent is often precluded by talking about a different issue and then carefully 'steering the discussion' to focus on the issue at hand. For example, an ex-pat manager should start the conversation on general issues before touching on the poor performance of the team (don't single out an individual) in a particular instance. This approach is considered more palatable to the receiver because it comes across as less threatening, saves face and does not disrupt or threaten team spirit.

Use of English

To Malaysians, English is a language of prestige, having been the language of administration during the colonial era. Being fluent in both spoken and written English is commonly the criterion for entry into a multicultural or global workplace. In other cases it could be a prerequisite for purposes of promotion. English remains the language which accords social status and elitism.

Due to the spread of satellite television, videos/CDs and Internet, the younger generation is increasingly exposed to Western values and English. The government is now emphasising the importance of the English language as an avenue for development. The older generation who lived under British rule are often fluent in English. Most educated business people speak English quite well.

Leadership

An expatriate manager should act somewhat paternalistically, behaving like a caring parent or wise elder who understands the needs and concerns of subordinates. Malays support and work hard for a leader who is caring and in whom they can place their trust. There is a moral component in the relationship between employers and employees which is similar to the relationship of a child with the extended family. There are mutual traditional obligations; on the side of the employer, protection of the employee, almost regardless of the latter's performance; on the side of the employee, loyalty towards the employer. This 'father and son' relationship can also be seen between a superior and a subordinate of the family or small businesses among the Chinese and Indians in Malaysia.

Through frequent face-to-face interactions, ex-pat manager–local subordinate ties will be built and the latter will feel a sense of belonging. Being seen to have a non-confrontational and compromising leadership style can help create a conducive environment where employees feel happy to come to work. Solidify relationships between employees by communicating vision and targets to be achieved on a group basis. Standards, if set, must be done by the group as their potential remains very much in their ability to function collectively.

Encourage co-operative ventures among employees so that they learn to work and support each other on both work and non-work matters. For all groups it is important that the manager attends functions when invited by their subordinates, even if it is just dropping by for a while. Or else send a representative such as spouse or an adult child. Personal visits, gifts and cards should be sent when close members of the family are hospitalised. Togetherness can be promoted by doing things such as eating together or entertaining, with the manager picking up the bill. It all promotes and emphasises the family group atmosphere.

Do not adopt an elitist attitude, but learn to be modest and humble. Avoid magnifying the difference in status by downplaying one's achieved symbols (car, big office, etc.) and reducing one's social and power distance from others. Managers have to create an atmosphere where subordinates feel comfortable to share their problems.

Motivating Malaysians

Malaysians of all ethnic groups have a strong affinity for group affiliation (families, friends, hometown (*kampung*) and if Malay, Islamic brotherhood). They derive their identity from being part of a collectivity in which traditional communal responsibility is cherished, hence the pursuit of self-esteem and self-actualisation is perceived as anti-social and even deviant behaviour.

They measure success in terms of rapport with family, friends and associates and are attracted by tangible rewards such as a piece of land, a house, pilgrimage to Mecca and a circle of friends and influential contacts. Each has an intrinsic value. They are secure when they are confident of receiving the respect of those they know. In corporate terms, they are also motivated if their job contributes to nation building. They respond better to efforts at productivity if they can see benefits accruing not only to the company but also to their family, community and nation.

Success among Chinese and Indian leaders is evident through their support for the family, clan or society. The Chinese will look for monetary rewards and would do their best when the needs of the family are provided for, while the Indians will be loyal towards the organisation that caters for their wellbeing and development.

Chinese philanthropists are highly respected, especially for their donation to education and religious institutions. However, as an individual, the Chinese are often modest in demonstrating their riches. When pressed for an answer they will describe their prosperity as *cukup makan* (enough to eat). The Chinese also believe that once success is achieved they will be able to acquire prosperity, thus ensuring a secure and happy future for the family.

However, this traditional communal responsibility (collectivism) is not as simplistic as it looks. Malaysians may be collectivistic within their own communities, but co-operation and trust is much lower with those in the outgroup, including overseas business persons, until the latter have developed a relationship such that it allows them access to the group.

Luckily, the work group or business entity is perceived as an ingroup, and most Malaysians are concerned to build and maintain good relationships with, and for whom they work. They are often contented at work if they have opportunities to show and receive appropriate recognition and respect from their superiors, peers and subordinates. For a Malay, it is the relationship with the manager that most determines motivation.

Thus in Malaysia, an overseas business person's power base must be both personal and positional. Credibility comes from perception of competence and in the manner they demonstrate their respect, trust and interest in their counterparts or employees. Personal decorum is a prerequisite for acceptance by subordinates as roles are modelled, not contracted, and the link between members of the organisation is more moral than calculating.

Given an environment conducive to group pride, and striving towards a common goal, team members are prepared to work beyond the call of duty. It is the motivation to be part of the group, to give loyalty and commitment to the leader and the task in hand, that enables the team to 'band' together. More important, it is the willingness and the spirit of 'give and take' that enables members to contribute their best efforts in order to accomplish the objective of the team, known as the spirit of *gotong-royong* meaning 'joining forces in carrying out a task'. When a mistake is detected, it is quickly rectified without putting the blame on one another. Instead the whole group will work to overcome the problem.

Working together to fulfil an external need can help 'push' members to work in unison. The government has formulated a 'Vision for the Year 2020' for the development of the whole country to which Malaysians all aspire and work towards vigorously.

Making contacts

Unlike other parts of Asia, you don't need an introduction in Malaysia, although an influential one will always help open doors. Your local counterpart is more likely to disclose more information about their company, products, and objectives if the third party is a trusted friend.

Unsolicited letters are also acceptable for smaller scale activities. But whatever approach you use, make sure that you know who the person or division is to deal with the type of activity, product or service you want to engage in. Try to preplan your meetings so that your schedule provides a measure of flexibility, as meetings can drag out sometimes in terms of Western standards, and in any case you will inevitably need to hold additional meetings and meet further contacts.

Given underlying ethnic issues, the likely success of your business endeavour may well hinge on which ethnic group you are negotiating or working with. In the government sector, but less so in the private sector, job offers and the selection of outside contractors, consultants, lawyers, accountants, bankers, and the like are underlain by ethnic considerations. Given the deliberate policy preference to develop Malay (*bumiputera*) businesses, it is an obviously wise, if unpalatable, decision to discriminate and appoint a local Malay as a partner. You may not wish to indulge in such practices and may want to seek the best arrangements for your organisation in the long term, irrespective of ethnicity, however this may cause subtle occasional impediments to arise when seeking permits etc. If you are interested in bidding on government contracts local Malay partners are mandatory. Again if using an agent you will find that a *bumiputera* agent will often get preferential treatment.

Meeting people

Greetings in Malaysia are essentially Western with a handshake, a warm smile, and a hello. Malays who are Muslim will touch their chest with their hand after a handshake to demonstrate that the greeting came from the heart. You are not expected to do that. Some conservative Muslim

Malay women may not wish to shake hands with a male, so don't pre-empt an expected reciprocation by sticking your hand out; wait until a hand is offered. If you are not offered a hand by a woman, give a slight bow of the head. Traditional Indian Malays may greet you with a *namaste*, which involves placing both palms together as in prayer at chest level and slightly bowing the head.

Names and titles—The polite system

Malaysians place considerable importance on names, titles and protocol. Titles must be used, as informality in using names is not acceptable. Malay Muslims use their given name as their first name and their father's given name as their last name. For example, if your name is 'Ali' and your father's name is 'Mohammed,' you would be called 'Ali son of Mohammed'. In Malay this becomes *Ali bin Mohammed*. For a female, *bin* is replaced by *binte* (i.e. daughter of) often abbreviated to *bte*. You do not need to use the entire name in a letter or conversation. For example, *Ahmad bin Ali* (Ahmad son of Ali) would be addressed in a letter as 'Dear Encik Ahmad'. Malays who have made the pilgrimage to Mecca (the *Haj*) are entitled to the prefix *Haji* (male) or *Hajah* (female) before their name. They should be addressed as such e.g. Haji Matussin or Hajah Rosnah. If you cannot remember the person's name it is quite acceptable to greet them as *Haji* or *Hajah* without any further name, as it is most likely they have been on the Haj.

Men with titles should be addressed as *Dato*, also spelled *Datuk*, followed by their given (first) name. It is similar to a British knighthood. For their wives use *Datin*. Common in Indonesia and Brunei as well, these titles are used for older and senior people and indicate respect. All members of Parliament are addressed by the honorific *Yang Berhormat*, sometimes abbreviated as 'Y.B.' in writing, which is the English equivalent of 'The Honourable'. They should never be addressed as 'you'.

For Malays, use *Encik* in place of Mr and their given name for men. Women are usually addressed by the prefix *Cik* in place of Miss or the prefix *Puan* in place of Mrs and the given name. Chinese names as usual start with the family name, so 'Sim Chee Kooi' should be called Mr. Sim. If the Chinese person has a Western name that will be placed first. If you are unsure how to address someone, politely ask them or their associate. For Chinese and Indian names as well as any others with family names, use the traditional Western salutations of Mr, Mrs and Miss.

The routine of presenting and exchanging business cards holds sway in Malaysia as elsewhere in the region. Typically they should be given and received with both hands. Never give or take with just the left hand, as Moslems consider this the 'unclean hand'. Read the card before storing it as a sign of respect. Your own business card should list your name plus job title, company name and even your major functional responsibility, as these all reflect status.

Women are not discriminated against as in Islamic societies in the Middle East and increasing numbers of women hold positions, sometimes quite senior professional ones, in the workforce. Women have always been well represented in the fields of medicine and teaching.

Nonverbal and verbal behaviours to be aware of

Appropriate body gestures in the communication process demonstrate one's humility and respect for the other person/culture. Nonverbal behaviours which you should remember are:

- Don't stand on or touch a prayer rug in a Muslim office or home.
- Don't forget to remove shoes when entering a Malaysian home.
- Always give recognition to an individual of high social status.
- Dress neatly and formally especially when meeting elderly folks.
- Never use the left hand to give or receive—it is the unclean hand.
- On most formal occasions it is considered very rude to cross your legs or put your feet up on the table or over the arm of a chair to reveal the sole to others. Showing the sole of your foot or your shoes is considered disrespectful and rude. Keep both of your feet flat on the floor and do not rest your foot on your knee.
- Never touch someone's head, as it is considered the spiritual part of the body.
- Standing with your hands on your hips implies anger.
- Beckoning should be done using the entire right hand with the palm facing down and the fingers pointing away from you, but moving toward you in a scratching motion.
- Pointing at inanimate objects should never be done with a finger, but rather with the thumb placed over the fist.
- Never make a fist and hit it against your open or cupped hand, for this is considered an obscene gesture.
- Never barge into someone's room without first announcing your arrival.
- Always remove your shoes when entering a mosque or Indian temple.
- Avoid the following verbal behaviours which are considered '*kasar*' (impolite or rough):
  - criticising another person publicly and causing them to lose face (*hilang maruah*);
  - using bad language, e.g. vulgarities in social conversation;
  - being blunt, outspoken and not diplomatic;
  - addressing elders without using proper pronominals and titles;
  - being insensitive to religious observances, e.g. making jokes about religious observances and food habits.

Getting down to business

Meetings

Meetings usually commence with small talk, particularly the first meeting. At subsequent meetings business will get under way a little quicker. You should talk about the enjoyable and interesting time you are having, what sightseeing you have done, your previous travels, and the weather. The sensitive subjects to avoid are religion, human rights, democracy-related issues and comments on the Prime Minister. Gifts are not expected at a first meeting, but something small with the corporate logo or a sample product is appreciated.

The Malays are hooked on rituals and ceremonies, so don't be surprised if an hour is 'lost' from a seminar, training course, or other meeting for an elaborate opening ceremony. Formal speeches of welcome from all and sundry in order of status, presentation of certificates of attendance, prayers, and food will all take precedence over the purpose of the meeting. This is seen by Malaysians as part of the hospitality and paying respect to those it is due. There will also be formal ceremonies at the end too.

Negotiation

While decision-making is not anywhere near as slow as in Japan or China, you are unlikely to receive quick decisions, or finalise transactions for large projects on the first trip, even with private businesses. Smaller projects may well come to a final decision after a series of meetings if you can spare the time for an extended visit. You should plan for at least two to three visits before business considerations will become serious. But all this depends on the ethnic group with whom you are doing business, as well as with the recognition and world placing of your organisation. Large, well-established international companies will find their passage smoother and quicker as they already have a large measure of credibility established. Unknown or smaller companies have to win their trust.

As Malaysia is a high power distance country with both Confucian and Moslem values that invoke hierarchical and authoritarian decision-making, there are few decision makers, particularly in family companies. Business decisions are arrived at in a very calculated approach, involving great attention to detail, analysis and research and deep thought. There is a high level of uncertainty avoidance, so that every attempt is made to avoid risk. This caution creates a reluctance to make difficult decisions, although decision-making often depends on the individual's international experience and status in their organisation. As a result, some decisions—even difficult ones—may be made quicker than expected. Overshadowing all this is the fact that Islamic Malaysians are fatalistic—if a deal is meant to occur then no matter what, it will. The Chinese are more entrepreneurial and astute; once a trusting relationship is established business often proceeds fairly rapidly if they see it is in their interests.

As maintaining face is an important element in relationship building, you must always be polite, courteous, never shout/lose your temper or embarrass your Malaysian counterparts in negotiations. You will rarely get a direct 'no' from a Malaysian, so if you think the rather obtuse answer you have just received implies a negative, then follow up with some indirect questions of your own to tease out the real situation. When a mistake is made, the Chinese are less likely to admit responsibility while a Malay and Indian business person will generally admit that they have made a mistake.

A trusting relationship and honour are the bases of creating a context for a successful business venture. While Malaysians find contracts quite acceptable, the contract may at times be interpreted by them as a malleable instrument which can be reshaped from time to time as circumstances dictate within a trusting business relationship. They prefer contracts therefore that are general rather than detailed so that any modifications can still lie within its covers.

Even though not much publicised, like the Thais and Koreans, some Malaysian business persons are likely to seek the advice of astrologers, *bomohs* (Malay witch doctors) and other occult fortune tellers before they make a decision. *Feng shui* factors will also affect decisions made by Chinese persons.

The social context of business

Dining out

Lunch and dinner are popular venues for conducting business. The breakfast meeting is rare as Moslem Malays will have been up since dawn, the first prayer time of their day. Overseas business women are expected to attend, while spouses and companions are always made welcome at these occasions. Meals, usually based round chicken, rice and/or pieces of meat, are sometimes served in large bowls or dishes, with everyone putting small portions on their plate. You will be provided with iced water or fruit drinks as alcohol is unlikely to be on offer in restaurants due to Islamic restrictions. There will be no pork products on the menu either. Do not drink or eat until your Malaysian host invites you to do so.

Should you be dining with Hindus, there will be no beef, but both they and the Chinese will eat pork and enjoy alcohol. Chinese restaurants are common in Malaysia, serving the usual range of dishes. In the major centres like Kuala Lumpur and Penang there are top class Western restaurants. The ethnic group with whom you are involved will affect what you are offered to eat and drink. You must be very careful in inviting your Malaysian colleagues or counterparts for an evening out as a result of these cultural food requirements and restrictions. You must never take Islamic Malays to a Chinese restaurant that has no *halal* food. When among the Malays and Indians, do not pass food or drinks with your left hand.

At Malay social gatherings , men may be split off into one group and women into another—even in different rooms. Occasionally meal tables at dinners will be allocated by sex so that all the men are at certain tables and the women at others. This can be a bit uncomfortable for married overseas couples who would normally sit together.

If you or one of your accompanying colleagues can play golf, you will be in a favoured position as golf outings have become an important activity for building business relationships in Malaysia.

The invitation home

It is rare for a Malaysian to invite business associates to their homes. You will be an honoured guest if that happens. The most likely occasion for that is at Hari Raya, the great feast and holiday period that marks the end of the month-long Ramadan fast. Most Moslems hold open house at this time and all your contacts/counterparts will invite you to visit them. These invitations should not be turned down, even if you end up on a Cook's tour, driving from one house to the next, tasting their offerings of food. Shoes should be removed before entering even though Malaysians hosts will not insist on it; the gesture is well appreciated and respectful.

When visiting a home, take a small gift, such as fruit, sweets, or cakes, and a token of your home country or firm. Malaysians will not open gifts in front of the giver. Remember not to give alcohol to a Malay, as most are Moslems and should not drink.

Giving gifts

While it is reported that corruption occurs in Malaysia, it is not always obvious to overseas persons. Leave these sensitive matters to your local representative or partner and keep it at arm's length.

While gift giving is not of the proportions found in Japan and Korea, because of Malaysia's mix of ethnic groups and religions, each having specific 'no-no's', normal gift giving can be quite difficult. White flowers, clocks, watches and knives all have negative connotations for the Chinese (see p. 55, chapter 2). You may receive an expensive and elaborate gift from your Chinese associate. Remember there may be pay-back time for this in terms of a favour of some sort. Don't give Islamic Malays alcohol or pork items. Be careful not to give an item to a Muslim that could be considered offensive, such as a calendar depicting scantily dressed females or famous Christian cathedrals. Omit a gift rather than risk offending your counterpart, although a somewhat bland company pen or some other gift with the logo will cause no harm. For Indian business people, items ending in 1 or in odd numbers are considered lucky. Gifts should always be given and received with both hands and never opened in the presence of the giver.

What to wear

For business meetings, the standard Western business attire is appro-priate—a suit and tie for men; a suit, dress, or blouse and skirt (not too short) for women. The Malaysians are far more casual at evening events when a short-sleeve colourful shirt without tie, and trousers are appro-priate except for the most upmarket restaurants. Women can wear trousers for casual situations. Yellow coloured dresses and/or skirts should be avoided as these are the royal colours. White denotes bereavement and mourning. A woman should never wear anything too revealing as the Muslim dress code for their own females is quite conservative and the less revealed the better. The preference is for even Western women to have their arms and legs covered to well below the knee.

Language

The official language is *Bahasa Melayu* (Malay). The official second language is English, which is spoken throughout the country by members of different ethnic and linguistic groups. Various Chinese dialects and Tamil, a language from southern India, are widely spoken in their respective communities. Bahasa Malayu is also spoken in Brunei and Indonesia although there are some minor variants in spelling and grammar, and different names for a few things like those differences found between standard English and American English.

Major holidays

January 1	New Year's Day
January/February*	Chinese New Year
December/January*	Ramadan (lasts a month)
January*	Hari Raya Puasa (feasting at end of Ramadan month)
May 1	Labour Day
May 6	Wesak Day
June/July*	Prophet Mohammed's Birthday

June 5	King's Birthday
June 21	Awal Muharram
August 31	National Day
early November*	Deepavali
December 25	Christmas Day

*These holidays are based on the lunar calendar and the date changes annually.

Brunei

General background

Politics

Brunei Darussalam lies on the northern coast of Borneo in the South China Sea. It is surrounded by the Malaysian state of Sarawak and one part—Temburong—is split off from the rest by a part of Sarawak. The capital is Bandar Seri Begawan.

Brunei received full independence from Britain in 1984. Since then, Brunei, or rather its hereditary autocratic monarch, Sultan Hassanal Bolkiah, and family, has quietly amassed enormous wealth through oil and gas industries, and overseas investments. The Sultan, along with family members and trusted courtiers, rules the country in a feudal manner, maintaining tight control. No criticism of his Islamic monarchy is permitted, with press and media censored. Parliament has not sat since its dissolution in the mid-1960s, and the emergency regulations proclaimed then to counter the Malaysian communist uprising have never been revoked.

Economy

Brunei has tremendous wealth in the form of gas and oil, extracted and sold mainly by Brunei Shell Petroleum. However, much else has to be imported. Due to the surplus revenue accumulated during the oil-boom decades, Brunei became an exporter of investment capital.

Lower world oil prices have resulted in decreasing revenues from the petroleum sector at a time when government policy has slowly reduced production to conserve this most valuable resource. Industries, such as fish farming, agriculture, forestry, tourism and financial services, have been developed to diversify the economy. The country plans to become the hub for trade and tourism in the region.

With one of the highest per-capita incomes in the world, Bruneians are income tax free. Their wage levels are the highest in the region while benefits such as pensions, free medical care, free schooling, free sports and leisure centres, interest free loans and subsidies for homes, cars, and religious pilgrimages (the Haj) to Mecca add icing to the cake. The infrastructure of dual carriage ways, upgraded power systems, and massive high rise apartment blocks and hotels continues to develop at a rapid rate.

Society and culture

The population of Brunei is about 300 000, the majority of whom are Islamic Malay (69 per cent); Chinese (18 per cent), indigenous peoples (5 per cent). Indians, Europeans, and other ethnic groups (8 per cent) complete the mix.

Islam is the state religion but religious freedom is tolerated, allowing Buddhists and Christians to follow their creeds. The Bruneian people tend to be very conservative, but are also warm, friendly, and hospitable.

The tourist industry is only just beginning, essentially focussing on eco-tourism (the flora and fauna of equatorial rain forests) and therefore Brunei has not been spoiled. However, it is impossible not to notice symbols of modern material success—expensive cars, homes, electronic appliances, and satellite dishes.

Getting down to business

Making contacts

Here, as elsewhere in Asia, introductions from respected third parties facilitate potentially useful contacts. It is critical to contact the right person in the company or ministry, otherwise a lot of time will be lost as the wheels of business and public service bureaucracy turn slowly in Brunei. Your initial contact, even if the correct person, may not reply speedily. Motivation is not high as the bread and circus mentality pervades. The handout of subsidies and the quality of life that is obtained without too much effort makes motivation a limited expenditure.

Your calm manner, polite and pleasant demeanour, and inevitable patience will be essential in succeeding in Brunei. Shouting, harassing others for action, and assertiveness will not pay off. You will be ignored, or made to wait even longer.

If you wish to set up a business in Brunei you must have a Brunei partner, even if of the sleeping kind (they will still want to be paid, of course). You also have to engage by law a local representative or agent if you are going to do business there. Some business people base their regional business in Singapore or Malaysia in order to minimise costs, and then only appoint a Brunei-based representative.

Meeting people

Much of the material in the section on peoples and culture in Malaysia is also applicable to Brunei. Brunei is however more focussed on, and more strict in its application of the Islamic way of life. There is a great stress on honorifics, titles and status, producing a highly structured society with a prescribed pecking order. It is seen as insulting to introduce a person without their correct titles. This poses a difficulty until you become familiar with the very complicated social hierarchy and a whole raft of 'nobility' with extremely long titles. Your hotel or the embassy/consulate can help you. It is best not to consult with a Bruneian, who may regard your ignorance of their culture as an insult. Appearing to know the social structure is very important. For everyday people, you place *Awang* (Mr) before the man's given name and *Dyang* (Mrs) before the woman's given name, e.g. Awang Ali or Dyang Rohani. The title *Haji* and *Hajah* precedes the name of those who have been to Mecca and should always be used. The male Hajis are distinguished by wearing a white cap.

Punctuality is not a prime characteristic of Bruneians, although if you are behind schedule, you should make sure to inform the people you are intending to meet, as they will see it as a reflection of your opinion of them. A handshake with a male counterpart is usual, but Brunei Malay women usually do not shake hands. Always refrain from any physical contact with Malay Islamic women. As usual with the Chinese, the family name comes first and they are best addressed by placing Mr or Madame in front of it. The business card routine occurs at the first meeting and is quite acceptable in English only, as most educated Bruneians can understand and use English.

Do not cross your legs when sitting Both your feet should remain flat on the floor and the sole of your foot should never face anyone nor should your foot touch anyone. Never touch a Bruneian on the head as it is considered the most spiritual part of the body. In fact it is better not to have any physical contact at all. Beckoning is done by using the whole hand with the palm facing the floor and the fingers pointing away from you, but moving toward you in a scratching motion. Point using the thumb placed over the fist.

Start the conversation with casual topics such as the steamy heat, the beauty of the mosques, your recent travels etc. Topics which should not be raised are the wealth of the Sultan, news reports in the foreign press about the activities of the 'local royals', democratic rights, religion, and/or what will happen when the oil runs out. It is not expected or appropriate to present a gift on the first meeting as this could be considered a bribe, although a simple item with company logo or sample product would not go amiss. Leave presents until the relationship is firm or at the conclusion of your business activity. After your meeting a follow-up letter should be sent to demonstrate your appreciation and interest.

The Bruneians are more into ritual and tradition than the Malaysians, so be prepared for most large formal meetings (particularly those involving government officials), seminars, etc., to start and end with speeches, maybe a prayer, and not get down to business very quickly. They love ceremony.

Negotiation

It is very important to establish contact with the appropriate ministry for government-related issues and with the right level of bureaucrat, for only the most senior people have decision-making authority. Overseas business persons must take the time to develop trust and to establish a good relationship with potential partners. Bruneians often take a long time to make decisions due to the many layers of the country's bureaucracy, a form of disguised unemployment to ensure all Bruneians have a job. Therefore, do not expect a decision on your first trip. There is little sense of urgency as time is more a framework than something to be mastered.

Bruneians are very conservative. It is important to maintain a calm, non-confrontational and polite composure throughout the negotiation process. Always try to preserve harmony. Allow all parties the opportunity to save face in the event of difficult decisions. Angry outbursts are frowned upon, as is public criticism. Bruneians may not say 'No' directly, so you will need to ask indirect questions to assess a situation.

Legal contracts are written out in detailed form. Once a decision has been made and a contract written and signed by both parties, that contract will be honoured and rarely changed. A gift of high quality would be appropriate at the end of negotiations as you will certainly be the recipient of one.

The social context of business

Dining out

Bruneian food covers a wide range of most of the cultures found in Southeast Asia, including Malay, Chinese, Thai, Korean and Indonesian food. There are very few Malay restaurants; Muslim Bruneians tend to eat at home or buy ready cooked at food stalls and take it home. Because the Chinese enjoy eating out there are numerous Chinese restaurants. No alcoholic drinks will be served as Brunei is a Muslim country, although some Chinese restaurants and major hotels will allow you to take your own (a small amount is allowed in through customs for the personal use of non-Moslem travellers), and may serve it out of a teapot into a cup to disguise the contents. The Bruneians do not consider it appropriate to discuss business over a meal. They do, however, see social meetings at lunch or dinner as an opportunity to get to know one another. Breakfast meetings are very rare.

Be more sensitive to Islamic religious practices in Brunei than in Malaysia or Indonesia. For example, do not eat in public in the daytime during the Ramadan fasting period. Muslims do not eat pork nor do they drink alcoholic beverages. However, the Chinese do both. Muslim Bruneians eat only with their right hand. You will be given Western-style utensils and it is appropriate to use them. At Chinese restaurants chopsticks are automatically provided, but you can request a fork and spoon. No knives will be offered however. In Brunei, more so than in Malaysia, the sexes may well be separated at social events. Be prepared for your wife to be escorted to a different room or directed to a different table from you.

Home visiting

Unlike many homes in Asia, Bruneian homes are generally large, luxurious and oversupplied with bathrooms. However, it is very unlikely that you will be invited to a Bruneian's home early on. Gifts are not required when visiting a home. If you wish to give a gift, remember that it is inappropriate to give Muslims anything containing pork, gelatins from unspecified fats, or alcohol. Suitable items include souvenirs from your home country, decorative items, expensive chocolates, and sweets. For the Chinese, refrain from giving clocks, knives, or white flowers, as mentioned previously. A follow-up thank-you letter after a visit is usually appropriate.

Giving gifts

There is little or no corruption or bribery in Brunei. Most Bruneians in senior positions are extremely well off and don't need to resort to bribery to enjoy a good standard of living. Bruneians do not exchange gifts as rigidly and methodically as do people in some other Asian cultures. For normal gift-giving situations at the end of negotiations etc, tasteful and elegant gifts are appreciated, e.g. expensive cut glass. The problem with giving a gift to a senior Bruneian is that they usually possess most things anyway.

What to wear

The Brunei dress code for business is quite conservative. Women should wear dresses or suits that cover their arms and legs to well below the knees. The appropriate attire for men is a suit and tie. Jackets may be removed during meetings, but ties should not be loosened and shirts should be long-sleeved. Evening events are usually less formal in dress for men who usually wear open neck highly decorated shirts. Women still must dress in a way that limits the revelation of arms and legs although colourful attire (but not yellow—the royal colour) is acceptable.

Language

The official language is Bahasa Melayu (Malay) although there are a few different words and spellings. English however is widely used, particularly in business, and Mandarin is also spoken. Most educated Bruneians and Chinese have taken English A levels and studied at tertiary institutions in Australia, UK, New Zealand or North America. Therefore while accent can be difficult at times, verbal and written material in English will be well understood.

Major holidays

(In addition to the common Islamic religious holidays noted in section on Malaysia)

February 23	National Day
May 31	Armed Forces Day
July 15	Sultan's Birthday

Summary

- Malaysians and Bruneians are not time conscious and demonstrate a laid back approach.
- They value traditions, so it is not easy to introduce change.
- They are loyal to authority, indirect and friendly people.
- To achieve business success in Malaysia and Brunei, you should:
  - spend time to build relationships and trust between yourself and your counterparts and subordinates;
  - promote feelings of togetherness. Loyalty and pride of working in a team is highly motivating;
  - be humble in manner;
  - promote harmony in social relationships. Be seen to be tactful, diplomatic and respectful. Always display good manners;
  - create a family atmosphere in the organisation. Malaysians value family and family ties. The workplace is seen as a second home where members embody the spirit of living together in harmony.

- show respect for elders;
- as an elder you are regarded as having a moral obligation to care for your subordinates and colleagues;
- avoid confrontation. Maintaining harmonious relationships is vital for success in any endeavour as it involves the importance of face-saving;
- never single out an individual for blame or lavish praise, even though both may be justified;
- using third party intervention to solve problems in negotiations or within a work team. Tapping the resources and energies of a third party who is respected by both parties can help relieve 'strained' ties.

- Be aware of ethnic differences and sensitivities of team members so as to avoid dividing loyalties based on ethnic identification.
- The values of harmony, face and relationships require the adoption of an open and friendly approach towards counterparts and employees. The ideal behaviour for an expatriate business person is low key, compassionate and unhurried, calm, polite and pleasant, being a benevolent autocrat if in a management role, showing concern for the welfare of others and exuding trustworthiness, honesty, fairness, and generosity.
- Never publicly criticise or make fun of the Islamic religion.

Activities

Try working out the solutions to these three problems, then check your responses with those in Appendix B.

1 Nathan Zammet, a real estate developer from a well known holiday resort area, had made a 2:30 pm appointment with Mr. Abdul Halim, a business person in Kuala Lumpur, Malaysia. From the beginning things did not go well for Nathan. First, he was kept waiting until nearly 3:45 pm before he was ushered into Mr. Abdul Halim's office. And when he finally did get in, several other men were also in the room. Even though Nathan felt that he wanted to get down to business, he was reluctant to get too specific because he considered much of what they needed to discuss sensitive and private. To add to Nathan's sense of frustration Mr. Abdul Halim

seemed more interested in engaging in meaningless small talk rather than dealing with the substantive issues concerning their business.

How might you help Nathan deal with his frustration?

2   Bill Chen, an executive with an international insurance company, was sent to Malaysia immediately after a severe earthquake in the Indian Ocean, which had sent huge tidal waves onto the Western coast, severely damaging several coastal hotels and businesses his company had insured. Back home Bill had the reputation of being extremely affable and sociable. The day after Bill arrived in Penang, he met with Mr. Mohammed, the manager of one of the insured tourist hotels. His previous telephone conversations with Mr. Mohammed were positive and had led him to expect that Mr. Mohammed was interested in getting the claims settled quickly and efficiently. His initial meeting with Mr. Mohammed went extremely well, with both men agreeing on most of the issues discussed. At the end of that first meeting they shook hands, and to emphasise the depth and sincerity of his goodwill, Bill grasped Mr. Mohammed's hand with two hands and shook vigorously. For reasons that Bill never understood, the subsequent meetings with Mr. Mohammed were never as cordial and friendly as that first meeting.

What explanation might you give to Bill?

3. Herb Wilson was the sales manager for a large Australian meat wholesaler. His firm had been invited to tender for a large contract to supply frozen meat as little meat is produced locally in Brunei. He was welcomed warmly by Ministry officials when he arrived and was invited to commence his presentation soon after introductions had been made in view of the specific reason for his visit.

In addition to a short video of his companies operations, Herb distributed a glossy brochure that depicted the company and its diverse operations in the fresh and processed meat industry. There were many pictures of quality breeding animals (such as cattle, sheep, pigs) and poultry as well as pictures of the hygienic conditions in which animals and poultry were raised, slaughtered, processed and packed.

He believed that the committee would recognise the ability of his company to supply high quality meat products with a high degree of reliability. However, when Herb was asked if any special consideration was given by his company to the fact that the meat products were to be supplied to Brunei, Herb indicated that the same high standards of hygiene and quality control would be applied as for any of their markets and their would be no slackening in these standards simply because the meat was being exported.

The meeting fizzled out at that point and Herb never heard any more from Brunei.

Can you explain why?

Conducting Business in

Indonesia

General background

Indonesia is collection of over 13 000 islands, of which about half are inhabited. Sumatra, Java, Sulawesi, Kalimantan (southern Borneo), and Irian Jaya (western New Guinea) are the main populated islands. They are generally volcanic and very mountainous, covered by forest and jungle.

Political structure

Indonesia is undergoing major political change at the present time. Indonesia is nominally a democracy, however, despite the recent resignation of President Suharto, the new President (President Habibie) still wields considerable power. The military has always played a major role in politics, and is still guaranteed seats in parliament even under the proposed new constitution, while opposition parties and groups continue to have difficulty finding a forum in which they can voice their policies, apart from street protests. This context will continue to create instability until the proposed elections are set in train, and the consequent election of a new president and government is achieved in a more democratic way.

While there is an apparent increase in some political freedoms, for example, limited tolerance for criticism by the press, you should stay clear of making any political comment when in the country as there is no way of knowing who will win out or what the political views of your contacts are. You will certainly lose your potential business by being outspoken.

Indonesia is not officially an Islamic state although most Indonesians are Muslim. The Indonesian state promotes a philosophy as national policy called *Pancasila*, which advocates five principles:

- *One supreme God* This is consonant with Islam, Christianity and Buddhism. Although the bulk of the population is Moslem, all religions are protected in law. Communism is totally rejected.
- *Humanism* This involves treating all others as human beings; respecting and helping them.
- *National unity* The nation is placed above self-interest. The nation's welfare and progress must be the primary goals of individual and organisational activity.
- *Democracy* The rights of the citizens are respected.
- *Social justice* This emphasises fairness in rendering justice to all, regardless of status differences.

The focus is on economic growth and maintaining stability and harmony among the various ethnic and religious groups rather than the provision of political democracy.

The Repelita, the country's five-year business plan, is drafted by Bappenas, the National Development Planning Council, which is charged with economic planning, co-ordination, and implementation, and is accountable to the president.

Dutch law provides the basis for Indonesia's legal structure. However, international business laws relating to foreign investment companies, specialised industries, and taxation have recently been developed and are still going through teething problems. As a result, practical application can be difficult, time-consuming, and inconsistent.

Most of Indonesia's laws do not come from parliament but are presidential decrees which have the force of law. Such decrees carry far more weight than those emanating from other sources.

Economy

The Indonesian economy has developed considerably over the past twenty years. Up to the recent financial troubles of 1997–98 inflation was under control and economic growth steady. Indonesia has reduced its dependence on oil exports and diversified its economy in the last decade. But it still remains a relatively poor country with gross inequalities of income between urban and rural areas, and between different islands and ethnic groups.

Indonesia is rich in natural resources such as timber, petroleum products, rubber and textiles. Petroleum products account for about 40 per cent of foreign revenues. Agriculture, in some places still little above subsistence farming, remains a major sector of the economy and employs about half of the population. The manufacturing and service sector are being developed as the government encourages more private investment, industrialisation and diversification.

The dominant role of the Chinese minority in the business activities of the country is a sensitive issue. With increasing economic liberalisation and privatisation the majority Moslem Indonesians fear that they will be left out in the cold while the Chinese prosper and increase their control of the economy. Ethnic rivalry is always an underlying tension in Indonesia.

Indonesia has developed strong and favourable relationships with the IMF and the World Bank and in its current economic problems are starting to adhere to the requirements of IMF loans. This will reduce the dominating influence of the Suharto family on the economy and open up the economy to real competition.

Society and culture

Indonesia is the fourth largest country in the world with approximately 200 million people, most of whom live on Java where the capital Jakarta (pop. 8 million) is located. Despite having a number of very large cities, most people still live in rural areas. In Irian Jaya (western end of Papua) and remote parts of Kalimantan (Borneo), the local tribespeople have barely moved into the twentieth century.

Indonesians are primarily Malay, except in Irian Jaya where they are mainly Papuan. The Chinese form about 3 per cent of the population. Despite the Malay predominance, there are around 300 different ethnic groups with a wide variety of different subcultures, social structures and languages, because of the geographical spread of the population across many islands. The national language, Bahasa Indonesia, a variant of Malay, is compulsory in primary school. Ethnic identity is usually as important as national identity and used as the primary basis for building and maintaining relationships. Geographic and economic distinctions among the rural, coastal, tribal, and urban Indonesians further the country's heterogeneity.

Religion

Indonesia is one of the most populous Islamic nations with around 90 per cent being Sunni Muslim. The rest are mainly Christian (6 per cent—

mainly tribal Iban), and Buddhist (2 per cent—mainly in Bali). Due to the Hindu influence, the Balinese have a very fatalistic attitude. Religious freedom is guaranteed and tolerance is highly valued by Indonesians. Nevertheless, as elsewhere in the Islamic world, there has been pressure to move toward Islamic fundamentalism, and there have been a few clashes between ethnic and religious groups as some people feel threatened and ambivalent about modernisation. There is a requirement for all offices and buildings to have a prayer room. However, few Indonesians have embraced fundamentalism.

Social behaviour

Like Malaysia, Indonesia is a high power distance collectivist culture with a traditional hierarchical and honour-oriented society. There is strong ingroup loyalty encompassing family, friends, and members of the same ethnic group. This provides a basis for the favouritism so rampant within the economic structure. Traditionally Indonesians have valued large families with extended families living together, supporting and helping one another. However, the increasing urbanisation and the need to move to where jobs can be obtained is breaking up this interdependence and extended family living.

Harmony and respect prescribe the relations between people. Conflict is avoided while values and behaviour in all aspects of life are directed towards smooth relations with others. Indonesian society is characterised by concepts such as 'consultation, agreement and solidarity'. 'Follow my leader' or 'bapakism' (*bapak* = father) is a well-known expression for this behaviour, as people find it necessary to honour older people, and those of higher status have the role of fathers in an organisation. Suharto has survived on the basis of this value. Bapakism is based on ascriptive considerations such as age, seniority, wisdom and class. Within organisations, loyalty is more important than efficiency. It is the role of the 'bapak' manager to maintain harmony and they will use organisational assets to achieve this goal. Managerial authority and power do not stem from Western considerations of contract or appointment. Subordinates will therefore not make decisions, and there is a wait and see attitude for senior managers to reveal what the decision is.

Similarly, Chinese business organisations are mainly family concerns, with non-family members only acting as assistants. The usual Confucian ethics apply in Indonesia to the Chinese who follow the principles of filial piety, obedience and loyalty.

Thus whatever the ethnic group or size of the organisation, the basis of enterprise is usually the family under the rule of the bapak (father/father figure). Most of the larger organisations do have professional managers, but they only provide advice, with the decisions still emanating from the top. These managers have to manage the company professionally, yet achieve the owner's objectives, which may be fashioned by factors other than those normally associated with sound business decisions.

Indonesians, like most modern societies, have become quite materialistic. A person's status is no longer solely judged on their family name/position, but increasingly on personal and family wealth and achieved status. Modern Indonesians have generally been motivated by status, which in turn is expected to lead to wealth. Jobs in the government service and military were highly prized by university graduates. These jobs brought benefits of status and respect, plus wealth in the form of gifts and bribes from people seeking favours. Now, business and other professions are sought by graduates as high rewards and status through material benefits accrue from those positions.

The literacy rate in Indonesia is about 62 per cent. Many children do not stay on at school, particularly in the rural areas and poorer parts of urban areas. About one-quarter finish primary school, and around 16 per cent complete high school, while 3 per cent finally graduate from college. The development of education, technical and skills training is one of the primary objectives at present to prevent Indonesia being left behind in the global economy. School dropout is often due to children having to help out with farming tasks, and the need for payments demanded as inducement for students to gain entry to higher institutions, receive school tuition and even receive their final certificates. Even admittance to public universities can require an under the counter payment, even if the student has an excellent academic potential.

Although Indonesia is a Muslim country, there are numerous female professionals in Indonesian companies. Indonesian women are not discriminated against and enjoy the vote, can obtain divorce, drive a car, and inherit or acquire property. They are not required to wear veils and few do. One of the few concessions to the religion is the closure of businesses at midday on Fridays in observance of Muslim worship.

Making contacts

You should try to gain an introduction to the party you wish to meet. This will speed up arrangements for a meeting and lead to speedier discussion. Cold calling, even if successful, will lead to the first meeting only being spent on establishing credentials and developing trust. Always address your letter or fax requesting a meeting to the most senior person of the company. They will then assess who should see you, particularly in terms of the level you hold in your organisation or the specialist knowledge involved.

Personal connections are often more important than economic criteria in making government and business decisions. Having the right connections is so important that it can be quite difficult in some areas to access senior persons or gain a meeting without them. Connections usually start with a person's family and filter down to the Indonesian-Chinese business person you really need to meet. The need to have these connections and the practice of paying people a fee to arrange them is so persuasive that even the World Bank has an informal taxation category in its cost estimates for Indonesian projects. There is also an overt favouritism with well-connected firms being backed by state-owned banks to finance pet projects. With credit in short supply and high interest rates, this favouritism creates difficulties for other companies. However the recent economic problems of Indonesia have resulted in shonky banks being closed and favoured deals ceasing for the present. Now that Indonesian business is opened up to foreigners, corruption and inefficiency is declining as reform and modernisation is led by Western trained technocrats.

You will prosper better in your attempts to do business in Indonesia if you have been able to arrange through trade shows, or other professional contacts, some local partner, representative, or agent to serve as an intermediary. This partner can be an actual business partner or a consulting or trade firm that acts as a formal go-between. If you are committed to doing business in Indonesia, the presence of a well-qualified Indonesian with good English skills operating your representative office is a valuable asset.

Your local partner, representative or consultant must have the 'correct' political connections, which implies access to senior state and other officials. Connections with socially acceptable people will have an undue significant influence on business interactions. Unfortunately, family, friends and contacts may prove more important in a business relationship than the quality of the product or service being offered.

The Chinese business community control many of the country's businesses, and there is considerable animosity towards this small group who appear to have prospered at the expense of the Malay Indonesians. However, there is emerging an indigenous Malay business class termed *pribumi,* similar in character to the *bumiputra* business persons and traders in Malaysia. This *pribumi* group is being encouraged to counteract the Chinese dominance. Hence they are another useful entree into a business venture in Indonesia.

It is important to remember that doing business in the private sector is vastly different from doing business with the government. The private sector works at a reasonable pace, but negotiations with government can be very slow. When doing business with the government it is important to start with the relevant department and work your way to the top, building relationships and strategic alliances all the way so that when you do eventually reach the top that person has already been given very positive noises about you and your proposals. Your lobbying has been done for you.

Communciation guidelines

Meeting people

The best time of year to schedule business trips is between February and June, and again between September and early December. July and August tend to be a major vacation period for Indonesians who can afford to travel. On no account try to get stuck into some involved and detailed business discussions during Ramadan, which occurs over a period of four weeks sometime during December and January—when energy and focus are distracted by religious observances and fasting. In Bali it is best to schedule a morning meeting as people like to get work done early to avoid the afternoon heat.

As both Malay and Chinese Indonesians have great respect for age, status, and position you should be equally sensitive to those factors at meetings and social engagements associated with business. Defer to older more senior people by standing when they enter and letting them sit down first etc. If a particular meeting involves a very senior Indonesian (often the final meeting), it is seen as respectful that your organisation has a very senior person available to attend.

You should be punctual at all times even though your Indonesian counterparts may not be so. Indonesians often use the phrase *jam karet*, ('rubber time') as an excuse for lateness.

Indonesians generally shake hands all round and give a slight bow of the head. You should do the same. They will smile a lot during these introductions, but during meetings can use smiling not just as a sign of pleasure, but to reflect sadness, nervousness and embarrassment. So don't always assume that a smile is an indication of positive feeling or approval. The handshake is usually less strong than a Western one and on occasions very similar to the Malaysian handshake which often degenerates into a touch of the hands. Additionally, the Muslim influence can be noticed after the hand shake as Indonesians bring both hands back to the chest, as if to symbolise that the greeting is from the heart.

Most Indonesians often have just one given name. Older, socially superior, or politically higher Indonesians may be referred to courteously by preceding the name with *bapak* for men, which means 'father,' and *ibu* ('ee-boo') for females, which means 'mother'. Both are similar to the English Mr or Mrs. Traditionally, these terms were used only between Indonesians, but overseas persons who have developed a close relationship may use the terms. It is also acceptable and safe to use the English Mr or Mrs, or a title. Conversely, as an honorific and courteous title, some Indonesians may call you *tuan* or *nyonya*, in place of Mr or Mrs respectably.

You should exchange business cards immediately following the first greeting. Since status, credentials and titles are important to Indonesians, you should make the most of your position in the organisation, and your professional qualifications. Overseas business women are generally well received if they have status and qualifications. However, there still a few more traditional and conservative Indonesians who may not regard a woman as the suitable representative of an overseas organisation. This situation should not arise among better educated and qualified internationally-oriented Indonesian business persons.

Following the Malay Islamic manner, people who are rude, boastful, impolite, aggressive, or pushy are not respected. You will make your mark with an Indonesian and improve your chances of success with your endeavour if you show polite, well-mannered, refined, and respectful behaviour and additionally demonstrate an interest in the country and its language and culture.

During the first meeting and at the beginning of all later meetings, it is important to engage in polite social and general conversation. Suitable topics include the weather, your travels, your appreciation of some aspect of Indonesian culture, or common contacts. Unlike other Asian cultures where personal questions are not only permitted but expected as part of the getting to know you routine, such questions are not the done thing in Indonesia. So stay off questions regarding your counterpart's salary and perks or his material goods, such as his home or car, and they will not inquire about your situation either. Indonesians prefer to discuss their culture and their national sporting activities such as badminton, soccer, volleyball, tennis, and bicycling. If someone compliments you, do not simply reply 'Thank you'. It is important to be humble. Try to invoke self-effacing responses like 'Thank you, but it was very little/not very important/no effort'.

Never raise issues concerning internal politics, East Timor, bribery/corruption, religion, or Indonesia's internal ethnic troubles/divisions, as these can be sensitive topics. At the end of every meeting, it is appropriate to say *terimah kasi, sampai jumpa lagi* which means 'Thank you. I look forward to our next meeting'. This helps in building and strengthening a warm business relationship.

Some nonverbal behaviours to be aware of

- In general men go through doors first or sit down first at a formal gathering. The most senior person goes first, with others following in descending order of seniority.
- Crossing your legs is usually inappropriate, particularly in the presence of senior people. However, if you choose to cross your legs, do so only at the knee or ankle.
- Never prop one foot on the other knee. The sole of your foot should never face another person, as the soles of the feet or shoes are considered dirty.
- It is considered rude to sit on a desk or to prop your feet up on desks or tables.
- Never touch an Indonesian woman except for the initial handshake.
- Members of the opposite sex may walk hand-in-hand, but public contact between the sexes is minimal.
- The left hand should never be used in any situation.
- It is considered rude and threatening to point your finger. If Indonesians need to point to something, they use their thumb held over the fist.
- Don't stand with your hands in your pockets or on your hips as this signifies a sign of defiance or arrogance.
- Beckon by using the whole hand, palm facing down and fingers pointing away from you, but moving toward you in a scratching motion. Wherever possible, avoid beckoning anyone except for a taxi, a *becak* (pedicab), or a child.
- Do not pat anyone on the head, for Indonesians believe that this is where the spirit resides. Backs are considered private as well.
- Indonesians sometimes show approval by a pat on the shoulder, but it is better to refrain from this gesture.

Getting down to business

Corporate structure

In line with the culture, Indonesian businesses have a hierarchical nature, are centrally organised, with decisionmaking controlled by top management, usually the firm's founder or key family member. Given this authoritarian structure and sense of obligation to the patriarch, there is very little accountability or delegation of work. The concept of professional management was introduced by multinational corporations and is only slowly extending to local organisations. The training of Indonesian managers continues to be an important objective for most foreign companies. Traditionally, because there is a higher regard for a person's social background and ethnic group than their ability, selection of staff is often based on irrelevant criteria by Western standards. Social harmony is also valued more than work efficiency. Thus the introduction of managers qualified by ability and training is still a difficult task. Of course the criteria used by Indonesians are not totally irrelevant since background and connections are just as important in advancing the company's line as quality of service/product.

Take care in interpreting the financial viability of an Indonesian company with whom you may wish to link up or do business in some form. They often maintain two sets of books—one to present to the tax authorities.

There is a vast bureaucracy which is undertrained, underpaid and ineffective. Many are part-time in their attendance at work, going to another job in the afternoon to earn enough for basic living. Low salaries have also been an inducement to petty corruption.

Negotiation

Much Malay Indonesian business is conducted informally on the golf course and over lunches and dinners. This is due to the importance of family and ingroup within the culture. Business is done between friends and does not require a formal setting. However, a more formal approach is taken by Chinese business persons, who believe that meetings and business meals must focus around a specific business purpose, and not be limited to or wasted on general relationship building. In Malay Indonesian culture time is regarded as limitless and to be savoured; to be spent with others and enjoyed. This leads to business, like other activities, being conducted in a rather leisurely manner.

This means that negotiations are slow and frustrating for the busy Westerner who wants to close this deal and move on, fearing on missing out on other opportunities. Too much time seems to be spent in listening and enjoying eating together and not moving towards any decisions. Patience is a virtue when dealing with Indonesians. Bargaining is also a way of life to them. For instance, they have bargained daily at the street markets and it becomes an automatic response to bargain and negotiate for more favourable terms. Your best role is to join in the bargaining. Don't make concessions quickly, but be ready to use a concession to extract a better bargain for yourself. The Indonesians will not rush into any decision simply because you show impatience. Plan to stay awhile or arrange several trips to negotiate a sizeable deal.

Decision-making is done by informal consensus, prompted by the senior decision-maker who has the ability to override the group. Most Malay and Chinese Indonesians will not question the authority of that senior decision-maker. To preserve group harmony and consensus Indonesians will strive to gain complete agreement without hurting anyone's feelings through bargaining, compromise and consensus. Indonesians with less experience of the international business world tend not always to be practical and realistic, but allow emotions and intuition to sway their judgement. They also need to believe that a business interaction feels 'right and is for the greater good' and a traditional belief in fate will show through in that 'if a deal is meant to be, then it will be'.

The important considerations in gaining a business contract appear to be a combination of product or service quality and personal relationship. Price is often less important than the financing terms. If the appropriate personal connections are involved the government will negotiate more on price than on quality. Other important criteria, particularly when doing business with the government, are follow-up service and specialised training for employees.

Indonesians rarely say 'no.' They will employ the word *belum* (pronounced 'b'loom') which means 'not yet'. It has less of a blunt finality about it. The keys to gaining business in Indonesia are patience and persistence. Even if you receive initial rejections, you and your organisation should continue to foster relationships and maintain a presence in Indonesia, either through a dedicated company representative or a consultant/adviser if you are really intent on doing business in Indonesia. It is likely that you will eventually be awarded a government contract. There are two reasons why it pays to soldier on. Firstly, Indonesians have an inability to say 'no' to a 'good' credible party who show interest in their country and appear interested in a long-term commitment. Secondly, in large contracts/projects the government attempts to maintain a balance by splitting the contract between companies from different countries. The private sector tends not to give in like the government. So while polite persistence is viewed as a positive sign of commitment, the probability is much less that the private sector will change its decision.

An acceptable personal demeanour is a necessary factor (although insufficient by itself) to assist, but not guarantee, gaining a contract. But if your personal demeanour is upsetting and discomforting to the Indonesians it will certainly lose you a contract. Indonesians appreciate tact, no shows of temper or frustration, a quiet voice, demonstrated respect and humility. Shouting, arguing, emphasising your status/skills, pointing out mistakes/lack of knowledge are frowned upon. If you believe they have picked up the wrong message, have failed to answer a question or made an error, you should ask further questions or make suggestions in an indirect and unassuming manner. Many Indonesians will be hesitant to ask you questions out of fear of being wrong. Because Indonesians rarely attempt to assign tasks or assume responsibilities, you should suggest that both parties identify responsibilities and outline the steps or actions to be taken and the corresponding time frames. Be careful not to appear commanding or patronising. Never say anything negative in public. Indonesians tend to understate issues—especially negative ones—and may not inform you of problems. The use of a go-between acceptable to both sides can help sort out major misunderstandings.

If you have local partners it is better to let them run the negotiation as they know 'the rules' and will probably win you a better deal than if you did the negotiating yourself. Local partners will also negotiate the appropriate 'commission'. This 'commission' is a common aspect of doing business in Indonesia. The speed of completion of a transaction and whether it is ever transacted at all, may depend on how 'financially satisfied' the relevant government officers are. Indonesians perceive the government not as a 'servant', as is typical in many Western countries, but as a 'partner' in facilitating joint activities for the good of the country. Therefore they argue that a 'commission' is appropriate for those who are doing you a favour by providing their support and official imprimatur. It is all part of a culture pattern in which who you know and whose support you have is the crucial factor.

You also need a local partner/representative/agent to ensure your transaction and company remains high up on the Indonesian counterpart's agenda. If there is no one there to keep contact and keep things moving, your project will lie dormant. Reference has been made above to the lack of concern for the passage of time. 'Out of sight, out of mind', is very applicable if your presence is not there in some form to jog the events along. E-mails, faxes or other long-distance communication efforts will tend to be ignored as Indonesians appreciate personal contact.

The legal contract is only a starting point for a business link and is most likely to be modified later as both parties recognise what is in their best mutual interests. Because Indonesians believe that fate or bad luck makes certain things happen or not happen, there has to be this willingness to massage the original agreement into something that is more realistic, given whatever new circumstances and constraints are arising. The cultural preference for consensus also means that litigation is rare and not the preferred action of choice. Thus the initial contract or agreement is simply a reference point for the current situation and does not always provide an accurate breakdown of responsibilities. This is why a continuing presence and close relationships are needed so that the progress of an agreement can be monitored, potential problem areas identified quickly as they arise, and early informal resolution achieved. Indonesians tend to take any major event associated with a contract— such as its signing, or the completion of a project—very seriously, and turn them into a celebration. They will invite eminent persons and senior officials to attend the celebratory feast. The Indonesians love to have an excuse to eat with their friends.

The social context of business

Dining out

Indonesians often conduct business over breakfast, sometimes as early as 6:30 am, after dawn prayers but before it gets too hot. Lunch meetings are rare and it is the business dinner that provides the venue for most for socialising and relationship development.

It is courteous to your Islamic Indonesian hosts to avoid ordering or drinking alcohol during your stay. It is quite appropriate to drink and invite Chinese business persons to drink, but on no account should you offer any to a Muslim. Some Indonesians may drink alcohol privately in their homes. Follow the lead of your host. If you are the host you should invite your guests to begin eating, because traditional Indonesians will wait for your invitation. It is polite to leave just a small amount in your glass or on your plate when you are finished otherwise your host will think they have not provided enough for you.

At large gatherings there may be welcoming speeches and you are expected to reciprocate. Stick to motherhood phrases in simple English such as expressing how pleased you and your company associates are at the event/visiting the country, thanks to the host, looking forward to further contact etc. Don't crack jokes as they will not be understood.

It is not usual for a woman to attend evening events alone. She should be escorted. Be prepared if you are male to receive invitations to massage parlours as part of the hospitality. You should decline politely (if you wish!).

A home visit

Most senior government and business people have some familiarity with Western dining customs. It is courteous to remove your shoes before entering a home. Although not required, you can take some small gift, often for the home or the spouse such as flowers, fruits, cakes, or a souvenir from your country. Guests generally rise when the host or hostess enters the room. A guest should not drink until invited to do so. To be polite, wait until your host invites you to drink a couple of times. You may eat the meal with a spoon and fork, or with your fingers. It is polite to sample any food or drink offered to you. When you are finished eating, place the fork under the spoon with the fork facing down. When eating with your fingers in the traditional manner, use only your right hand. It is respectful not to eat or drink in public during the fasting month of Ramadan.

Giving gifts

Gift giving and graft may be difficult to separate, as gift giving is a normal part of Indonesian life, in both social and business situations. In order to win contracts, gifts need to be presented often, although they are not usually given at a first meeting. Senior company officials who want a 'commission' will have their requirement communicated by their juniors to your local partner or agent rather than to you directly. Some claim that in government areas this bribery is essential to prevent documents and permits being left unsigned or being lost.

Indonesian counterparts will often hint about or even suggest what they would like to receive before serious negotiation starts or an agreement is signed. If the hint isn't clear, you should ask whether there are any 'additions' they would like to make to the contract. Do not offer money gifts but leave that to your agent, whose fee can be increased to cover 'extra expenses' that have to be paid. If you are requested personally to provide something as a commission or a 'goodwill' gesture, be diplomatic, discreet and non-judgemental.

Do not give alcohol and spirits as gifts to Muslims. Gifts for all ethnic groups can include designer wear ties and athletic shoes, silk scarves, hand bags, sunglasses etc. For more prestigious gifts consider small household appliances, top level international design wear. A very acceptable gift for a senior person in a large transaction is an air ticket to your country to facilitate a fact finding visit to your company. They are of course unlikely to go anywhere near your company location unless you are a sand excavating company at a beach resort or a golf course design group.

If you are offered a gift, put on a humble and deferential air, and do not open it with others present.

What to wear

Men should wear a suit and tie for formal meetings and a shirt and tie for less formal events. As Indonesia is an Islamic culture, women should dress modestly and cover their arms and legs. Shorts are definitely not to be worn by a woman; even trousers are considered too casual by some. A dress or suit is appropriate. Makeup and perfume should be used conservatively. The evening attire for men is often batik shirts and dark pants.

Language

Bahasa Indonesia, the common language among the many subcultures is a variant of Malay. English is generally taught as a third language (after the main ethnic language and Bahasa Indonesia). Most business people speak Indonesian, Chinese and/or English. As Indonesian is based on Malay, many of the words and phrases are the same as those given for Malaysia.

Major holidays

January 1	New Year's Day
December/January*	Ramadan
January*	Ascension of the prophet Mohammed
January*	Eid el Fitr—end of Ramadan fast
March*	Nyepi—national Hindu holiday celebrated as a day of silence in Bali
May 21	Waisak—anniversary of birth and death of Buddha
May*	Eid al Adha
June/July*	Birthday of prophet Mohammed
August 17	National Independence Day
December 25	Christmas Day

*These holidays are based on the lunar calendar and vary widely on an annual basis.

Summary

- Indonesia is the world's largest Islamic nation.
- The country is currently passing through an economic and political crisis which is tending to remove some of the patronage and nepotism that has marked Indonesian life.
- It is a high power distance collective culture with a strong focus on hierarchy, social order and veneration of the elderly.
- Personal connections are often more important than economic criteria in making government and business decisions. Having the right connections is so important it can be quite difficult in some areas to access senior persons or gain a meeting without them.
- Following the Malay Islamic manner, people who are rude, boastful, impolite, aggressive or pushy, are not respected. You should show polite, well-mannered, refined and respectful behaviour and additionally demonstrate an interest in the country, its language and culture.

- Negotiation is slow and patience is needed.
- You need a local partner who has good contacts and who can handle the commissions necessary to government officials.
- The contract is only a means of starting a business link.
- Follow Muslim dress and food customs. Meetings will tend to be formal and you should dress appropriately.

Activities

Try working out the solutions to these two problems, then check your responses with those in Appendix B.

1   Don de Carlo, an up-and-coming accountant, was on contract in Jakarta, Indonesia, for three months setting up an accounting system for a local organisation. Since he had never been overseas before, he was interested in learning as much as possible about the people and their culture. He was fascinated by the contrasts he saw between the traditional and the modern, relations between the Malays, the Chinese and the Europeans, and the influence of the Arabic language and the Muslim religion. Every spare moment he had the company's driver take him to see the interesting sites both in town and in the rural villages. To document the sites for friends back home he filmed wherever he went. Although Don was able to get a number of good pictures of game animals and buildings, he became increasingly frustrated because people turned their backs on him when he tried to take their picture. Several people actually became quite angry.

What advice could you give Don?

2   Marc Heffernan, a construction supervisor for an international engineering firm, was a forceful person who always spoke his mind but he also had the reputation of being fair-minded if tough. He never hesitated to carpet any worker who he regarded as performing poorly. Marc had never worked outside Australia so he was delighted to be asked to supervise construction on a new hospital project in Indonesia where he would supervise the work of about a dozen Western ex-pats and nearly 200 local labourers. He soon started to think that the Indonesian workers were nowhere as reliable as the workers he had supervised at home. He became increasingly annoyed at the seeming lack of competence, poor attendance

records and general low motivation of the local labour. Using the leadership style that gave him such a good reputation for completing projects on time at home, he started reprimanding any worker who was not doing his job properly, and did it publicly so that it would serve as an object lesson to all the other workers. However, the problems seemed to be growing worse and more numerous.

What advice might you give Marc?

Conducting Business in

Singapore

General background

The island of Singapore is at the southern tip of the Malaysian peninsula. It is a city-state, linked to Malaysia by several road connections across the Johor Strait. It was a flat swampy island until Stamford Raffles established a trading station there in 1819. It became a Crown colony and later in 1963 became part of the Federation of Malaysia. Within two years a dispute over racial rights with the largely ethnic Malay Federation led to Singapore separating from the Federation.

Politics

Singapore has been a shining example of political stability and policy continuity, compared to other small Southeast Asian countries, through strong central leadership. Although elections have been generally above board, the government tends to be intolerant of criticism, and has stifled the formation of effective opposition parties resulting in one-party rule with excessively large government majorities in nearly all constituencies. Criticised abroad for its emphasis on social order and social management, Singapore argues that totally Western style democracy and political liberties are a luxury it cannot afford. There is a widespread view among those in power that 'Asian values' (so-called) must be promoted and that more permissive Western behaviours and attitudes be held at bay. The tough autocratic style has brought considerable economic growth and social benefits such as a low crime rate, cleanliness and political stability. The lack of a significant opposition has enabled decisions, even unpopular ones, to be made on the basis of need rather than any pandering to the whims of pressure groups.

Singapore is governed by a single house of parliament. The President, elected directly by the electorate, has extensive powers, and the right to make key appointments in the judiciary and civil service as well as appointing the Prime Minister from the majority party in parliament. The judiciary is legally independent of the executive branch of government. Overall, the government has developed and promoted an efficient administration that places sound economic policies first, with 'beneficial' social control practices a close second.

Economy

Singapore has become the premier hub of commerce for Southeast Asia, based on a large deep water harbour, strategic location, a reputation for high standards and honesty, and a well-educated English-speaking population. It is the major entrepôt for the Asia-Pacific region, re-exporting a third of its imports. Favourable tax/investment conditions and a well-educated professional workforce have resulted in some major multinationals placing their regional headquarters in Singapore. It has boomed over the last few decades, although the current economic downturn throughout Asia has reduced its performance minimally.

Large businesses are generally in the hands of the Chinese who are well educated. The Malays and Indians are less well educated and hold down lower tier jobs with little influence in international commerce, although fairly strong in the 'corner shop' variety.

Education

As good education is a priority in Singapore there is a free and effective education service. All families give great encouragement to their children to do well at school as there is an extensive competitive examination system that regulates movement through the system and controls entry to tertiary studies. After ten years of compulsory education, a considerable segment of the Chinese students in particular proceed to a two year college matriculation preparation, the majority of whom continue to tertiary level, sometimes overseas in the UK or Australia. Education is the key that unlocks the door to leadership and social standing.

Society and culture

Ethnicity

Singapore is a multi-racial society of over 3 million people. Within the mix of ethnic groups the Chinese predominate (nearly 80 per cent), with 14 per cent Malay, 6 per cent Indian (mainly Tamils), while the remaining 1 per cent are of varying ethnicities. This range of ethnicity leads to four major languages being in regular use: Malay, English, Mandarin Chinese, and Tamil. The national language is Malay, with English strongly promoted because of its neutrality and its international role in business, administration, and education. All Singaporeans have to be at least bilingual, speaking English plus their own ethnic tongue to maintain their culture.

While the use of English cuts across ethnic and religious divisions, the government strives to ensure that its people's ethnic heritage will not be lost in the process of modernisation by mandating a second language. Most of the population is largely multilingual, with many mixing the languages to form a hybrid, as in Malaysia (in Singapore it is termed 'Singlish'). Mandarin has been established as the official Chinese language over the other Chinese dialects.

Malaysia and Indonesia have been the source of the Moslem immigrant community, particularly the former as there was free movement from Malaysia to Singapore when both were British. Now Singapore is very strict about immigration, accepting on a temporary basis only those individuals whose skills are critical to the economy, usually unskilled, low-paid workers or professionals employed by multinational corporations.

Many Singaporeans retain ethnic links by joining ethnically and/or religiously exclusive organisations. Among the Chinese, certain communities tend to be concentrated in specific professions and trades with specific trade organisations reserved for those who speak a particular Chinese dialect. While hierarchies exist within each ethnic community based on ancestry and religion, the elite political, business and social groups are all well educated, English-speaking wealthy Chinese.

Religion

No official state religion is prescribed and Singaporeans follow a variety of religions that reflect their ethnicity and historical trading associations. Buddhism (28 per cent), Christianity (19 per cent), Islam (16 per cent), Taoism (13 per cent), and Hinduism (5 percent), form the major faiths with the remainder (19 per cent)—mainly Jews, Jains, Parsees and Sikhs—following their own religions. As elsewhere among the Chinese community *feng shui* is also predominant so that locations, buildings and spatial arrangements within buildings have to be in accordance with requirements to repel the negative energy *chi*. As part of the balance between national identity and support for ethnic/religious freedom, Singapore celebrates Muslim religious days (see chapter 4 on Malaysia), Chinese New Year (chapter 2) and standard Christian religious days. The major additional holiday is National Day on 9 August.

National identity

Given the diversity of cultures and the worry that this could be a divisive factor, there has been a deliberate attempt made by the government to create a Singapore identity that overarches the different ethnic and religious groups. There is considerable concern about any possibility of splintering national identity in such a multi-ethnic multilingual state. There is tolerance and encouragement of ethnic/religious activities and celebrations, but ethnic divisions are feared and avoided. The emphasis on English is part of this process, and the education system brings young people of all groups together as Singaporeans to understand that their national identity is far greater than their specific ethnicity. In these ways cleavages are prevented while preserving and honouring a variety of customs which become the customs of all.

The role of the family

In all the ethnic groups the family is the focus of most social life and behaviour. However, the nuclear family is far more prominent than in other Asian countries. This is because of the density of apartment living on a small island, plus personal wealth and government social provisions removing much need for extended family support systems. However, while families may live apart, the smallness of the island has helped retain an underlying strong Asian culture of collectivism and high power distance; elderly members of families are highly respected and patriarchies flourish in business.

Many women hold middle to high level posts in commerce and government, although the more culture-bound and religious beliefs of Moslems and Indians still restrict women from full involvement in society, unlike the Chinese.

Communication guidelines

Verbal and nonverbal behaviour

As a result of the variety of ethnic groups, it is difficult to generalise these two forms of behaviour, and reference should be made to the two chapters on China and Malaysia for full details. In general, Singaporean society is very polite, conservative and reserved. Remember not to rest your foot on your knee, as showing the sole of your foot or shoes is considered disrespectful and rude. It is best not to cross your legs unless you are seated behind a desk or table. Beckoning should be done using the whole right hand with the palm facing the ground and the fingers pointing away from you, but moving toward you in a scratching motion. Avoid pointing with one finger; either point with your knuckle or use your whole hand. Refrain from physically touching anyone. The head is considered the spiritual part of the body and should not be touched. Excessive compliments on a person's appearance, particularly a woman, are inappropriate and not appreciated.

In all ethnic groups, the Western sense of humour is not properly understood or appreciated. It is better not to tell jokes, particularly those with a political or sexual connotation. Likewise, comments on national political issues and religious behaviours must also be avoided, as Singaporeans believe that only ill-educated and socially inferior people would talk in such a way. As usual, tact and diplomacy are required. Do not speak too positively and proudly about your skills, achievements and possessions. A lack of modesty and humility is offensive to Singaporeans. They will downplay their talents. At interview, a Singaporean may say 'yes, I have had a little experience with that particular computer program and had some experience in sales'. This should be translated as 'I have had considerable experience using that program and possess extensive on-the-job and administrative experience in a sales department'. Highly qualified Singaporeans often fail to get jobs with Western companies because they do not speak up positively about their abilities and experience. In selecting staff you must probe a little deeper to find the real truth about their career experience.

Always think before you act in Singapore as there are very strict laws affecting public behaviour. You must not smoke in public, chew gum, litter, spit, or jaywalk. Even failing to flush a public toilet after use is an offence. Luckily, most toilets now flush automatically as you leave. Drug running and the possession of weapons usually result in the death penalty. Strict laws also regulate gambling, fireworks and the sale of counterfeit/pirated goods. Singaporeans respect these laws because they have protected the island nation from some of the worst excesses of anti-social and criminal activities so common in the rest of Asia and the West. When in doubt, don't.

And do not comment on the laws as you will be regarded as a person who has no standards and is willing to tolerate anti-social activities. This will not earn you respect.

Tipping is strongly discouraged as Singaporeans believe that if overseas persons tip, this will make it more difficult for locals to get good service and attention without also tipping.

Making contacts

While referrals and introductions from known third parties will always lend credibility, in Singapore you can contact businesses and potential clients directly and even set up set up appointments within a few days of arrival if your business is straightforward, such as export and trade-related transactions. For larger projects and joint ventures, more time will be needed to establish trust and it is here that third party introductions and networking is necessary. The usual Chinese *guanxi or connections* system operates, particularly if you wish to be involved on a continuing basis, with a sizeable project, or need specialised contacts.

A local representative or partner is essential if you wish to continue doing business in Singapore, though is not necessary for a short one-off activity.

Meeting people

In such a hygienic and well-organised society, punctuality for pre-arranged meetings is expected. Lateness is seen as disrespect. So if unforseen delays occur, make sure you contact your counterparts/clients well before time. The Singaporean business community is prone to take long lunch breaks as these are used for conducting business, so do not fix meetings between noon and 2.30 pm. Most meetings are held in the local person's business office or in hotels. Business is less frequently conducted over dinner and business breakfasts are rare, although urgent meetings could be held at a top hotel's coffee shop. Most Singaporeans are aware of Western business practices and will be accommodating. However, you must be respectful, courteous and polite, especially to an older Singaporean business person.

Singapore is a culturally conservative society. People should be referred to by their title, or Mr or Mrs, and the family name. First names should not be used unless you have been specifically invited to do so. It is feasible to invite your counterparts to use your first name after establishing a good relationship with them. This will then allow them to reciprocate. Names can be somewhat confusing in Singapore given the ethnic diversity. As usual, many Chinese place the surname first, followed by one or two more names. However, more Westernised Chinese, particularly those with daily connections with Westerners, will adopt a Western first name such as Mary or Danny and place it first, switching the order of their name. Most Chinese women retain their maiden family name.

Only a first name is used by the Malays. To this is added *bin* (son of) and *binti* (daughter of) followed by their father's first name. As a result, Malay women usually keep their maiden name after marriage. Malays also use *Encik* in place of Mr and *Cik* for Miss or *Puan* for Mrs. This means that you will greet and refer to a Malay as Encik Osman or Puan Jamilah. You never need to use the whole name in speaking to them, but the full name should be written at the top of a communication or on an envelope to be posted.

Many Indians in Singapore do not use their family names. They use their father's initial before their own name. Some Indians use Mr or Mrs and others may add 'son of'(s/o) or 'daughter of '(d/o) after their first name and before a family name. As business cards are not always reliable indicators of how a person prefers to be addressed, it is acceptable to ask.

The Western handshake greeting is common, though often lighter than one might expect, accompanied by a warm smile and 'Hello'. If greeting an older person, give a slight nod of the head as well. Direct eye contact is not common amongst Singaporeans as it is considered a sign of disrespect. Formal verbal greetings are exchanged, usually in English. When introducing people say the name and title of the senior person first. In general, show respect and deference to elders.

Muslims, particularly Malay men, will bring their hands back to touch their chests after shaking hands to symbolise that the greeting comes from the heart. They are pleased when a foreigner returns the gesture. Women are not expected to follow suit. Some Malay women may not offer their hand for a handshake to a Western male. So wait for them to make the first move. Some traditional Indians may greet you with a *namaste*, in which both hands are held in a prayerlike position at chest level with a slight nod of the head.

You will be expected to exchange business cards at the beginning of a meeting. These should be given and received using both hands. Make sure you are seen examining your counterpart's card carefully to show respect. Particularly when with Moslems, never use the left hand only, as it is considered the 'dirty hand'. Consider having your cards printed in Chinese on the reverse, given the high probability that you will be meeting Chinese business persons rather than any other.

The usual casual conversation should fill the opening minutes of your first meeting. Suitable topics include your trip to Singapore, your counterpart's experiences overseas, and positive remarks about the country. Remember to keep off political and religious topics. You may be asked questions about topics such as age, weight, and money, which you may feel are too personal. If you are uncomfortable answering, be polite and vague. Singaporeans believe that people who disclose too much personal, family, and emotional information lack self-control. You will find that most Singaporeans are anxious to discuss business far more quickly than other Asian countries.

Getting down to business

Corporate structure

Most Singaporean traditional firms are family-owned with the senior person usually the eldest male family member. Non-family professionals will be employed as needed but can never become the top person. Outside the family members, promotions are based more on merit than on connections.

Negotiation

There are always serious attempts made, however difficult the negotiations, to preserve harmony and personal relationships. No party to negotiations should have to lose face. Anger, raising the voice, or criticism are not expected behaviours of business persons who wish to be respected. The focus is on co-operative behaviour and teamwork. Individual competition must not come at the expense of the group.

The Chinese business people tend to be tough negotiators and you may find yourself pressured into making concessions, however negotiations will proceed fairly rapidly. Don't be misled by Western-dressed, Western-educated Singaporeans who speak excellent English. The are still Asian in mindset and attitude, relatively conservative and are focussed on the long-term perspective.

The senior persons in the business will make the decisions which will generally be based on rationality and the amount of information they have been able to glean from you.

The typical roundabout way of expressing 'no' will be used to avoid the face loss and embarrassment it conveys. Substitutions will include, 'we will consider it', 'It is difficult . . .' or 'I would like to, but . . .'. Equally, a 'yes' may simply mean 'I understand' rather than 'I agree'. It is essential you follow up all these phrases with delicately phrased items of your own to tease out the real meanings and intentions. Only when a 'yes' response is accompanied by details can an affirmative response be inferred. The sucking in of air or a hissing sound are used to indicate difficulty, discomfort or even upset with what you have said or want. Use these signals as an opportunity to change your response/offer etc, as one who is willing to compromise and maintain harmony is more likely to gain their objectives than one who is unwilling to bend.

The use of silence may bode well for you. It indicates that thought is occurring and does not indicate lack of interest. Don't feel you have to fill the silence. Indians often indicate acknowledgment or agreement with a slight bob of the head from side to side which a Westerner may assume means 'no'. Watch for a grammatical change in meaning with the phrase 'isn't it?'. It can mean 'Isn't it right?'

As Singaporeans may not ask questions or indicate when they are uncertain out of fear of losing face, it is necessary for you to ask polite questions to monitor progress and verify agreement. Ask indirect questions, rather than closed 'yes–no' questions, to make sure everyone understands and is in agreement.

Should you need to point out errors or disagree, you should do it discreetly in private to prevent loss of face. Criticism focussed at a person is considered highly personal and objectionable. Conversely, avoid handing out excessive compliments, for these (and by implication you) will be perceived as insincere. The culture extols modesty and humility. Never boast about your abilities or previous successful hard dealings; let your abilities to conduct negotiations in a friendly, professional way speak volumes for you. Don't criticise competitors either. Prove your worth and your organisations worth by your behaviour and the quality of what the organisation has to offer. The Singaporeans want to make their own judgements and resent having a biased judgement foisted on them. It implies they are naive simpletons unable to make rational decisions.

Contracts are regarded as binding, unlike other parts of Asia, and therefore should contain all essential details that permit all parties to benefit from the transaction or negotiation.

The social context of business

Dining out

Business breakfasts are not common and business dinners are not popular apart from the Chinese banquet, as detailed in Chapter 2. Business lunches are common and are usually held in restaurants. It is usual to have a lunch together once a business relationship is developing. When eating with Indians and Malays, remember to use only your right hand to eat. Don't empty your plate or glass or else your host will think they have not provided enough. Follow your counterpart's lead in whether business is to be discussed over the meal.

The home visit

Singaporeans rarely entertain at home for business. If you are invited to a home, be punctual. It is acceptable, but not expected, to bring a small gift. In Chinese homes, leave some food on your plate to indicate when you have had enough to eat. In traditional Muslim homes, the hostess may not join you, as women keep a low profile. Remove your shoes before entering most homes, particularly those of Malays and Indians (also remove your shoes when entering mosques and temples).

Giving gifts

Corruption is unlikely to be met in Singapore, given the strong social and financial controls within a conservative highly ethical context. There are strict directives aimed at preventing individuals from accepting large gifts, particularly in the public service, and it is wiser never to offer money to government officials, even at New Year. Only people such as children, servants, grocers, and delivery people should receive the traditional red envelope with money at the Chinese New Year.

Gift-giving to individuals, even in a moderate sense, is therefore quite uncommon and not expected, even in the private business sector. To avoid misunderstanding, it is preferable to present a group gift to the company or section, rather than expensive gifts to an individual, which may be misinterpreted as a bribe. This could be either one gift that can be shared by everyone or a series of similar gifts for each individual. A group-centred gift of something that can be seen, used and remembered by many people for some time is appropriate. The group gift should be a formal presentation at the end of negotiations and be seen as a gift from your group to their group.

For individuals in the group, token gifts, such as pens or items with a company logo, or fruit, sweets, and cake, small toys for children, souvenirs from home are appropriate, provided that they are obviously inexpensive, and should be wrapped in red or gold (good luck colour). Never single out an individual in public with a gift. Not only may it be perceived as a payment for a favour received or to be performed, but will incite envy and disharmony, reducing group morale. Most Singaporeans will accept gifts even for a work group reluctantly to indicate humility. You will need to gently insist that they accept your gift, adding that you are pleased or honoured to present the gift. As is common in Asia, the gift will not be opened on receipt in your presence. It is the gesture you have made, not the value of the gift that makes it mark. Always use the right hand or both hands to present the gift.

When giving gifts, it is important to take into account the ethnicity of your intended recipient. Red, yellow, gold and pink are auspicious colours for the Chinese, but avoid white flowers and clocks as these have connotations of death. Cutting items like scissors and knives symbolise the severing of a friendship. Items for the children are particularly welcomed, such as sweets and cakes, and around Chinese New Year a little money in a red envelope is a traditional children's gift. This recognition of their tradition will be greatly appreciated should you be around at that time. Always provide things in even numbers for good luck, except the number 4 which has a connotation related to death. Money gifts can be given for weddings and should be in odd amounts, particularly ending in 1, such as 101.

For Malays and Indians, sweets, fine chocolates, and souvenirs from your home country are welcome, but remember not to give Malays any gifts containing alcohol or pork. As Malays can be quite touchy about anything that may offend their religion check very carefully any company calendars, brochures, books etc to ensure no girls in skimpy bathing suits, dogs, or photos of famous cathedrals illustrate the material. Avoid white and black colours for Indians who prefer brighter colours, such as red, yellow, and green.

Other useful information

What to wear

Climate dictates that business dress is generally informal with men wearing a long sleeve shirt and tie without a jacket. For women, a jacket and skirt or professional dress is most appropriate for daytime appointments. In the evenings, men often wear short-sleeved shirts except in the most expensive restaurants. In these restaurants, long-sleeve shirts and ties are appropriate. On some occasions, jackets may be required for cocktail parties. Women should wear trousers only on casual occasions. Avoid black, white, or navy blue to a party or wedding because these are traditional funeral colours.

Language

There are four official languages: English, Mandarin Chinese, Malay, and Tamil. The language of business is English. Children are required to learn English as well as their native ethnic language. You should speak in English, especially if your counterpart is doing so, bit speak a little slower and more clearly than normal as your pronunciations will probably differ from that of the Singaporean due to the influence of that person's mother tongue on English.

Major holidays

These consist of the usual Chinese, Moslem, Indian and Christian festivals already noted in chapters 2 and 4.

Summary

- Singapore is a multi-ethnic country whose culture is mainly Chinese, with minority Malay and Indian cultures. English is used as a unifying language medium as part of the drive to create a national identity.
- There is strong social control imposed, and observation of correct social behaviours is vital. For example, gifts may be seen as attempts at bribery.

- The long exposure of Singapore to Western commerce has made business activity more akin to Western approaches than Asian. Introductions are not necessary, decisions will be made quickly and contracts are written and honoured. However, some formalities still remain, such as deference to the senior family member of the family firm, the need to be polite and calm, and be willing to compromise.

a Activity

Try working out the solution to the following problem, then check your response with Appendix B.

1 Stephen Jorgensen, recently appointed to manage his firm's office in Singapore, was anxious to do well in his first overseas assignment. Shortly after his arrival he called his first staff meeting to outline the objectives for the coming fiscal year. He had already met with his staff individually and was feeling quite confident about the prospects for having a good relationship with them. Toward the end of the staff meeting, Stephen, in his characteristic upbeat fashion, told his employees that he looked forward to working with them and that he anticipated that this would be their best year ever. To emphasise his optimism for the coming year Stephen punctuated his verbal remarks by slapping his fist against his palm. The reaction was instantaneous: Most people laughed, giggled, or looked embarrassed. Unfortunately, he felt that the point of his dramatic climax was lost amid the laughter.

How might you explain the cause for the hilarious outburst?

Conducting Business in

The Philippines

General background

The Philippines is composed of an intricate web of 710 islands and sea passageways. The islands are characterised by rugged mountains, including some active volcanoes, and frequent earthquakes. Floods, typhoons and volcanic eruptions are natural disasters that form regular events in the lives of many Filipinos. Virtually all the population resides on the largest islands, the main ones being Cebu, Luzon, Mindanao, and Palawan. Manila, the capital is located on Luzon. Other major cities include Cebu, Iloilo, Cagayan de Oro, Quezon City, Davao, and Iligan.

Politics

Until the late 1980s power was held by a limited elite of wealthy landowners and their extended families. After the fall of the Marcos regime, this hierarchy had its power somewhat curtailed as Corazon Aquino restored the democracy with the 1987 constitution. Unfortunately, she failed to reduce the ingrained historical legacy of human rights abuses, inequitable distribution of wealth and power and corruption that mar life for most Filipinos.

Fidel Ramos, the current president, has been a strong and effective leader, further consolidating democratic stability and promoting economic growth to ensure continuing liberalisation and internationalisation of the Philippine economy. The required presidential election in 1998 is expected to continue the democratic transfer of power to the electorate and no signs of overthrowing a popularly elected government seems likely.

The Roman Catholic church exerts a great deal of social, educational and political influence. The judicial system is strongly influenced by Spanish and American law, as well as by indigenous Philippine customs.

Economy

Under democracy there have been significant strides made to promote economic growth by encouraging foreign investment and international trade, promoting privatisation of public entities, and reducing bureaucratic control. Private enterprises, many still family managed, are starting to dominate the economy. But despite a large sprawl of urban settlements the Philippines remains an essentially rural society with agriculturally-related activities providing the work and income for about half the labour force. The country produces much agricultural produce such as timber, rice, bananas, pineapples and sugarcane. There are significant mineral resources too, such as copper, nickel and chromium. As a result, food processing, wood products, electrical machinery and electronics are important export earners. However, as in most larger economies, the service industries are starting to burgeon and become major players in the national economy.

There have been problems with the infrastructure, particularly power generation, but new power projects, plus improved transport and communications are opening up the whole country to development. Unfortunately, little can be done to control the natural disasters that play havoc at unpredictable times and places.

Society and culture

Around 68 million people live in the Philippines. Nearly all are of Malay stock, blended with the many groups who have visited, traded, or colonised the islands over many centuries, such as Malay and Chinese traders, Spanish (essentially Mexican), and later American colonial governance. There are a few Chinese, and remnants of inland indigenous hill tribal groups. Due to the island nature of the country, which encouraged variations in culture, language, history and rate of development, regional and ethnic and religious rivalries continue to have a small but significant impact on political stability and economic development. However, the predominance of the Roman Catholic church in most parts of the country and a focussed emphasis on Filipino national heritage are now creating a basis for allegiance that overcomes more limited local issues.

The major cultural groups now comprise of Christian Malays, Muslim Malays, the Chinese and the indigenous tribes. The Filipinos have produced a remarkable synergy among the diverse groups despite some remaining internal dissension from leftover business with communists and tardy resolution of regional autonomy issues with Moslems.

Unlike other Asian countries, around 90 per cent of the population is Christian, mainly Roman Catholic, a legacy of Spanish influence. About 5 per cent of the population is Muslim; the rest are tribal animists, Buddhist, or Taoist. The Muslim communities are limited to the southern part of the Philippines, notably the island of Mindanao and in the Sulu Archipelago, which are the closest parts of the Philippines geographically to the Islamic nations of Malaysia and Indonesia (Kalimantan) with whom trade has been done by the short sea crossing for many centuries. Although racially the same as other Filipinos, this Muslim group lies beyond the mainstream of national life, due to religious, linguistic, and regional differences. Economic grievances, general government neglect, and perceived religious prejudice have encouraged the rise of militant groups, fighting for the establishment of an Islamic state in the south. Some are still continuing their struggle, despite an agreement with Islamic leaders that the central government will provide greater regional autonomy for them and develop the economy of the region. As usual the Chinese have traditionally dominated certain commercial sectors and as a consequence have periodically met with discrimination.

Up to the beginning of the twentieth century Spanish, the language of the colonists, was generally spoken, taught in the schools and most of the local hierarchy took Spanish names. Since the American influence began in 1898, English became a main language along with the local language called *Tagalog*. The education system provides a literacy rate of 90 per cent and 25 per cent of the nation's budget is spent on education. As a result, while many of their underlying values are still Asian in tone, the Filipinos provide the major resource of an educated, relatively inexpensive, and English-speaking workforce. The Filipinos are hospitable, friendly, loyal and happy people. They are not nearly as formal as other Asian societies as a result of their centuries old association with Spanish and American cultures.

The Filipinos are very fatalistic. They suffer many environmental disasters as well as the usual personal happenings. They simply accept what comes and bear it with fortitude, hope and patience, or as they say, *bahala na* (God wills it). Success is therefore very much in the lap of the gods rather than based on personal merit, motivation or skill. There is acceptance of social status since fate has allocated their position. Expressions such as 'it does not matter' or 'it was my fate' greet personal problems stemming from epidemics, floods and earthquakes. This belief in luck has lead to an inordinate interest in gambling and the playing of games of chance.

Traditional beliefs about spirits and ghosts abound. These are used as excuses for doing or not doing things. Such irrational behaviour is difficult for an overseas business person to understand when the failure to keep a promise is said by the Filipino to be due to the uncontrollable influence of a spirit that forced them to do something else. It is almost like a Freudian explanation using unconscious motivation 'I don't know why I did that'.

The family is the focal unit in Philippine culture and its wellbeing supersedes all else. The village or *barrio* forms the community unit. There is considerable respect for those older than oneself and for those in authority. Specific names indicating respect and status are used between family members. The Filipino does not strive to obtain money and other resources for themselves but for the family group. There are large extended families that operate like clans, with a strong sense of obligation to assist one another in all matters. One's first loyalty is to the immediate family, this then extends outwards to the extended family, with friends and community members last.

Despite a strong religious bent, most Filipinos do not interpret right and wrong through a moral code. What is correct behaviour will be regarded as that which relates to family and other reciprocal obligations. It is the failure to live up to the expectations of tradition and family that brings shame and guilt.

Four basic concepts exert a considerable influence on Filipino behaviour :

- *hiya* or embarrassment/shame/loss of self-esteem. This occurs when someone is unable to meet their own expectations or the expectations of others. Accordingly, most people will refrain from showing anger or displeasure, and will seek to control their emotions and maintain a sense of social propriety. *Hiya* is a combination of inferiority, shyness, alienation and embarrassment. It is an important social force and the concept is instilled into children at an early age by parents. This ensures that their children will understand the threats of experiencing it and therefore take steps to avoid it. You must never criticise a Filipino in public as it is the greatest insult. The negative implications of *hiya* are that Filipinos will resist change, innovation and competition simply because the result could be failure which could bring shame to the person and their family or work group.

- *amor proprio* or self-esteem. It reinforces the concept of *hiya* by emphasising the need for self-confidence, maintenance of face, self-respect and pride. The Filipino has a deep sense of personal dignity, requires to be treated like a person, and is very sensitive to any violation of this. Difficult situations must therefore be handled gently with a personal touch.

- *utang na loob* or obligation. This refers to a bond between people that creates a sense of obligation and interdependency, as well as a need to repay debts of gratitude. This is the feeling that you get when another person has done you a favour. It is a debt of honour and cannot be repaid by money, but by actions. The Filipinos also differentiate between outer self, *mukha*, or 'face' and inner self, or *loob*. These values permeate into the business context. For example, a person who repeatedly utilises the personal network relationships of another colleague to accomplish work or to find employment has obligated him or herself, creating *utang na loob*, or inner debt, and is obligated to repay the debt at some point, although not necessarily immediately. While we also feel obliged to repay favours, we have not got the Filipino's degree of concern for keeping the scale of obligation in balance over the long term.
- *pakikisama* or getting along together. This is the Filipino desire to enjoy smooth interpersonal relations. They will sacrifice efficiency to avoid confrontation. Frankness and outspoken expressions of opinion are uncultured and individuals doing this are ostracised. A go-between is often used to avoid confrontation and loss of face. As a conforming people the Filipinos are willing to go along with any situation rather than change it. As a result, the true feelings are often hidden behind an agreeing facade and an overseas business person needs to be able to read hidden signals and nonverbal mannerisms to detect the real feelings.
- *Suki* relationships are personal bonds and relationships often derived from *utang na loob* obligations. In *suki*, personal bonds and obligations are created because of favourable business interactions and feed back into that commercial relationship. For example, *suki* relationships are commonly established when a buyer, over time, continues to patronise the same supplier as each feels obligated to the other and each provides special treatment for the other, binding them together in a web of mutual obligations. Thus in exchange for special treatment, such as reduced prices or better credit terms, the purchaser will stick to one supplier and even increase their orders.

The collectivism and solidarity learned and practiced within the family ingroup extends in a natural way into the work group, which is often family-based. This unfortunately can result in loyalty to the work team, business, clique or faction taking precedence over loyalty to the overall program, business or nation. Within the group there are *bata* relationships. The *bata* is the protegé or favoured individual.

As a result of these social control values, any individual is usually cut down to size if they attempt to take more credit than the group to which they belong. Individual privacy is discouraged and anyone who questions the status quo is branded as simply being a smart ob-structionist.

Education is valued as the main method for achieving upward economic and social mobility. Filipinos have been exposed to Western ideas, lifestyle and products through the American influence. Numerous Filipinos have migrated overseas or spent time working abroad. These experiences have made them more open to accepting different cultures and ways of doing things. They are therefore not as rigid or as narrow-minded as other Asian cultures, show more tolerance of risk-taking and are a little less hierarchical in their structures and degree of deference. Their exposure to American attitudes has also led them to be somewhat materialistic, and tangible wealth such as expensive watches, electronic equipment and cars are flaunted.

The Spanish heritage has left a machismo attitude, to which male Filipinos are greatly attracted. Many married men also maintain a 'lady friend' or *'casa chica'*. Generally, in the workforce women (or Filipinas) are considered equal to men, and some hold senior positions in the government and the private sector.

Filipinos enjoy telling jokes, particularly at each other's expense, and appreciate a good sense of humour. You must not join in and make personal jabs. Never tell any jokes that reflect on local political or religious (strongly RC) issues.

Making contacts

There is much less formality and considerably more flexibility in dealing with Filipinos than other Asians. The American influence and the use of English by most Filipinos has made the country a relatively comfortable and satisfying environment in which Westerners can undertake business activities. However, the possession of an introduction from a person known and trusted by the Filipino you wish to meet remains an important part of doing business. Only if you work for a large, well-known multinational firm is it possible for you to gain entree to the better companies and higher government circles without an introduction. The best introduction is one from someone who has done business with you before, or a Filipino trade mission/ diplomatic representative working in your home country who can vouch for your credentials. Filipinos are very impressed by titles and respect protocol, so an introduction from someone with a title/status will open many doors. Your own status/title in the organisation you represent is also a factor in assessing whether you are worthwhile seeing. Always verify the credibility of a potential local partner or representative by ensuring that they have the 'correct' political, social and family connections and by researching their existing clients and track record.

Communication guidelines

Meeting people

It is always better to arrange your appointments ahead of your arrival through third parties, or by direct communication with your potential counterpart. You must arrive on time for any appointment, even though your host may well be late. Should you be delayed, be courteous and phone ahead using a very acceptable and undeniable excuse (if in one of the major cities)—that of being caught up in a traffic jam. You must try to arrange your meetings for the mornings only. Most Filipino business people and senior government officials often take long lunch breaks filled with large lunches and alcohol. Afternoon meetings therefore always begin late and drift into lethargy, particularly in view of the effects of hot sticky weather on a full stomach.

You should make the first meeting a courtesy visit, enabling both sides to get to know each other. Filipinos will shake hands and present you with a large warm smile. This initial greeting can be ended by presenting business cards. Your card should emphasise your status, title and qualifications etc. This will enable your hosts to select persons from their side who match your level of responsibility. Where titles or profession is known, you can refer to your Filipino counterpart as Dr Ramos or Attorney Ramos. When you are unaware of title or status, the Western Mr, Ms, or Mrs is quite acceptable. In the initial meetings use a formal title and a surname. Between themselves Filipinos commonly use first names, but you should wait until you have been invited to do so. When you are invited and they start using your first name you know you are accepted and business dealings are most likely.

The usual small talk precedes business talk in an effort to develop a relationship. Relationship formation is vital as elsewhere in Asia, but Filipinos are loyal once a relationship has been formed. In the small talk and at lunch times keep off controversial subjects such as local politics, birth control, corruption, and insurgency by Islamic fundamentalists. Many Filipinos have travelled to the United States to visit relatives and friends and often enjoying chatting about their experiences. Later in the meeting, you can generally state your objectives for interacting with the company or person. This will be followed up at later meetings. Be careful not to appear pushy or boastful. Emphasise wherever possible, the benefits your company can offer to the Filipino firm. Small gifts are acceptable and customarily exchanged at the first meeting. You could give some sample product, something with your corporate logo on it, like a presentation pen set, or some small item from home that typically reflects your culture.

Nonverbal communication

The Filipinos use a range of body language. They will often greet each other with an 'eyebrow flash' (slightly raised eyebrows) or a small nod of the head to signal recognition. If this body language is accompanied by a smile, it is a friendly hello. A frown would signify a challenge. Filipinos tend to smile often in a wide variety of situations. A smile is used in several emotional circumstances, including to cover up discomfort, sadness, or nervousness. Smiles are a very important part of the culture and should be used liberally by foreigners.

They employ a jerk of the head upwards to indicate 'yes' while a jerk downwards means 'no'. The Filipino, reluctant to say 'no', will verbally say 'yes' while simultaneously jerking their head downwards. Watch out for this important nonverbal clue to the real meaning. Other nonverbal signals include:

- Staring at someone, which the Filipinos consider quite rude.
- Standing with your hands on your hips, interpreted as anger or a challenge.
- Do not point at someone or beckon with just your index finger. Use your whole hand with your palm facing down and fingers pointing away, but moving toward you in a scratching motion.
- Filipinos also point by shifting their eyes in the relevant direction or by pouting their mouth in the indicated direction.
- In comparison to people in other Asian cultures, the Filipinos tend to be more physical and may extend a pat on the back. It is best not to initiate such gestures. Physical contact in public may exist between people of the same sex, but never with someone of the opposite sex.
- To attract the attention of a waiter you should hiss.
- Filipino women often use fans and have developed a nonverbal signalling system employing various fan movements.

Getting down to business

Corporate structure

The larger Filipino companies are run by members of a few key ruling families. A paternalistic style of management therefore predominates, although a more professional style of manager is developing at the middle and senior employee level. This blending leads to benevolence and patronage underpinned by a solid professionalism. The corporate structure is usually similar to the American corporate system with the most senior person (often a senior family member) as the president. Overseas business persons should target at least group or division heads, who usually have decision-making authority. Titles can be misleading so that senior managers and assistant vice-presidents may not have the authority you think they do. Only the senior-most people have authority and responsibility.

Having contacts in high places is essential for cutting through the masses of red tape. Most bureaucrats and some business people will work a '*mañana* system' with few things done to time but will always promise 'tomorrow'. Things do eventually get done. Most Filipinos will make every effort to meet their deadlines, although they will organise their work schedule to reflect the *mañana* attitude. For example, even if a project deadline is two or three weeks away, most Filipinos are unlikely to commence work on it until two to three days before the end of the deadline. You must plan for this *mañana* approach to life in your time schedules. It is sensible idea not to reveal the actual deadline that you must have. It is better to set earlier deadlines, and sub-stage deadlines to keep things on track and to allow for several lapses.

Negotiation

Filipinos are willing to take the time to develop a smooth interpersonal relationship before business negotiations are commenced. You will find trust builds quickly if you arrive with a favourable and credible introduction. The concept of *pakikisama*, considered above, is invoked in the business relationship, as in any other relationship. It is both a value and a goal. Achieving *pakikisama* can even take precedence over accomplishing a specific task.

As authority is concentrated into the hands of few, or even one person in each company, particularly family ones, decision-making can occur speedily or drag, depending on the level of your counterpart and the size of the deal. You must not be misled by pompous sounding position titles, as they can be misleading and the person may have no authority at all. The answer is to ensure that you know who the decision-maker is and cultivate them if at all possible. If the decision process seems to be stagnating, contact your introducer who can act as a go-between to determine what the problem is. You must take with you appropriate technical staff who can answer detailed questions if you are selling products or seeking a contract. The Filipinos like to know all of the details. Delays can occur because the Filipinos want to know which individuals support specific positions before negotiations begin, particularly if government departments or political issues are involved. The 'who' can be a critical part of the decision-making. As in everyday life, business negotiations are part of what fate has in store for a person. The Filipino counterpart is likely to believe that 'if a deal is meant to be, then it will'. Of course, the concept of *bahala na*, or 'letting God take care of it', can also be used as a pretext to avoid making hard decisions as indicated earlier.

As the Filipinos are non-confrontational, they have an aversion to saying no, their response of 'yes' can mean all things to all people from 'yes, we have an agreement', through 'yes, I understand, I'm following what you are saying', and 'well, yes, if you say so', to 'yes I would like to but can't' or 'yes I will try and will let you know' (hoping if they wait long enough the matter will have ceased to exist as you will have gone home) and 'yes, I hope my lack of enthusiasm for what you propose conveys to you that I really mean no'. In the light of this you must always confirm a response several times. The Filipinos will not convey bad news and will often just not do anything in such a situation. Sometimes a go-between will be used to bring up matters that would embarrass the Filipino (to avoid *hiya*). They will also avoid admitting they have made a mistake or do not know the answer to a question. Here they are trying to preserve *amor proprio*. Junior level Filipinos will wait for explicit instructions to ensure they do the task properly and avoid losing face through making mistakes. While Filipinos will rarely admit when they have made a mistake and will rarely take blame, they are often quick to blame someone else. However, if something goes well, everyone will attempt to take credit.

Should you get a positive decision, the delight unfortunately soon becomes tempered by the time lapse in implementation. A slow inefficient rubber stamp bureaucracy takes over. An array of signatures and documented approvals are required after a decision has been made. Do not lose your temper, shout or become demanding at the delays in decision-making or bureaucratic procedures. Let your local representative or partner monitor progress and problems. If you must criticise, do so gently and indirectly, and do not make it personal. Face saving is the rule.

Filipinos are patient negotiators and enjoy making flowery arguments. They tend to make greater concessions as time passes. Try not to accept the first offer. Legal contracts in the Philippines are detailed and honoured by business people.

The social context of business

Dining out

As a happy and lively society, Filipinos enjoy business socialising and developing relationships. Business breakfasts are common in hotel coffee shops. Some regulars actually have established tables and 'hold court' there, receiving business visitors. These are 'must attend' breakfasts, where strong alliances are developed and business deals can be cemented. Politicians also engage in similar breakfast gatherings.

Business lunches are more casual, while business dinners or cocktails are reserved for a more mature stage in a soundly developing relationship. A Filipino will only accept a dinner invitation if they feel comfortable with you. It is quite socially acceptable to be late for dinner appointments. You will be considered over eager if you are punctual. Aim at a time about twenty or thirty minutes later than on the invitation if you are the guest. If you are the host you should be punctual. If possible, check with your local associate for the appropriate time delay. The Western habit of having a drink at the bar before sitting at the dinner table is common.

When you are being entertained during business times you may be asked to join in a karaoke session. Just try and go along with the fun. Sing-along or karaoke bars are very popular in the Philippines.

A home visit

You will only be invited home if a Filipino really feels a strong bond has developed. It indicates acceptance. Again, punctuality can be considered rude. Arrive at least fifteen minutes after the designated time. Filipinos are very generous hosts and will go to great lengths to extend their hospitality.

Flowers, a cake, perfume, a bottle of wine or whisky, are all appropriate gifts to take. A hearty appetite is viewed as a compliment to the cook. Your willingness to try new foods will gain you instant acceptance, although you should feel comfortable declining something if you really do not want to try it. You should leave a small portion of food on your plate to indicate that you are finished and that the host has provided more than enough food.

Gift giving

Although it is illegal to bribe someone (called *lagay* locally), some claim it is a normal part of many business interactions, particularly those with the government. It is reported that bribery is virtually a mandatory cost of doing business in the Philippines in order to speed up the provision of a permit, expedite goods through a port, gain an essential signature, smooth out a complication of business etc, with kickbacks often already built into the contract price, often representing 5–10 per cent of the value of the contract. Never give cash; this is considered an insult. Do not try to manage this aspect of business yourself. Ask your local partner or representative to deal with the problem.

In normal business interactions it is appropriate to give something before and after the signing of a contract; the after-signing gift should be more expensive. A dinner invitation to an expensive restaurant or club after closing the deal is appropriate. Other appropriate gifts would be crystal or an item from an internationally recognised store. Be sure that the item has significance, quality and value. This is not considered a *lagay,* as described above. Prior to the signing, appropriate gestures could include nice lunches, or a local weekend vacation disguised as a working trip. In order to avoid entering into an unwanted obligation, most Philippine companies will not accept a gesture of this magnitude unless they are comfortable with you and feel that the deal will be completed.

Christmas gifts are appropriate to colleagues and employees as well as to people with whom you have regular dealings. You can give small gifts such as company products, or calendars. The Asian habit of never opening gifts in front of the giver or in public is followed. Opening a gift publicly suggests a materialistic nature and may cause embarrassment and loss of face to all parties.

What to wear

For first meetings and meetings with very senior persons a suit is appropriate. However, a male visitor must take the opportunity of dressing with local flair and buying and wearing a traditional heavily embroidered open-necked shirt, called a *barong tagalog*, made of pineapple fibre, *jusi*. This type of shirt is worn by Filipino males on most occasions—the more expensive and ornate the better. In fact, visiting politicians and diplomats often wear the shirt when meeting with the Philippine president. Make sure you purchase one that is heavily embroidered and looks expensive. Open-necked white shirts or business shirts with ties are also acceptable. *The barong tagalog* is even suitable for formal dinner occasions in place of a suit and tie.

Businesswomen tend to dress in brightly coloured dresses or suits rather than dark ones. Trousers are not usually worn for business appointments by women, who are always expected to display modesty.

Other useful information

Language

The official languages are Filipino, or *Tagalog* (used widely), and English, in which most Filipinos are fluent. There is rarely a need for translation in normal business and social encounters. Spanish and Chinese have limited currency.

National holidays

	January 1	New Year's Day (*Bagong Taon*)
	Thursday before Easter	Maundy Thursday (*Huwebes Santo*)
	April*	Good Friday (*Viyernes Santo*)
	April*	Easter (*Pasko ng Pagkabuhay*)
	April 9	Bataan and Corregidor Day (also known as Heroism Day)
	May 1	Labour Day
	June 12	Independence Day
	Last Sunday in August	National Heroes Day
	November 1	All Saints' Day (*Todo los Santos*)
	November 30	Bonifacio Day
	December 25	Christmas (*Pasko*)
	December 30	Rizal Day

*These holidays change from year to year.

Tipping

Due to the extensive US influence, tipping is common and expected throughout the Philippines.

Transportation

Whenever using a taxi, always insist on using the meter or agreeing to a fixed price prior to entering a taxi. Air-conditioned taxis are at least 50 per cent more expensive. For hotel minibuses and shuttles, arrange for a pickup when you reserve a room prior to arrival.

It is not advisable to drive in Manila due to the heavy traffic. First-time visitors to the Philippines are advised to rent a car and driver. The subway, known as the Metro Rail or Light Rail Transit, is an easy, efficient, and cheap form of transportation within Manila.

Summary

- Filipinos are generally less formal than other Asian cultures, although there is still a strong respect for elders and those in authority. This is evident in the paternalistic style of management in the private sector and the slow red tape bureaucracy which blocks up the government sector.
- Enabling a Filipino to have self respect, maintain face, avoid shame, and fulfil obligations to others, are important factors in building up relationships and negotiating with Filipinos.

- Collectivism is strong, particularly in relation to the family.
- Negotiations can take a long time as only very senior persons have authority to make decisions.
- Bureaucracy is slow and many permissions are needed. These can be sped up by 'greasing the palm'. Some claim that bribery is endemic, particularly in the public service. Slowness is compounded by a *mañana* attitude. Deadlines become hard to meet.
- Filipinos dislike saying no, and 'yes' can therefore mean a variety of things.
- There is a strong belief in fate—what will be, will be.
- You do not need a translator as most business people speak English.

Activities

Try working out the solutions to these two problems, then check your responses with those in Appendix B.

1 Within the past decade Robert McGowern had worked hard to become the top salesperson for the entire East Coast district of his company. When his company received an invitation to make a marketing presentation to a large distribution firm in Manila, Robert's excellent salesmanship and mature personality made him the logical choice for the assignment. He efficiently had set up an appointment to make his presentation on the same day that he arrived in Manila. But upon arrival the marketing representative of the host firm, who met him at the airport, told him that the meeting had been arranged for two days later, so that Robert could rest after the long trip and have a chance to see some of the local sites and enjoy their hospitality. With his conscientious and hardworking personality, he desperately tried to assure his host that he felt fine and was prepared to make the presentation that day. Robert could see no good reason not to get on with the business at hand. Eventually the marketing representative (somewhat reluctantly) intervened on his behalf, and the meeting was reset for later that afternoon. But once the meeting began Robert noticed that the Filipino executives never really got beyond the exchange of pleasantries. Finally, the vice president in charge suggested that they meet again the next afternoon. Robert was feeling increasing frustration with the excruciatingly slow pace of the negotiations.

a

How could you help Robert gain some clarity on this cross-cultural situation?

2   Angela Capaldi, the managing director of a publishing company, had been working for several months with a Filipino architectural firm that was designing the company's new printing facility in Quezon City. However Angela was becoming increasingly frustrated with the many delays caused by the architects. When the preliminary plans for the building—which the architects had promised by a certain date—had not arrived, Angela called them to inquire when she would be receiving the plans. The architects, somewhat indignant that she called, felt that Angela doubted their integrity to deliver the plans. Angela was equally annoyed because they had missed the deadline, and what was worse, they didn't seem to be the least bit apologetic about it. By the end of the phone call, Angela was convinced that her company's relationship with the Filipino architectural firm had suffered a major setback.

How might you explain the conflict in this case?

Japan

*If you have a joint venture
with a Japanese company,
they'll send 24 people here to
learn everything you know
and you'll send one person to
tell them everything you know.*

Kupfer 1988

General background

Japan is an island nation. The major cities of Tokyo (the capital),
Yokohama, Osaka, Nagoya, and Kyoto are on Honshu, the largest island.
Japan is an amalgam of volcanic mountains, short, rapid rivers and small,
agriculturally rich plains. Japan has been heavily influenced by the
Korean and Chinese cultures.

Politics

Japan has been a parliamentary democracy for over a hundred years.
The legislative power resides in the *Diet*, which consists of the House of
Representatives and the House of Councillors, both of which are elected
by the citizens of Japan. The emperor is the official head of state as a
constitutional monarch. The House of Representatives selects the prime
minister from the majority party.

The bureaucracy exerts a great deal of power in policy development
and implementation as well. It possesses a continuing cohesive identity
and political voice with influence outliving any government. There is a
long tradition of group rather than personalised leadership in both
political and business worlds.

Society and culture

Ethnicity

Virtually all the population of 125 million is ethnic Japanese, the remainder being mainly Ainu and Koreans. The Japanese distinguish clearly between things foreign and things Japanese, with a preference for the latter. If you are not a Japanese you are an 'outsider' or *gaijin*. Strict immigration and citizenship rules keep Japan's population as 'Japanese' as possible.

Religion

Shintoism is the main Japanese religion. It teaches respect for nature and counsels harmony between human beings and nature. A large number of shrines characterised by red wooden archways dot the cultural landscape, dedicated to a plethora of Shinto gods (*Kami*), as everything possesses its own *kami*.

Confucianism and Buddhism have also influenced Japanese society, providing two focal values of loyalty and obligation and themes of strong family, social hierarchy, ritualistic behaviour and politeness. While there are few Christians, the Japanese celebrate Christmas with commercial decorations and Christmas carols due to its importance in the West. There are also rituals for special occasions such as births, weddings, and deaths. Many follow the beliefs and practices of different religions for different life events. Each Japanese home is likely to have an altar where respects are paid on a regular basis.

Decision-making, saving face and hierarchies

Japan is a high power distance, collectivist, and high context culture. The Japanese have a great respect for fixed hierarchical relationships. A Japanese person will usually obey people of greater age, seniority, social position, political position, or rank at work. There is no reward for individuality; group unanimity and consensus is the prime motivation of behaviour. In Japan 'we' comes before 'I' and being excluded from the group is serious punishment. A child being punished may be sent out of the house; in the West they would be grounded in the house. The high consciousness of social order and group feeling with its obligations and responsibilities stems from Confucianism. Attempts are always made to maintain harmony (*wa*) in all things, therefore the Japanese are generally non-confrontational, preferring to establish unanimous consensus when making decisions.

Hierarchy is evident in the language where, for example, there is no simple word for brother or sister but words to indicate whether the sibling is older or younger than you. Even in school younger students use a polite form of address to older students. The junior person always bows first and lowest.

'Saving face' and maintaining dignity are also absolutely critical. The Japanese go to great lengths to avoid calling attention to anything that might cause embarrassment to themselves or others to maintain face. As a result, they are not likely to act spontaneously, and will carefully consider all possible implications before acting. They rarely single out an individual for praise or criticism if it is likely to separate the individual from the group.

Social reciprocity is an important Japanese cultural trait. This reciprocity is called *kashi* and *kari* or literally, loan and debt. When a person does a favour towards another it creates an expectation that the person helped will reciprocate at some future date. This has obvious implications in the business world.

However, younger professionals exposed to Western value systems are now trying to break free and demonstrate more individuality within business life and create a better balance between their professional and private lives. Significant generational differences are emerging in Japanese society. However, at the core, these individuals usually retain their Japanese character and these changes do not yet extend to the family, where upholding the family name and showing respect for the senior members still holds sway.

Inflexibility

Linked to their collectivist nature, the Japanese are rule bound, methodical and meticulous in their approach to daily activities, following procedures to the letter. Bending rules is something that hardly ever enters a Japanese mind. This may explain why the Japanese have excelled in areas such as manufacturing and producing high quality products. However, the Japanese are also rather practical and unsentimental about the past and show a willingness to gradually adapt to new situations and ideas. School children are taught in a way that stresses interdependence and reliance on others, and are discouraged to be independent self thinkers.

Male domination

Male domination continues to mark Japanese society. There is an old Confucian saying that a woman should obey her father in youth, her husband in maturity, and her son in old age. Women are the primary caretaker to children and elderly parents, as well as managing the household. Those who work tend to be allocated menial or 'lower' tasks. However, Japanese women are gradually becoming more assertive, both politically and socially, as more gain degrees and pursue careers particularly looking for work with foreign firms, which offer more equal opportunities for advancement than local ones.

Economy—The keiretsu network

Japan's post-Second World War development has been the result of an alliance of business leaders and politicians. *Keiretsu* refers to the financial and non-financial relationships between companies that links them together in a pattern of formal and informal cross-ownership and mutual obligation. Two major ones are Mitsui and Mitsubishi. Each *keiretsu* has significant holdings in the fields of banking, manufacturing, mining, shipping, and foreign marketing. There is a high proportion of corporate cross shareholding. These related companies provide each other with support in finance and trade, and with strategic co-ordination, assisting each other on new products, markets and projects. Within each cluster there are companies drawn from every industrial sector. This provides diversification, access to technology, economy of scope, the possibility of winding down inefficient operations to free up resources and employees for other parts of the group, and a secure financial base. Companies can subsidise another within the '*keiretsu* family' when necessary. The functioning of *keiretsu* is facilitated by employees at the same level in different companies in the *keiretsu*, knowing each other through school and university so that they are comfortable doing business with each other.

The *keiretsu* nature of Japanese business has made it difficult for foreign companies to penetrate the commercial sector. The use of high level local advisors and hiring of senior Japanese managers who have good contacts assists in manoeuvring into relevant business networks. Careful selection of an appropriate entry mechanism is essential as there is a strong degree of lock-in. Shifting alliances are regarded poorly in Japan, so first impressions count and there are no or few second chances.

The lifetime employment, employer paternalism, long-term relationships with suppliers, and minimal competition that has characterised the economy is starting to decline. The influence and control of the *keiretsu* will also decrease as government and businesses recognise the need to restructure and deregulate parts of the economy, particularly in the financial sector in response to the global economy.

Making contacts

One of the first steps in entering the Japanese market is to establish contact with potential partners, distributors or buyers of one's product. A letter or phone call will usually not be sufficient to elicit a response regarding the possibility of establishing a business relationship. However, this does not necessarily signify a lack of interest, as it would in many other countries. Instead, there are a host of factors that can impede the formulation of a response. Among such factors are:

- *A lack of foreign language capability* which may impede under-standing of your communication. While most larger firms possess comprehensive resources for conducting business in major langu-ages, the average small or medium-sized firm is not accustomed to direct contact with non-Japanese companies and may not have access to multilingual capabilities. In general, the onus is on you to come prepared to communicate your information, if necessary, in Japanese.
- *A lack of familiarity with your company or product.* Having a well-established name in overseas markets is no guarantee that a company or product will enjoy a similar reputation in Japan.
- *A lack of information.* Making a commitment to negotiate with an overseas firm is a big step for Japanese companies, and many are unwilling to do so without detailed information concerning the pro-posed business venture. Sending annual reports, corporate broch-ures, and other data about your company may help eliminate this problem.
- *The complex decision-making process* implemented by Japanese companies. The time required by a Japanese company to formulate a response to initial contact may substantially delay communication.

The personal introduction

In business, the Japanese place considerable importance on personal interactions and devote much time to building relationships and developing trust. The preference is for face-to-face contact with poten-tial partners. A formal introduction to a person or company must be made by someone of an equal level to the person whom you want to meet, or by someone who has done a favour for that person. There is an unwillingness to discuss matters of importance over the telephone or through written correspondence. This applies particularly to small and medium-sized firms, which are accustomed to personal contact.

Thus third party personal introductions are an integral part of conducting business in Japan. A direct approach by someone completely unknown (cold calling) is uncomfortable for the Japanese and will usually prove futile. A highly respected third party introducer will increase your chances of achieving business success, especially if the person you want to meet has a sense of obligation to your introducer. The introducer (*shokaisha*) becomes a trusted and respected go-between, who may also act as mediator during difficult negotiations. Be careful not to require too much of the introducer and place them in an awkward position with the person to whom you have been introduced. In your business dealing you must ensure that you continue to be 'worthy' of your introduction, as your introducer has essentially guaranteed your worthiness by introducing you.

It is not absolutely necessary that an introduction come from someone especially close to or familiar with the party being contacted; however, any introduction is better than none. For instance, contacting a local overseas branch of a Japanese company and asking for an introduction to its head office is a more effective means of establishing initial contact than merely sending a letter directly. Serving the same function as an intermediary, the branch representative will be responsible for facilitating correspondence with the head office.

There are several other potential means of arranging introductions, including embassies, trade representatives, and other official government organisations. Fostering and maintaining good relationships with your company's Japanese banks can also be fruitful. Whenever possible, it is helpful to have a local agent, representative, or distributor manage local issues for you. JETRO, the Japan External Trade Organisation, helps foreign businesses enter Japan by hosting trade shows in Japan and by facilitating meetings between specific companies and industries.

However, do not be discouraged from making a direct approach if no other means of contact is available. This practice has become somewhat more acceptable in recent years, as corporate managers re-evaluate traditional Japanese business practices in recognition of the need for new approaches to a changing business environment. When making a direct approach, however, at the very least you are advised to ascertain in advance the name of the person in charge of the section with which you wish to make contact or conduct business.

You must try to interact with a person of similar status after the initial introduction, but also pay attention to all members of your counterpart's team or office; they are all likely to be involved in the decision-making. The structure of large Japanese organisations is intricate, and understanding the hierarchical arrangements is an important key to achieving good communications with the right people. You must be aware of the exact positioning of each person and make sure information filters both up and down. A tendency exists in Western business to go straight to the person with the highest position, since that person can usually make a decision single-handedly. In Japan, however senior the person is, it is likely that considerable consultation will take place before the final decision is made. That is why it is so important that communications be a multi-level endeavour.

The Aisatsu

For negotiations of considerable significance it is important for the chair person or a high-ranking person in the non-Japanese company to establish initial contact with his or her counterpart in the Japanese company. The Japanese word for this procedure is *aisatsu*, which literally translates as 'greeting' in English, but conveys a much deeper meaning in Japanese. Rather than for discussing specific points or business matters of substance, this initial *aisatsu* serves to break the ice, allowing you to make your company known to the Japanese side and get acquainted with the Japanese firm. Although this procedure is not considered necessary for such activities as the export of small quantities of a product to a trading company, it is still a good idea to take advantage of all opportunities to develop relationships and expand your network of contacts.

Corporate structure

There is a well-defined corporate structure with specific management roles and titles. Although Japanese organisational structures often appear to be the same as those in other countries, some key differences are not always readily evident. A notable example is the existence of formal and informal mechanisms for communication. Because of these mechanisms, a lower-ranking employee in an important division may at any given time have more active influence than a person in a high-ranking position. Thus titles may not accord with the locus of decision-making. Areas of authority and influence may overlap in a very nebulous way.

Japanese white-collar professionals join a company directly after leaving university/college, often making a lifetime commitment. The top companies recruit from the most prestigious schools and universities, the key selection criteria being the ability to fit in with the 'company' and give it loyalty and allegiance. Many companies recruit from the same universities or geographic region annually and keep the year group together to continue the camaraderie. This increases the harmony, loyalty and collective nature in the enterprise. A young employee will be rewarded through their lifetime of service not on grounds of merit but for loyalty, total involvement and service that enables the company to prosper. In return the employee gains a huge range of company benefits and facilities.

This paternalistic attitude of companies toward their employees stems from the close-knit conformist historical feudal village, which helped to foster Japan's well-known teamwork concept. It reflects Japan's collectivist, high power distance culture. Companies became the substitute 'feudal lord' requiring loyalty but offering security in return. Employers gained by retaining labour on which they had spent resources training and skilling. The wage system also encourages employees to stay with one firm, as financial rewards are delayed until a worker's senior years.

Although talent and capability are considered to a much greater extent now than in the past, seniority is still the foundation of most corporate hierarchies. Thus, an individual's status within a company is often closely related to age. As well as age, marital status may influence a male's career path. There is distinct social and professional pressure to find a wife at least by one's early 30s. As marriage and family are perceived as symbols of stability and maturity, a bachelor over the age of 30 will have difficulty gaining promotion and will be given postings or assignments lacking in prestige. Even appearing to work hard is more important than actually accomplishing anything substantial.

Gradually, as a result of global economic challenges, these policies are starting to break down, and with recent changes in the economy and corporate restructurings, more Japanese professionals are considering switching companies at mid-career. There are the beginnings of a discernible shift from a traditional, seniority-based promotion system to one based more on performance and ability, as companies restructure to meet the changing economic environment. Efficiency and effectiveness are becoming valued characteristics as Japanese businesses realise that they will need to soften their traditional belief in hierarchy to enable young, creative, and capable professionals retain the competitiveness of the company.

Getting down to business

The first meeting

It is essential to provide written information on your company as well as your proposal at the beginning of a meeting, or prior to it, with essential parts translated into Japanese, as few Japanese really understand spoken English well. They tend to understand written English better than spoken English. Clear, colourful professional presentations and graphics, and technically detailed material impresses and is expected from companies seeking business in Japan. The presentation skills and quality of material tell the Japanese about the quality of your company, its products and reliability.

The first meeting is used essentially to establish a relationship. Your Japanese counterpart is likely to be accompanied by several associates. General talk will dominate, such as remarks about the weather, your trip, and your experiences since arriving. You should ask your counterparts about their experiences in other countries. Increasingly the questions will be 'get to know you' ones—about place of residence, city/country attractions, children's schooling and activities, sports, hobbies, world travel, and arts/culture. Developing knowledge of each other helps to start a friendly relationship. It is acceptable to gradually shift the conversation to the purpose of the meeting.

The Japanese do not respond well to aggressive manners, and display soft speech and quiet manners which they identify with wisdom, experience, and age. So do not appear brash and demanding in your attitude, speech or mannerisms, or so pressed for time that you appear uninterested in your counterparts. Some Japanese, particularly older ones, may close their eyes during a meeting. This does not mean that they are sleepy or bored, but rather that they are deep in thought, reflecting on the topic. The Japanese are a high context culture and their conversation content assumes the other person has an indepth knowledge of the subject matter.

At a meeting the place of honour is usually that furthest away from the door or that nearest to the *Tokonoma* (the alcove with the scroll in it). Custom dictates that the visitor makes a show of initially refusing the place of honour. All others will wait for you to sit before taking their seats. At the end of a meeting you will be formally escorted often as far as your car. Reciprocate if they are visiting your offices/hotel and escort them to their car. Make your goodbye somewhat formal and polite, accompanied by a bow.

There are several key things to keep in mind at the initial and later meetings with a Japanese business person, including how to address them, presenting your business card, and bowing.

Addressing your counterparts

The suffix -*san* is added to the end of a person's family name as an honorific title. For example, 'Mr Frank Brown' would be called 'Brownsan' by his Japanese colleagues. This is the English equivalent of 'Mr' or 'Mrs', and you should use this suffix in place of these titles when referring to Japanese persons, but never place -*san* at the end of your own name when you refer to yourself. You may also refer to a person using the English 'Mr' or 'Mrs'. Professional titles may also be used like 'Dr' but never use both the title and the family name together; use one or the other. First names are never to be used between business colleagues and are reserved for close family. Many Japanese who have worked together for many years have never used each other's first names.

Greeting a Japanese in their own language is regarded as courteous and they will be favourably endowed towards you for taking the trouble to learn some basic phrases. Every syllable is pronounced exactly as it is written in Japanese. A standard initial greeting is: '*Hajimemashite.*

Watakushi no namae wa Ross desu. Dozo yoroshiku', which means 'This is my first time to have the pleasure of meeting you. My name is Mr. Ross. Please feel kindly toward me'. Bow or nod your head, then present your business card. People should be introduced in order of seniority.

The business card

An integral part of Japanese business etiquette is the exchange of business cards. Japanese business people exchange cards when meeting someone for the first time who may have significance in the future. As Japanese business becomes increasingly internationalised, those Japanese business people most likely to interface with non-Japanese are often supplied with business cards printed in Japanese on one side and a foreign language, usually English, on the reverse side. This is aimed at enhancing recognition and pronunciation of Japanese names, which are often unfamiliar to foreign business people. Conversely, it is advisable for visiting business people to carry and exchange with their Japanese counterparts a similar type of card printed in Japanese and their native language. It is wise to have cards printed in Japanese on one side and English on the other (see Figure 8.1). These cards can often be obtained through business centres in major hotels.

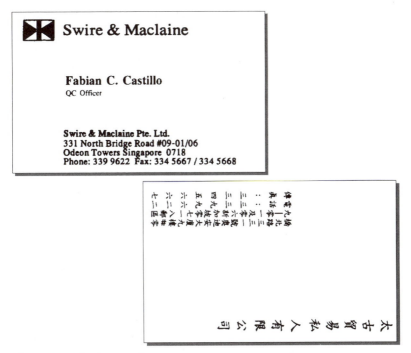

Figure 8.1 A business card

In Japan, present and receive a business card with both hands. The words should face the receiver. When you present cards written in *kanji* (Chinese characters), make sure the cards are facing in the correct direction. Japanese text is written from right to left and read downward. Accordingly, some Japanese business cards may be written vertically. On receiving a business card you should appear to read it slowly and carefully to demonstrate full respect for the other person, even if you cannot read a word of Japanese. If you are sitting at a conference or other type of table, the cards can be placed on the table in front of you for the duration of the meeting. This also helps to locate who is sitting where. It would be considered rude to put a prospective business partner's card in your pocket before sitting down to discuss business matters. The presentation of the business card (*meishi*) is actually an acknowledgment of a person's identity.

When receiving a card, it is considered common courtesy to offer one in return. Not returning a card might convey the impression that you are not committed to sowing the seeds that could blossom into a meaningful business relationship in the future. Never hand over a creased business card.

Bowing

Although the handshake is increasingly common in Japan, bowing remains the most prevalent formal method of greeting, sending off, and expressing gratitude or apologising to another person. Bowing allows greeting and courtesy without invading the other person's space. It also allows greetings at a distance when verbal communication is impractical. When meeting foreign business people, however, Japanese will often use the handshake as a way of greeting or a combination of both a handshake and a bow. Even handshakes can be awkward as many Japanese cannot refrain from the conditioned reflex of a bow as they greet someone, and when it comes to hugs and kisses they have no idea how to react. Be careful to keep your handshake light, and do not judge a person by the strength of his or her grip.

Bowing is an art form, with different angles and styles of bowing, depending on the relationship of the parties involved. For example, the more junior person always bows first and with a greater depth and angle. If you are meeting a professional at the same level as yourself, you may bow at the same angle, though if your Japanese counterpart is older than you are, you should bow slightly lower than he does. Foreign business people are not expected to be familiar with these intricacies, and therefore a deep nod of the head or a slight bow will suffice in most cases.

The Japanese accept that foreigners have considerable difficulty learning the nuances of who bows first and lowest and do not expect foreigners to bow. So don't try to imitate Japanese bows, as your good intentions may result in an improper bow that offends someone.

Some other cultural issues

The Japanese are quiet, traditional and reserved people for whom etiquette is important. It is considered rude to display an open mouth. Accordingly, most Japanese women will cover their mouths when laughing or expressing shock or disbelief. The Japanese will maintain smiling faces even when talking about a recent death in the family in order to maintain composure. They may also laugh to express a negative attitude such as 'you must be kidding'. They do not appreciate jokes. In public it is not done to blow your nose—keep sniffing! Nor should you eat while you are walking in the street. Carry some kleenex with you as the public toilets, while clean, do not have toilet paper. As the Japanese think the passing of money is distasteful, when buying something, look for a little tray on the counter; this is where you put the money and where your change will be placed.

You should maintain a straight posture at all times. When you are seated, place both your feet firmly on the floor with your arms resting in your lap or on the armrests. Traditionally, junior people tend to sit with their hands in their laps, and also with a slight forward tilt of the head and shoulders, out of deference to the senior people present. Senior people usually sit with both arms resting on the sides of a chair or table. When you are standing talking to someone, your hands should never be placed in your pockets. Don't cross your legs or bring one foot up to rest across your knee.

As women do not feature strongly in Japanese business circles, few Japanese are comfortable dealing with women in business situations. They will certainly find it difficult to socialise with a woman on a business level. It is not meant personally, but stems solely from their lack of cultural experience of such a situation. Try to avoid any situation or confrontation that may cause embarrassment to your counterparts. With patience and gentle persistence you will be able to gradually win their respect and business, but as a woman do not expect to be able to develop close relationships with them. Some of the younger Japanese, particularly those who have had some time overseas, will be able to deal with you better than their older colleagues.

Building business relationships

Business relationships are characterised by a well-structured hierarchy and a strong emphasis on nurturing personal contacts. Relationships in Japan are built up over a long period of time and often have common roots such as birthplace, school or university. Ingroup social activities add further cement to the bonds. It is not surprising that looking in from outside, many overseas companies fear that the Japanese business world will be hard to break into.

Japanese businesses generally put a premium on stable long-term relationships with business partners. In addition to price and product they want to understand the backgrounds, personalities and business strategies of prospective associates and their companies. The Japanese place high importance on loyalty, honour, and spoken commitment, as these are central elements in developing long-term relationships through which trust grows. As a result, many business decisions are initially verbal ones, followed up later by a written agreement which functions more as a formality. As a non-Japanese, a *gaijin*, you will always be regarded as a foreigner, no matter how hard you work at building your relationship. A close business relationship in Japan will therefore always have a strong formal dimension permeating it. You will rarely be allowed to become part of a counterpart's inner circle, no matter how long a profitable and amicable a business relationship lasts.

Making use of existing relationships while striving to form new ties can be an effective means for companies seeking to enter the Japanese market, as successfully developing close ties may require a long period of time, and patience is essential. Making the effort to nurture these relationships, however, will demonstrate a serious approach to the Japanese market and can prove to be rewarding over the long term. The Western short time-frame requirements for achieving objectives, with managers moved around if a business deal does not look like taking off, is counter to building the necessary relationships. The Japanese find it impossible to deal with an everchanging overseas partner. Keeping core people involved over the long term can facilitate negotiations tremendously, since relationships are built up slowly with a personal touch. Staying power is of prime importance and overseas businesses have to be financially prepared to carry the burden of non-profitable involvement for some time. The positive side of the process is that once the business ties are firmly cemented, they are invariably solid and long lasting.

The Japanese have an eye for detail. Therefore all documents must be accurate and thorough. There is a mania for information and you are expected to have valid answers. Avoid draft documents that look like draft documents with poor formatting and grammatical or spelling errors. Although final contracts may be vague, the discussions are detailed. Everything you do must exude quality, whether it is in a fax, a proposal or advertising. Technical details must be spelled out. Any sloppiness is seen as a reflection of your performance standards and business acumen.

In addition to quality of communication, frequency of communication is also important. Putting forward a proposal and then not following it up quickly is regarded as lack of real interest. By keeping a steady stream of faxes, e-mails, memos, agendas, proposals for meetings etc, an overseas company makes it commitment clear. Always give any communication from the Japanese side an immediate response to indicate the matter is being pursued, even if an answer isn't available immediately. It is an indication of acknowledgement and action. It is also essential in demonstrating commitment to modify products to the local preferences, and produce promotional material and packaging etc in Japanese. Japanese customers also demand a local office that can deal with servicing, delivery and other problems that can arise.

Consensus building and the ringi system

One of the organisational features peculiar to Japanese companies, that can affect the conduct of negotiations, is the group decision-making system known as *ringi seido*, or consensus in decision-making. It is a multi-step procedure for building consensus and often involves a complex set of negotiations through which divergent viewpoints are considered and accommodated. Under this system the *ringi-sho* or written proposal is circulated around the company, finally moving upward through the chain of management command. The original proposal will probably be written by a junior employee, with others adding comments or their approval as the proposal is circulated. The proposal will be redirected back to the original group for changes if there is no approval or serious reservation at any level.

Only when proposals/reports have received total support will they move to the next, higher level. For most medium- and major-level issues, final approval rests with the most senior executives.

The *ringi* system is very time consuming and there can even be informal discussions before a *ringi* is prepared, so that no reviewer is completely unaware of a proposal before it reaches their intray. The aim is to build consensus so that a proposal is finalised that meets with total approval.

For the foreign business person waiting for a response the process can be frustrating due to the seeming inability of the Japanese negotiator to make a firm commitment. But from the Japanese perspective, building consensus and group decision-making is critical and precludes disagreement over the eventual decision. These decisions are easier to implement than those rendered by a president alone, or by other high company officials acting on their own, since everyone affected has had input into the final proposal.

In short, do not expect a definitive response until the decision-making process has been fully completed. If you are unable to remain in Japan for an extended period as this process is played out, appoint a local representative to deal with any issues that arise.

Japanese staff also expect an expatriate manager to run their operation in this consensus approach. Japanese employees are more motivated and effective with if you use *ringi* consensus-based decision-making, clearly defined office rules and targets, and a clear line of hierarchical command.

Negotiation

The emphasis on consensus-based decision-making means that Japanese delegations are usually much larger than their foreign counterparts, encompassing representatives from various sections and levels of management. The Japanese characterise the bargaining table with polite manners, ambiguous objections, restraint and hidden emotions. They take a long-term perspective on negotiation in which the long-term relationship is more important than maximising immediate profit. In fact, Japanese companies are more concerned with long-term market share than immediate profits, often driving down prices to repel competitors and capture a larger share of the market. Deeper market penetration is effected at the cost of a slow return on investment. In other respects they are not rational in the economists' sense, in that they will sacrifice their interests as purchasers for the interests of the nation as a whole, and will often make spending decisions on the basis of who is selling, not on the basis of price.

The Japanese have two concepts of truth. *Honne* is the real or inner truth of an issue, but *tatemae* corresponds to the diplomatic, official or public position. This dichotomy assists the Japanese to maintain harmony by avoiding the expression of their true feelings or *honne*. As a result, words do not always truthfully express what a person is thinking in a culture where polite indirect behaviour is valued. You need to ask more indirect non-offensive questions to get a better sense of their true opinion on an issue without causing embarrassment to your Japanese counterpart.

In communication, a logical, intellectual approach is insufficient; the emotional level is important too. The Japanese sometimes complain that the overseas person is always doing things to achieve their purpose; the Japanese prefer to allow things to 'become' and happen through natural progression.

We have already noted that age is synonymous with wisdom and experience in Japanese business. The Japanese will be more comfortable negotiating or conducting business with an older person. If your counterpart appears significantly older than you, you will have to work even harder on establishing a level of mutual respect and trust through a patient, soft-spoken, gentle demeanour and a respectful deference to the older person. Always pay attention to the oldest person present even if they speak no English, as they will usually be the person with most influence and would be insulted if they were ignored.

As the Japanese are a low uncertainty tolerant culture, they tend to be cautious and thorough in their decision-making. Their collectivism also demands that negotiation must be performed such that the team as a whole receives credit and praise, not a single individual. There are, of course, some Japanese international firms that do not fit the typical pattern and employ aggressive executive managers who are quick decision-makers. But generally, for the methodical Japanese, the results can be less important than the way in which the negotiation and business activities are conducted.

While bargaining over price and terms is usual in Asia, the Japanese do not fit the pattern with concessions being made slowly. So do not make concessions quickly, for the Japanese may question the sincerity of your original proposal. They will negotiate on one issue at a time, rather than opening up debate on the whole proposal. This again is time-consuming, but it allows you to hold the rest of the cards close to your chest and not be required to show them all at once.

A permanent presence

A permanent market presence is indispensable. The challenge is to maintain close relationships with all elements of the market including retailers, distributors and end user to demonstrate commitment. Japan is not the place for the spot sale of goods as the Japanese value long-term commitment, reliability and quality of service and goods to a far higher degree than Westerners. Japanese customers simply will not deal with a company which does not have a local office able to deal immediately (in Japanese) with servicing, delivery problems, ordering and the like, all of which indicates trustworthiness. Thus a local competent agent must be appointed who can deal with all these issues as well as produce promotional literature and manuals in Japanese. It is also expected that distributors, retailers and customers will be motivated by the provision of gifts and prizes etc, such as tickets to sporting events and free holidays. The seasonal gift giving detailed below is also part of the means to reaffirm close ties with distributors, retailers etc.

Communication guidelines

Verbal and nonverbal communication

As is common in Asia, the Japanese—particularly junior persons—often avoid sustained eye contact as it can be considered intimidating. Silence is common when the Japanese are thinking deeply about an issue, and should not be interrupted.

The Japanese can maintain smiling faces when they are talking about a death or serious accident in order to maintain composure. They can also laugh when expressing a negative attitude.

As a high context culture, indirect and vague communication is more acceptable than direct and specific references. Sometimes sentences are left unfinished so that the other person can conclude them in their own mind. Thus conversation can be a shadowy activity, never definite enough to preclude personal interpretation, but clumsy for science, technology and business.

A Japanese who is too specific may be viewed as rudely displaying superior knowledge. The Japanese can communicate with a wide palette of communicative expression—what they call 'belly·language'—conveying their intentions through penetrating stares, appropriately timed grunts and quick glances. For example, a guttural moan with the tilt of head will often occur in a situation in which they feel uncomfortable. Anytime you hear a laugh or see a smile that appears inappropriate, it may be hiding some discomfort over an issue or situation.

The high context communication can cause problems for Western business people who are confounded by the meaning of what is being conveyed and by the use of 'yes' and 'no' in the Japanese language. For example, the appropriate negative answer to the English-language question 'You don't want any coffee, do you?' is 'No, I don't'. In Japanese, however, the appropriate answer is to confirm this statement by saying 'Yes, I don't', which appears contradictory in English. This feature of the Japanese way of answering questions should be kept in mind. It is best to simply refrain from using negative interrogatives.

One should also always keep in mind that various equivalents of the word for 'yes' in Japanese, such as *hai*, (pronounced 'hi'), do not necessarily indicate agreement with what has been said. They merely confirm that what is being said has been heard or understood, not necessarily that it is agreed with. When you hear a 'yes' watch for verbal clues that might indicate enthusiasm, caution, concern etc.

Another factor to consider is the cultural aversion of most Japanese to answering a question with 'no'. As a negative reply, 'no' implies disharmony with the position of others, which is avoided if possible, especially as 'no' reflects on the person as well as the idea. If a negotiating position is unclear or if opinions within a group are diverse, a Japanese business person may reply affirmatively just to maintain a facade of unity and harmony. The best way to overcome this difficulty is to ask directly for the other party's opinion and clearly state that one would prefer to have opinions expressed frankly to avoid disharmony later.

When negotiating with the Japanese, keep in mind that they do not always say what they mean. The very positively sounding 'we will consider the matter in a forwarding looking way' implies 'probably not'.

Similarly, the Japanese are rarely candid about their opinions, as frankness may cause discomfort and confrontation. Instead, they speak in a roundabout manner utilising gentler phrases. For example, expressions like the following can mean no:

'I will try'	'I will think about it'
'It is an interesting idea.'	'I am not sure'
'It may be difficult'	'We shall make efforts'
'I would like to, but . . .'	

A Japanese will signal that they 'don't know' or 'don't understand', by waving their own hand in front of their face. If you have to say 'no' do it in the same roundabout way to avoid confrontation and loss of face, like 'yes I hear you and understand what you are saying but . . .'

If possible have your second in command handle the chore of delivering bad news to the Japanese number two. In this way there is no loss of face for the Japanese chief negotiator.

Iken

In the West we all have opinions on most things and voice them aloud, even if they are not well thought out. In Japan, people who voice their opinions are seen as annoying. The word 'opinion' and the Japanese word '*iken*' mean the same on the surface, but the *iken* is formed as a result of lengthy consideration rather than as an immediate or subjective response. Similarly, while Western people expect to have different opinions and views and agree to disagree, the Japanese perceive a different view as indicative of a problem, mistake or poor relationship. This occurs perhaps because the word for differences in Japanese has connotations of 'mistake', whereas we see it as a neutral concept. We will 'agree to disagree' but the Japanese want harmony and are unwilling to halt discussion till all agree. One overseas person who worked for a Japanese company for a number of years cites a personal case where after a number of hours discussion at a meeting realised that their preferred course of action was not to be taken, even though they believed it was the right one. Accepting their Japanese colleagues decision, they maintained their right to disagree. The Japanese were very uncomfortable with this and were unwilling to halt their discussion until the overseas manager agreed, which the latter did simply to keep the Japanese onside.

Contracts

In Japan, the basic assumption is that both parties to any negotiation are honourable. The contract is secondary in importance to the trust built up between the companies/negotiators. Therefore some Japanese may be offended by an insistence on written contracts. The Japanese concept of *amae* denotes the mutual dependence on each others' goodwill and kindness; that both parties to a negotiation are honourable people. This explains why contracts are seen as a sign of distrust. The Japanese see contracts as a means of trying to maximise the interest of one party without considering the interest of the other party. The relationship is the commitment, not the business contract as in the Western world. A contract is seen as impeding flexibility in maintaining the relationship in the face of changing circumstance.

For example, in an economic downturn the Japanese may not order as many components as stipulated in the contract, but their expectation is that once business picks up they will order in excess of those in the original agreement to restore the balance. Alternatively if the purchaser was committed to an inflexible order level during temporary slow down that would sour the relationship.

Thus when problems arise later the Japanese company is likely to look beyond the terms of the contract in its search for a solution. While an intransigent attitude to the terms of the contract might succeed, the long-term benefits for other deals will be nil. Thus flexibility is invaluable as is the willingness to compromise. You can certainly indicate that while you are willing to be flexible, this will entail some sacrifice, but you will make every effort to work towards a solution acceptable to both sides. The long-term benefits of this approach will be great.

However, the international Japanese companies are aware of the need to document terms and agreements. If there is reluctance, politely explain that it is standard procedure for your company to detail specific terms, and it in no way reflects on the trustworthiness of the Japanese company. It is always best to point out how written contracts can also protect the Japanese company. Even though international Japanese companies are starting to use contracts, they dislike exit clauses, due to a profound distaste for discussing unpleasant eventualities before a relationship has had time to develop. They see it as almost inviting trouble.

The Japanese are not very litigious and generally prefer arbitration and compromise. As far as a Japanese company is concerned, using lawyers for problem-solving means that something is already very sour in the relationship. There are no known instances of happy endings between Japanese and foreign companies after litigation; so use the courts only as a last resort. This fits appropriately with their preference for non-confrontation. In fact, the desire to settle a problem amicably is so engrained in Japanese tradition that foreign lawyers have expressed frustration at the unwillingness of the Japanese to fight in court even when they have a very strong case. However, the Japanese have a great deal of respect for laws, rules, and regulations, with private and public entities meticulously observing all rules in the most minute detail.

The social context of business

Dining out

Business lunches and dinners are common, although business breakfasts are rare. These occasions are times when you can get to know your Japanese counterparts. Eating is ritualistic, communal and time consuming; the food is less important than the interaction. The Japanese trust those with whom they socialise, so never turn down after-hours socialisation. Even though you are socialising you must still not over-disclose about yourself, nor ask personal questions about your Japanese colleagues' background or family. The Japanese get quite uncomfortable about these matters if probed in depth.

Although most business people will begin work at 9.00 am, they will dine out late into the evening, often until midnight, spending most of the evening dining and drinking with customers and/or colleagues within the firm or the industry at large. This form of social interchange is considered to be a vital part of the professional workday for white-collar professionals. You can expect a lot of late-night socialising with Japanese business people. For the most part, Japanese spouses do not participate. You would not be expected to bring your wife along either for this night on the town with the boys.

Some employees may even go back to the office to finish tasks or simply to put in 'face time' after business socialising. Junior executives feel this pressure to be 'seen' as hard-working, diligent, and conscientious and rarely leave the office before their superiors do. You thankfully will not be expected to work as late or as long as this. But you can gain respect if you do keep the hours of your Japanese counterpart.

In traditional restaurants, the males sit cross-legged and the women sit with their legs tucked neatly to one side on *tatami* mats. Your shoes should be removed. Never leave your chopsticks standing in your rice: this is part of a funeral ritual. It is usual to hold or touch your glass when the host is filling it otherwise it is presumed you don't want any.

The Japanese drink before and at dinner, providing a context in which both parties can feel a little freer and an ideal opportunity for you to increase your acceptability. You should participate but not drink sufficient to make errors in judgement. When entertaining your counterparts on a return visit to your country you will be expected to return the lavish entertainment (dinners, golf, theatre and sporting event tickets etc).

The karaoke bar is becoming very popular. You should join in, as participating enthusiastically and singing when it is your turn is a perfect way to show that you are a team member. Don't worry about your singing ability; no one else sings well either: participation is more important than talent. The same goes for company sporting activities. Although the star player will always be the office hero, those who do not play at all are the 'outcasts' as compared to those who play poorly. Participation is the key.

A home visit

The Japanese will rarely invite you home, as their homes are usually small and modest compared to Western homes. Remove your shoes before entering a house. Most homes have an area just inside the door for removing shoes. You will usually be provided with slippers. Another pair of slippers in used in the bathroom. A gift should be taken, but not flowers. Most good department stores in Japan will assist you in selecting an appropriate gift. During the meal men tend to sit cross-legged while women kneel. Touch or hold your glass when it is being refilled otherwise it is presumed you do not want any more. Send a thankyou letter or make a phone call, much the same as you would in Western countries several days after the event.

Giving and receiving gifts

The giving and receiving of gifts plays an important part in Japanese social life with about $A8 billion each year spent on gifts. This is the measure of its seriousness in Japan, particularly as a way of maintaining relationships, but as recent scandals have unearthed, there can be an ulterior motive. In a gift giving culture, it is easy to disguise a bribe as a gift. Some people give gifts out of obligation and duty, others because they are after a favour, and at others times it simply signifies a thank you or condolence. You may view this excessive gift giving as corruption, but in Japan it is just part of the social system. Money may be given to bereaved persons, children, and sick people, but never do it in business circles.

If you are meeting with your counterparts for the first time, or are re-visiting clients after overseas travel, you may want to present a small gift, souvenir/regional speciality, or company product. Generally, these are not expected at first meetings. If you choose to present gifts, they should be presented toward the end of a meeting or visit. Always have enough gifts for everyone present in a meeting. Senior people should not receive the same items as junior people. It is advisable to carry a variety of tasteful items such as leather goods, wine or fine china with you just in case you need them, but avoid gaudy, heavily emblazoned items with blatant advertising of your company, although golf shirts or baseball caps can be exceptions. If you have a gift for only one person, present it privately after your meeting. If you have a group gift, make its group nature known prior to presenting the gift. If you give expensive pens, make sure that they have fine points which are more suited to writing in *kanji*. Flowers are only given in the event of a death or illness.

The Japanese usually give visitors gifts and it is considered polite to reciprocate. During successive rounds of gift giving, present gifts of equal or slightly greater value than the previous round. Don't upset the balance or start with expensive gifts. This will only create an increasing financial obligation for both parties. This obligation to reciprocate creates a potentially dangerous 'money go round' for public figures. For future gifts, note the likes and dislikes of your counterpart. Giving items linked to a hobby or an activity is much appreciated and communicates respect and friendship. Giving copies of the group photograph is also much appreciated.

Gifts must always be wrapped, but never in white because it is the funeral colour. Wrapped gifts are often kept in the shopping bag during a meeting to prevent excessive attention being attracted to the gift. Gifts are given and received with both hands and accompanied with a slight bow, and should not be opened in the presence of the giver. A gift should always be presented in a humble way, so as you give a gift, you should say 'Please accept this small item' (*'Tsumaranai mono desu ga'*).

Gift giving even has specific occasions, particularly at *oseibo* (year's end) and *ochugen* (midsummer). For businesses in Japan these are *must give occasions*. *Oseibo* gifts are given to thank clients for their business, for loyalty and gratitude of earlier favours in the first half of December. *Ochugen* occurs between mid-July in Tokyo and mid-August in other regions, falling two weeks before *obon*, the holiday for honouring the dead. This period of gift giving was originally an occasion to provide consolation, including financial support to families who had suffered bereavement in the first six months of the year.

If you are involved in business in Japan at these two times it is appropriate for you or your representative to ensure *oseibo* and *ochugen* gifts are exchanged with those with whom you have dealings. However, if you are on a short first time visit for a specific purpose it is not expected that you exchange *oseibo* or *ochugen* gifts, but simply the visit gift. Convention has established a price level for gifts at each corporate level. At the most senior levels, it is not uncommon for people to exchange gifts worth A$500 (US$300). Such stores have displays of appropriate gifts, will advise on choice, and gift wrap for you in their own trademark paper. The store will also deliver as these gifts are usually not delivered personally. Appropriate gifts for these two occasions include elaborate packs of whisky or other liquors, condiments, specialty fish and meats, and other food treats, such as dried seaweed. Buy internationally known brands of high grade products as the Japanese are very materialistic and brand conscious.

Items should be given in odd number quantities, or in pairs if giving gifts that consist of less than ten items, as this represents good luck. Ten is acceptable because it is a multiple of five but avoid four and nine for those numbers have homonyms relating to death. Red paper and ink is considered auspicious and red is used for wrapping paper and ribbon, particularly at Christmas. But do not use red paper or ink for gifts or cards to those who are sick or suffered bereavement as the colour signifies blood. If you are invited to a wedding the minimum you should give is 30 000 yen (A$270 or US$120).

Other useful information

What to wear

Your policy, whether you are male or female, is to be neat, orderly and conservative in dress. Most Japanese business people wear dark or navy blue suits, although slight variations in style and colour have come to be accepted in recent years. As a general rule, what is acceptable business attire in virtually any industrialised country is usually regarded as good business attire in Japan as well. If unsure about what constitutes appropriate attire for a particular situation, risk being dressed too conservatively. Above all, garish or ostentatious clothing or jewellery should be avoided, as the wearer is likely to be perceived as lacking seriousness. Choose clothes that will avoid an impression of excessive wealth or individuality. Colours have significance in Japan where white is for sorrow and black for joy. Men should refrain from wearing earrings. The Japanese take care to appear neat and well groomed at all times and they expect this of others.

Japanese companies frown upon employees making outward displays of wealth that might create distinctions among them or disrupt the harmony of the workplace. This is readily evident in most Japanese factories, where all employees, including top management, wear company uniforms to promote both safety and harmony.

Language

Standard Japanese is spoken throughout the country with some regional differences in accents. English is taught in many schools and is the most common foreign language. While many young people speak English with ease and fluency, older Japanese in senior business positions are unlikely to have any English, so it is advisable to obtain the services of an interpreter.

Major holidays

January I	New Year's Day
January 15	Adulthood Day
February 11	National Foundation Day
March 20/21	Vernal Equinox Day
April 29	Emperor's Birthday (Greenery Day)
May 3	Constitution Memorial Day
May 5	Children's Day
mid-August	Obon Festival (held in July in some cities)
September 15	Respect for the Aged Day
September 23/24	Autumnal Equinox Day
October 10	Health and Sports Day
November 3	Culture Day
November 23	Labour Thanksgiving Day

Avoid scheduling meetings during the three main holiday periods and adjacent weekends:

- Year's end and the New Year, from December 27 to January 4;
- Golden Week, from April 29 to May 5; and
- the Obon Festival at mid-August.

Summary

- A familial and group-oriented society. Propriety, a sense of order, self-control and appropriate behaviour are important, while individual initiative is unwelcome.
- A personal introduction is essential for a foreign business.
- Personal relationships score high and future relationships depend on how you are perceived to respond to the first encounter. Cut and dried business relationships are inadequate.
- The Japanese system of management is firmly rooted in collectivism and high power distance that emphasises harmony through consensus and is supported by a hierarchical structure of seniority-based promotion and wage increases. Although certain aspects of this system are now changing in line with shifts in the structure of Japanese society, a reliance on consensus continues to guide most corporate activity in Japan.
- Decision-making through the *ringi* system is time consuming but the answer will be one all agree on. You must think long-term.

- The Japanese tend to be formal, conservative, and meticulous in their approach. The use of introduction cards, bowing and posture are essential parts of business etiquette.
- Face saving, harmony, trustworthiness and long-term commitment are more important factors in gaining business than possibilities of achieving higher sales and profits.
- The Japanese are high context communicators and Westerners must be careful in interpreting what they mean, particularly 'yes' and 'no'.
- Gift giving is taken seriously with respect to cost, packaging and occasion.
- Business dinners and evening entertainment are popular in Japan and regarded as part of the work activities.

Activities

Try working out the solutions to these five problems, then check your responses with those in Appendix B.

1 Directly after completing his MBA, Sam Rosenberg was moved to a subsidiary of his company in Tokyo. He had studied Japanese for a year and was most interested in immersing himself in Japanese culture. Within the first month of his arrival he was invited to an office party. As was the custom, most of the employees were expected to entertain the group with a song, poem or joke. Knowing the keen interest the Japanese have in baseball, Sam recited a poem 'Casey at the Bat', which seemed to be well received. He was having a good time at the party and was secretly congratulating himself on his decision to come to Japan. In fact, he couldn't help thinking how informal and playful all his colleagues were, including the upper-level executives, a far cry from all the descriptions he had read of the Japanese as austere and humourless business people. Later in the evening Sam found himself talking with two of his immediate superiors. Wanting to draw on the informality and good humour of the moment, Sam casually brought up some plans he had for a new marketing strategy, only to be met with near total indifference. For the remainder of the evening Sam felt as though he was not being included in the party.

What advice could you give Sam?

a

2　Liz Jacobi, a corporate lawyer for an international accountancy firm, was responsible for property, negotiating leases for their new branches overseas. Because she had been particularly successful in similar negotiations in Europe, she was looking forward to securing attractive leasing agreements from a shopping mall developer in Tokyo. She was especially optimistic because of her successful telephone communications with her counterparts in Japan. But when she arrived with her two male assistants, she was told by her Japanese hosts how surprised they were that she should come to negotiate in person. Liz was usually not included in the after-hours socialising, and frequently the Japanese negotiators would direct their questions to her two male colleagues rather than to Liz herself.

Can you explain why Liz was treated as she was?

3　Tom Buckley, marketing manager for a timber company, was making a sales presentation to a plywood wholesaler in Tokyo. Tom had just proposed what he considered to be a fair price for a large shipment of first quality plywood. Much to his amazement, the three Japanese executives did not respond immediately, but rather sat across the table with their hands folded and their eyes cast downward, saying nothing. Fifteen seconds passed, then 30, and still no response. Finally, Tom became so exasperated that he said with a good deal of irritation in his voice. 'Would you like for me to repeat the offer?' From that point onward the talks were stalled and Tom never did successfully negotiate a contract for plywood.

What advice would you give Tom for further negotiations? What went wrong?

4　Ken Burns was a chief engineer for a machinery manufacturer which had recently signed a contract with one of its largest customers in Japan to upgrade the equipment and retrain mechanics to maintain the equipment more effectively. As part of the contract, the Japanese company sent all ten of their mechanics to Melbourne for a three-month retraining course under Ken's supervision. Although Ken had never lived or worked abroad, he was looking forward to the challenge, for he had been told that they were all fluent in English and tireless workers. The first several weeks of the training went along quite smoothly, but soon Ken became increasingly annoyed with the constant demands they were making on his personal time. They would seek him out after the regularly scheduled sessions were over for additional information. They sought his advice on how to occupy their leisure time. Several even asked him to help settle a disagreement that developed between them. Feeling frustrated by all these demands on his time, Ken told his Japanese trainees that he preferred not to mix business with pleasure. Within a matter of days the group requested another instructor.

What was the critical issue operating here?

Some useful further reading

Holden N. & Burgess M. (1994), *Japanese Led Companies: How to Make Them Your Customers, Maidenhead, McGraw Hill.*

March, R.M. (1990), *The Japanese Negotiator*, Kodansha International, London.

Woronoff, J. (1991), *The No-Nonsense Guide to Doing Business in Japan*, Tokyo, Yohan Publications.

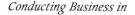

Conducting Business in

South Korea

General background

South Korea, the Republic of Korea (ROK), occupies the southern part of the Korean Peninsula; communist North Korea, a backward xenophobic country teetering on the brink of agricultural and economic collapse, forms the larger northern part. About 50 per cent of the terrain is mountainous and only about 20 per cent of the land is arable, located mainly in the West. After the Korean War in 1953, a buffer zone called the Demilitarised Zone (DMZ), was established as a boundary between North and South Korea. The capital of South Korea is Seoul and is located in the northern portion of the country just 35 miles (56 kilometres) south of the DMZ. Other major cities include Pusan, Taegu, Inchon, and Kwangju.

With the death in July 1994 of Kim Il Sung, the dictatorial leader of North Korea for forty-nine years, a period of uncertainty began. However, given such huge political changes as the reunification of Germany and the collapse of the USSR, South Koreans now believe that reunification of the two Koreas is a future possibility. Currently, discussions to end the hostility are underway, forced on the North by the devastating famine. Given the uncompromising beliefs in the North, any positive conclusion is doubtful.

With an average population density of nearly 140 per square km (about 1 110 per square mile)—greater than that of either Japan or India—South Korea is the fourth most densely populated nation in the world. More than 70 per cent of South Korea's citizens live in urban areas, and this percentage is increasing. Some 25 per cent of the country's people already live in or around the capital of Seoul, and nearly half reside in the country's six largest cities, each of which has a population of greater than 1 million.

South Korea was, up to late 1997, one of the world's most dynamic economies and had built a modern, internationally-oriented industrial economy largely from scratch after the Korean war. This economy, the third largest in Asia, has historically been an exporter of high value goods. South Korea relies on the export of high-value-added, clean, capital intensive products. South Korea is also making the transition to a more open and democratic political system after years of authoritarian rule, although it maintains a core of stability within its pro-business government.

As a disciplined, fervently nationalistic country, Korea has a uniquely indigenous value system and world view which affects their business culture. The spirit that has seen them survive as a nation through years of Japanese rule and later depredations by North Korea, inserts a strong work ethic and a willingness to get the best for their country out of any business deal into the underlying Asian Confucian tradition to lift the country to great heights. In many ways they are as tough in business as the North Koreans are in politics.

Society and culture

Ethnicity

South Korea is extremely homogeneous ethnically which creates a highly developed sense of national identity. The only sizeable minorities in Korea are resident Chinese, variously estimated to number between 20 000 and 50 000; a shifting contingent of United States military personnel, numbering around 40 000; and several thousand foreign business and technical people centred in Seoul. The total foreign minority population is estimated at around 100 000—about 0.2 per cent of the total.

While political differences prevent reunification, most Koreans view themselves as a homogenous ethnic group with a common culture, language, history and destiny. Despite their country's physical proximity to China and Japan, South Koreans have a strong national identity and are at times quite xenophobic. Like the Japanese and Chinese, they perceive citizenship or nationality as being the equivalent of membership in a homogeneous ethnic group and feel that their culture is so truly unique and superior to other cultures that it is well beyond the comprehension of any mere foreigner. The concept of multi-racial and multi-ethnic societies such as Australia and the United States is hard for them to understand. This deep awareness of common heritage and culture is one reason that both South and North Koreans believe the current division of their country to be unnatural and wrong.

Religion

The traditional religion is Buddhism, but currently Confucianism, Shamanism and Christianity are prominent. Over 40 per cent of the population are Protestant Christian, but it is the two contrasting beliefs of Confucianism and Shamanism that have really been the mainsprings in shaping the conflicting cultures that often seem to tear apart modern Korean society. There is a considerable belief in fortune telling too. This will impact on business decisions which may succeed or fail, not on the rationale of acceptable business argument, but on the basis of a visit to the fortune teller. This practice exists right to the top of Korean society.

Confucianism

Korea is the most zealously Confucian society in all Asia, including China. The basic tenets form a social code promoting obedience to and respect for superiors, including parents and elderly, duty to family, loyalty to friends, humility, sincerity and courtesy. In this way a harmonious society will be achieved.

Confucius, of course, had in mind that enlightened, benevolent superiors would take wise and altruistic care of their subordinates in the natural order, avoiding the temptations to use power in less than honourable ways for less than honourable ends. The more cynical Western view challenges this ideal with the adage that absolute power corrupts absolutely.

The ideal person is one who can control their emotions in order to fulfil social obligations. To be sincere means not to express what one really feels but 'reflect' on one's thoughts and feelings until they conform to the traditional norm. Social relations are not conceived in terms of happiness and satisfaction of the individuals involved, but in terms of the harmonious integration of individuals into a collective whole that mirrors the harmony of the natural order and promotes a hierarchical social structure. Correct behaviour is determined by age, gender and social position. Throughout history, two enduring principles of Korean society have been:

- the importance of authoritarian centralised control, and,
- the significance of a social system that makes a clear distinction between the rulers and the masses. Thus, individuals' rights are less important than community/family obligations.

Thus, vertical and horizontal relationships must be observed to retain the stability and harmony of society. For example, filial piety extends to loyalty when serving the country, and order and harmony in the workplace. Filial piety in which the son owes the father unquestioning obedience still is for many Koreans the cornerstone of family life. The father is a true *pater familias* with absolute authority over family members; traditional rituals are conducted to show respect for ancestors and family obligations. The elderly are always honoured, respected and appeased. Family lineage is also important, with the main function of marriage being to produce a male heir to carry on the family line. Genealogy is a family interest and families maintain detailed family trees.

The business environment reflects the Confucian culture. The main effect has been in the development of a strictly hierarchical working environment in which workers are dedicated and industrious, productivity is high, and labour relations mostly harmonious. In a company, the boss is paramount and looks after his employees, making certain all their needs are met. Workers unquestioningly follow all orders to the letter and work hard, even working overtime without additional income to guarantee company success.

Employees of greater status and age command the respect of their juniors who are expected to defer, open doors, not disagree, be polite, and so on. In return juniors gain benefits and rewards from work well done by the senior staff and from any promotions that the seniors receive. To annoy a senior person causes serious damage, as their status and age allows them to influence others irrespective of the rights and wrongs of the matter.

The negative side of Confucianism is that:

(i) Koreans are the most naturally polite people when etiquette is followed precisely; they are conformist rather uncreative people, unwilling to think about new ideas that could challenge the status quo; and,

(ii) women play a distinctly inferior role to males. Although on occasions a woman of exceptional skill or talent has gained career success in business, most fill secretarial type roles, or work on assembly lines as low paid yet highly skilled employees. As cheap labour women have been the backbone to the success of the Korean economy. In reality there is no seriously acknowledged role for women in Korean corporations and few find really challenging or creative positions to match their education or talents. Yet behind the scenes women yield a lot of power, managing the family finances and taking responsibility for the family wellbeing and their children's education. In public, women may appear quiet and submissive, as public display of a woman's power is socially unacceptable, even when holding a management level position. Males' priority in Korea is exemplified by the man walking through a door first, walking ahead of a woman and being helped on with their coats by the woman.

The Confucian belief that scholar-officials should lead society has always been strong in Korea. Until recently, as only the children of well-to-do and well-educated families received the benefit of education, the status quo of society was retained and upward mobility was incredibly difficult. After the end of the Second World War, with most Koreans in the south living in poverty, education became the key for personal improvement. The literacy rate now lies at over 90 per cent. Young people are pushed by parents and drilled by teachers and cram schools to absorb extensive amounts of knowledge. Education also builds important lifelong bonds and networks. Universities and schools are training grounds where young people develop close relationships that will sustain later networks and engender career success. For example, most future leaders of government and industry are recruited from graduates of Seoul National University. Social classes in South Korea are now based on education, profession and wealth, as these become greater determinants of promotion in the business world. Accordingly, personal improvement is now an important cornerstone of Korean culture. Intensely competitive, Koreans perceive wealth as a positive sign of success.

Shamanism

Shamanism, Korea's oldest religion, is based on the premise that the world is inhabited by various spirits who are placated by the Shaman priest through rituals involving incantation, music and dance. The ecstasy, euphoria and free flowing emotion of Shamanistic religious practices contrasts sharply with the severe self-control of Confucianism. The frequent student riots within a culture that is generally self-controlled, deferential and meticulous, are explained by the volatile and emotional elements derived from Shamanism added to the Confucian belief that rulers who misuse their power lose the right to rule. This schizophrenic behaviour has earned the Koreans the title of 'Irish of the East'.

This religious mix has been infused by Western ideas concerning democracy, equality, and respect for the individual, inculcated by Western missionaries, American involvement and the effects of greater integration into global, political and economic activities. This is leading contemporary Koreans away from some traditional culture and practices. For instance, complex extended families are being replaced by the nuclear family structure. Further, there is more equality among family members, including women. Nevertheless, Koreans continue to place the family above all other concerns. As in many Asian societies, sons are expected to financially support the family and to carry on the family name by marrying and having sons of their own. Koreans are often preoccupied with family honour and with maintaining dignity at all times. Recent scandals have led to senior family members publicly apologising for the shame brought by some errant relative. Many Koreans attend university in the United States, particularly for postgraduate work. Their experiences and the economic modernisation further erode the post Korean War military's view of a disciplined society and promoted the emergence of a more contentious and pluralistic society than the military would consider desirable. Westernisation however is still only a thin veneer for most Koreans.

Therefore Korean social and religious values are a complex mix that extend beyond an authoritarian Confucian tradition. The values that permeate modern Korea are like a kind of yin-yang opposition and synthesis, with tension between self-control and explosive volatility, between veneration of age/seniority and merit, between dutybound family obligation and democratic notions.

Hahn

This is the word for the pent-up energies and frustrations that developed under conditions of extreme deprivation and subjugation which constantly afflicted Koreans through the requirements of the Confucian code, foreign domination—in particular the brutal colonial Japanese rule—sexual discrimination, family vendettas and debilitating poverty. It is the release of this repressed *hahn* in the last few decades of greater freedom that has enabled the Koreans to focus their natural desires and creative energies towards recent economic success.

Today, the *hahn* of the past shame of foreign domination manifests itself as a fervent nationalist spirit and an overly paranoid concern about foreigners and their business interests in Korea. Many Koreans today still don't want to get too entangled with foreigners and their endeavours. This attitude hampers the development of positive co-operation with foreign business interests. The *hahn,* stemming from the difficulties of social immobility, drives students to work hard to gain university entrance and motivates businessmen from lower social levels to work long hours. It is only since the massive economic growth from the 1960s that the average Korean could, through dedicated study and a myopic focus on the job or business, achieve a lifestyle previously unimaginable. The *hahn* energy has been like a volcano erupting after centuries of pressure, driving the economy and individual performance ever upwards.

However, there is still pent-up tension in the system which has not yet been released: one stems from minimal democratic practices, and the other from female inferiority. These are currently simmering and evident in massive street demonstrations against corruption and abuses of power in government.

Work ethic

The *hahn* translates itself into the legendary Korean work ethic. Even the Japanese complain that the Koreans work too hard!! The average working week for an industrial worker is around 53 hours per week, about 2 800 hours per year compared to 1934 per year in the USA. The Korean worker on average takes 4.5 days vacation each year compared to the 20 plus in most Western countries. Not only do the Koreans work hard, they are highly achievement-oriented. However, the motivation is different from that in the West. The Korean is motivated to succeed for spiritual reasons, rather than financial or individual ego enhancement. Work effort is also defined in terms of the group, not the individual. The collective focus is on the company's success. In Korea if the group succeeds it takes credit for the success; if it fails the manager gets the blame.

The Kibun factor

Koreans place the highest premium on harmony and the maintenance of good feelings. *Kibun* (pronounced kee-boon) literally means mood or inner feelings. If one's *kibun* is good then one functions smoothly, easily, and feels like a million dollars. If one's *kibun* is upset then things come to a complete halt and one feels depressed. Koreans, through their social etiquette and behaviour, aim to maintain a harmonious environment in which a person's *kibun* can stay balanced.

Kibun is therefore involved in business activities, for to damage *kibun* damages the relationship. This leads to very formal business relationships. Koreans may appear quite helpful, friendly, and polite on a personal level to ensure good feelings, but they will tend not to do or say anything which would upset *kibun,* leaving you somewhat unaware about the reality of the situation. You will be frustrated and confused, wondering why middle management Koreans always say 'yes', never say 'no', never give a straight answer, and never assume personal responsibility for anything. In Korea the buck never stops anywhere; it always floats around somewhere else. Handle these situations by not demanding yes or no answers, by reading between the lines, and by patiently accepting the Korean need for consensus decision-making.

The Koreans are somewhat schizophrenic in character. The release of *hahn,* their history of frustration and subjugation, have all combined to create a culture with tension just beneath the surface. Yet this conflicts with the alter ego which has to meet social demands for harmonious relationships. Personal dislikes and grudges have to be kept veiled by a veneer of everyday courtesy. Don't take it for granted that this latter is true friendliness, believing that all your counterparts seek a positive resolution to your discussions. Some may not.

Face

Having face is very important to Koreans; they are extremely sensitive to all aspects of face in social and business relationships and must always be treated with respect. A person with face has high status in the eyes of their peers; it is a mark of personal dignity. You must never insult or criticise a Korean, especially in front of others, or even unintentionally make fun of them in the good-natured way that is common among friends in the West. Your business prospects would wither. Another way to cause a Korean to lose face is to treat them as your inferior. Koreans must always be treated with proper respect.

The converse is that you should try to give face, for example by praising or thanking someone in front of peers or superiors. By doing this you earn respect and loyalty, and it should be done whenever the situation warrants. But don't overdo the praise as the appearance of insincerity is equally damning.

Helping the other person avoid embarrassment saves their face and you should help out in these situations. For example, don't point out mistakes in public which they and others probably realise they have made. In playing golf allow your business counterpart to win, even if you are clearly the better player—but don't make it too obvious. The other person will not forget the favour, and it will be repaid. Given the collectivistic nature of the culture, a person's face is not only their own but that of the entire organisation that they represent.

As there is little concept of equality in Korea, face is also given by knowing one's place in the order of things and lower oneself in to give honour and respect to those of higher standing. This means that you should become aware of the status of people and while not overdoing deference, show them respect and courteous recognition while avoiding boasting or pride. Even a senior, well-respected Korean will often assume the attitude of self-negation and self-effacement in social and business contacts. If you have to appear in public to speak, perform or whatever, bow to the audience, then to the chairperson. The Koreans are very concerned about social standing, and anything that you can do to enhance their regard for you is a plus. Be careful not to appear arrogant or haughty, as Confucian morality condemns such behaviour.

Corruption

Business and political dealings are mainly based on the twin pillars of ingroup loyalty and relationships. Filial piety, one of the foremost tenets of Confucianism, sees loyalty and obligation to one's family group as the highest of all virtues. With this in mind, a Korean who has attained political or other power is obliged to provide the family group with the benefits of special privilege derived from their position. Indeed, denying a favour that is within your power to grant to a family member (or friend or colleague representing an extension of the family), regardless of the issues of ethics, public policy or trust, fiduciary or other responsibility involved, is regarded as contemptible in Confucian society. Rather, gift giving and seeking favours from family members and acquaintances in power is simply a cultural norm. However, using relationships to one's advantage has developed into a national sport. Some percieve that the current economic crisis emerged from a tight collusion between big companies and government that meant credit was extended using political rather than economic criteria.

Although politicians in the West are not generally depicted as wearing halos, most Western societies have not experienced the degree of patronage and favourtism prevalent in the Korean government, business, and other sectors of its contemporary society. Millions of dollars of hidden assets are now being revealed among Korea's people as a result of new laws. What began with Confucius as paternalism in the best sense of the word, has evolved into a complicated web of obligation and opportunism that reaches into all sectors of Korean society, and even the Koreans have become uncomfortable with some of its more extreme manifestations.

Gift giving has evolved from a means of showing respect and confirming reciprocal relationships into a means of obtaining business, political election, favours, and so on. It has been exacerbated by the Confucian emphasis on submission to authority that has caused many lower level employees to go along with it all at the behest of their superiors. Some claim that large businesses have bribed government officials to avoid paying substantial taxes or gain lucrative contracts and that companies have bribed bank officials to get loans. Sons of officials have reportedly obtained university places and jobs in companies denied to other better qualified but less well-connected candidates. In the military, promotion kickback scandals have been uncovered. No sector or group seems to be untainted by this endemic problem.

The current President, President Kim, came to power with a number one priority of rooting out misconduct and corruption. For many Koreans, true justice seemed quite remote in a land where many government and leading officials have traditionally risen through a system of patronage and favouritism to reach the top. By making the attack on corruption his top priority, he indicated both the severity of the problem in Korean society and that he was staking his reputation on his ability to handle it. Unfortunately, recent events have revealed that even the President's own family may have been involved in corruption. It has been reported that the current economic crisis is in large measure a function of the financial instability resulting from the corrupting effects of patronage and favouritism. Despite recent modernisation, the nation's economic and social system still reflects the strict hierarchy of the small village. This system is to be considerably altered in future as the large and favoured conglomerates (*shoebills*) break up and have to compete on even terms with other businesses. This is good news for younger executives who see that the traditional emphasis on seniority may yield in favour of ability and will be able to take over from elders who are strong on loyalty but weak in efficiency. The *kiss* system of rating employees by seniority by labelling each yearly group of entrants—a tag that remains through the person's career with the firm—is now vulnerable.

Another element of corruption can be cooking the books. In order to maintain face for the employer/organisation it is claimed that accounting practices are highly irregular and it is reportedly common for companies to practice incredibly creative accounting to ensure a profit is shown at year's end. This maintains investor and consumer confidence. Be extremely careful when checking on a potential associate's or joint venture partner's financial viability.

Getting down to business

Corporate structure

In contrast to Western companies, the Korean economy is still dominated by large business conglomerates or *chaebols,* which resemble the Japanese *keiretsu.*

The characteristics of the *chaebol* are:

- A family affair with clear paternalistic autocratic lines of control, ownership and management, e.g. Daewoo, Samsung, Hyundai, Goldstar. The Chairman of the group is usually the most senior family member. Most *chaebols* have not yet begun the transition from family management to professional management as has already taking place in Japanese *keiretsu.*

- *An authoritarian management style.* The chairperson's decisions are absolute. The social distance between the chairperson of a group such as Samsung and one of the constituent companies is about as much as the social distance between that company chairperson and a newly hired department manager. As in Japan, senior people are expected to take the blame for corporate misdeeds or poor performance by resigning, thereby protecting the company's reputation.

- *The school tie plays a strong role in recruitment.* For example, 80 per cent of Daewoo's senior executives attended the same high school and university as the Chairman of the group. Nine major family business groups were reported to be linked by marriage to two presidents, two prime ministers, and other senior ministers (*Business Week,* 1 June 1992).

- *A wide range of business activity.* Each *chaebol* is composed of many independent companies—some 20–30 strong—with interlocking directorates and shareholdings. Within the group subsidiaries support each other similar to the *keiretsu.* The Daewoo group, for example, not only makes cars but also ships, textiles, chemicals, computers and supplies financial services.

- *Close and mutually beneficial relationship with government.* The government has traditionally used these large companies to put into effect national development goals and aid the country's economic development. In return, the government has officially and un-officially supported the *chaebols* by offering them special privileges and lending rates. However, failure to attain government set targets can lead to termination of funding or access to favourable bank loans with eventual bankruptcy. The Japanese *keiretsu* are better placed, having banks as a subsidiary to provide stability of finance.

The influence of *chaebols*, their reckless business activities and their involvement in high level graft will be checked by the requirements now imposed by the IMF. The recent events, commencing with the failure of a large steel making conglomerate, illustrate the financial linkages within a group and how special financing arrangements lead to bribery and corruption in high places in Korea. The corollary is that small businesses fare poorly when competing with these preferentially treated conglomerates. This interactive relationship between government and business is the major reason for the economic miracle that has occurred in Korea.

Management and human relationships in business

Confucian influences

Confucianism has a great influence on organisational behaviour, management systems and human relationships in business. Enterprises are managed by the same principles as those applied to private lives, and reflect the basic ideology and values of society, pursuing harmony, unity, co-operation, stability, devotion and diligence. Specifically it is reflected in the loyalty and collectivist feeling of employees, and the acceptance of high power distance relationships.

- *Collectivist group harmony.* The Korean work environment is based on the belief in preserving group harmony. The individual subverts their own interests for the good of the group.
- *High power distance, paternalism and exclusivity.* Most employees obey their seniors and superiors because they are just that, ir-respective of the actual performance of those people. There are strong feelings of loyalty on the part of employees to the person who brought them into the company, rather than to the company itself. In social life consanguinity and social status create a socially

exclusive and closed way of thinking. Where continuity and prosperity of the family is paramount, it is natural for this to be extended into the workplace. Discrimination is offered to those not part of the ingroup, so that employees who are not in the clan can never aspire to any position. Relationships between superiors and subordinates are characterised by a high degree of paternalism. While the manager in a Korean company has the right to be boss and issue orders, there are mutual commitments and obligations. It is expected that a manager or business owner will assume personal responsibility for the development of subordinates and they will respond by showing the proper amount of obedience and respect. Exclusiveness and centralisation of power are the bases of what appears to be nepotism and shady dealing within business and politics, as the power structure is retained, monopolised and secured in the distinct favour of those who are of the right connection. What is more valuable and realistic than to do favours to help one's family and close friends?

Career success

Career progression is for most still not based on job performance. Age, blood line and seniority remain important criteria. This stems from the Confucian tradition for harmony. It is unseemly for younger persons to supervise older ones. Management rights do not go to the competent, as the eldest son is not necessarily the one with ability to follow the father. However, as Korean firms are now moving towards greater professionalism to maintain their global position, more emphasis is starting to be placed on performance.

Changes in society

As South Korea enjoys the fruits of its labour in a global economy, and for political reasons seeks ties with the West, the form of society is changing. Social class is still based on education and occupation but income is becoming important. Social class is no longer hereditary and there is increasing social mobility. Public service is no longer seen as the most desirable occupation and the Confucian scorn for commerce is dead. As a stronger economic feeling develops individuality is starting to awaken in the younger set. The biggest changes are coming in the role of women with the growing realisation that a large and educated part of the nation's workforce has been underutilised. But as yet, equal property rights and equal opportunity laws are only loosely enforced and many women still have low expectations and aspirations. Even female graduates are expected to leave work on marriage to raise a family, or on reaching the age of 30.

Contacts beat contracts—cultivating relationships
Who do YOU know?

Without personal connections, conducting business in South Korea is virtually impossible, as personal and business relationships are one and the same. A Korean saying sums it up: 'Make a friend first and a client second'. Relationships in Korean society are based in terms of closeness of blood, school ties and geography (coming from the same town). Your first and continuing aim must be to cultivate close personal ties with business associates and earn their respect and trust. Koreans will only do business with those they respect, trust and honour.

South Korean firms are known to pay 10–15 per cent more if they know or have had a good relationship with a company previously. Another Korean saying is that 'you get a contract not because you are qualified, but because you know someone'.

Profit from networking

The South Koreans are great networkers. Since the most acceptable way to arrange a meeting is through a mutual friend, the wider your group of friends, alumni and co-workers, the easier it is to open doors. This makes it even more necessary for overseas persons to work hard to build up positive and trusting relationships, as they are well behind the eight ball in knowing a range of South Koreans. Korean executives will work hard to retain and develop further networks of contacts at a highly personal level in order to access other companies and individuals. To cultivate friendships in business circles you need to pay close attention to the needs and expectations of others, anticipating these with favours and help, but above all never failing to demonstrate integrity and sincerity towards all those with whom you have relationships.

So, Koreans spend considerable time on business socialising, accepting social invitations and reciprocating. You must do the same. However, it is important to remember that just because your Korean counterpart entertains you, it does not automatically imply that a deal has been agreed upon. Further, be careful not to let your business judgment slip by allowing the pleasantries to affect your negotiations. Business in effect is done with someone you know and trust, and often concluded with a handshake. Most Koreans reserve trust, respect, and honour only for those people whom they count as personal friends. A Korean who does not know you will back off any business relationship until he has sized up your character and intentions. Strangers have never been good news for Koreans. You need to lose that tag before any Korean will touch in as a business associate.

While the ingroup is awash with trust, reciprocal favours, and support, outgroup foreigners can be discriminated against without any sense of ethical impropriety. Some claim that contracts will be broken and promises will not be delivered because it is acceptable to cheat someone foolish enough to enter into a business relationship without having first established a personal relationship and being accepted into the ingroup amongst whom those behaviours are unacceptable.

The third party matchmaker

Cold calling or letters 'out of the blue' are unlikely to be effective. An introduction or referral from a trusted third party who has a close relationship with both sides is essential. This third party will act like a sponsor and take responsibility for your behaviour. Anyone who can vouch for you such as common acquaintances, suppliers, accountants, lawyers or consultants and who has worked in Korea or who has co-operated with Koreans in the past could be a key third party and source of business contacts. If you are seeking an introduction to a large Korean firm, check to see if it has a subsidiary in Australia, the USA or other country where your company also has an office. If you can develop a relationship with the Korean subsidiary, it can serve as your introducer.

Presenting letters of introduction from well-known business leaders, overseas Koreans, or former government officials who have dealt with Korea is also an excellent way of showing not only that you are a person of high standing, worthy of the trust of the letter writer, but also that you are sincere in wanting to do business. If your search for acceptable third parties and personal contacts fails, you will have to seek out a consultant based in Seoul who specialises in bringing business interests together (for a fee of course!).

In most business circumstances it is very helpful to have a local partner. If you need an agent, use one who is approved by the Korean government. Prior to going to Korea, you should have made contact with the firms that interest you and scheduled meetings. Do not expect to arrive in Korea, contact those companies then and expect to meet with them. It won't happen!

Meeting the company

Once you have convinced your third party to act for you and provide the introduction to a company in Korea, you must ensure they get you to meet people from the appropriate levels who make important decisions. These people will be at middle and junior management levels in the company hierarchy since you need to build up good relations at all levels to ensure every part of your business proposal is approved before final decisions at the top are made. It is often difficult to access the company boss, as Korean CEOs are often jealously cloistered by levels of gate keepers of vice president and junior executive status. A whole raft of managers will need to be 'wooed' with dinners, gifts, visits and small favours to facilitate and strengthen personal relationships. It will be costly and time consuming but it will not go unnoticed. If you don't, you will have damaged their 'face' by not demonstrating their importance to you. The consequences will be that they will ignore you and your requirements, negotiations will stall and the atmosphere will be quite cold and unwelcoming. However, if the Koreans really want something such as your advanced technology, that will take precedence over any personal allegiance.

You must always have potential local partners and the potential market checked out carefully. Some Korean companies will deliberately encourage links with overseas organisations solely to tap their technology and copy their products, withdrawing once they have learned what they need. It is advisable to establish relations with several firms so that if one partnership breaks down you will have other business relationships. Korean business people can be opportunistic and will drop you like a stone into water if a better deal comes along. It is also advisable to assign someone from your firm to represent you on a permanent basis, or at least visit the country regularly to supervise the implementation of a venture. The Koreans like to deal with the same individual, treating each interaction as a personal one. Any replacement should overlap and be introduced by the existing representative. Frequent visits by senior members of the organisation will also assure your Korean associates that you are committed to them and to the market. One trustworthy and loyal Korean advisor is also a must; they should have social credentials, have been to the 'right' school and university, as well as possessing required management skills and a good command of English.

Clans—The family business

Personal connections have their origin in the collectivism of the traditional Korean culture, particularly the concept of family cohesion within which identity, protection, and companionship are located. In the brutal and subsistence level existence of the past, the Korean family was the only trustworthy body around. Families linked together in clans through arranged marriages etc, enhancing the support system. This has left a powerful legacy of a sense of collective trust as the basis of life and now encompasses the new business world where the company (often a family one) has become the new clan.

Those outside the clan are perceived as either of no importance to the clan or a potential danger. Thus loyalty, co-operation and trust is required on a reciprocal basis among all those in the company. Such moral obligations do not apply to strangers within the Confucian social code, so those on the outside are fair game. However, to enter into a close relationship as required for effective business activity has its negative side. It entails responsibility and commitment to all other members of the network. You cannot simply be a fair weather friend to the person whose influence and decision-making you need; you may well take on a whole raft of other obligations. Moreover, when a Korean has a close relationships with you, you will always be a foreigner to them.

In summary, the Confucian form of business is male-dominated and rigid. The boss is all-powerful, involved in most aspects of his subordinates' lives, from cradle to grave. He honours their devotion by trying to do his best for them. In return they honour and respect him as if he were their own father. Add to this a nationalism even more extreme than Japan's, and doing business in Korea becomes a cross between inviting yourself to become a member of someone else's family and invading their country. You are manifestly not part of the family and don't really want such a commitment, nor do you want to be treated as the enemy. Thus intermediaries are essential to help you to get a foot in the door.

Hiring

When recruiting local managers—given the complexities, language problems and relationship networks in Korea—you should attempt to recruit someone who has attended Seoul National University, as they alone have the necessary contacts with influential people in government. Other influential universities are Yonse university and Koryo University. Another reason why a blue ribbon educational background is needed is because subordinates will not respect or work diligently for a person not 'educated' at a prestigious university.

Communication guidelines

Names and forms of address

Koreans generally have three names: two given names and a surname, with the latter appearing first in Chinese. For example, Park Young San's family name is Park, his generational name is Young, and his personal name is San. The name may sometimes be inverted when written in English. Ask how a person wishes to be addressed if you are unsure—it is better than making an error since Koreans do not like those outside very close family using their personal names.

More than half of all Koreans are named Kim, Lee (or Yi), Park (or Pak), or Choi. In large organisations where there may be hundreds of people with the same family name this can cause confusion for both foreigners and Koreans. This is further complicated by the fact that people outside the family almost never call each other by their personal names, even if they are very close. The use of names in Korea has a different connotation to that of the West. To a Confucian, using a name is presumptuous and impolite, as a name is to be honoured and respected and never used casually. To call someone directly is an affront. In Shamanism, to write a name calls up the spirit from the spirit world; this brings bad luck.

To distinguish between many similarly surnamed persons, Koreans in the workplace are referred to by positions and department. For example, a manager in the drafting office will be referred to as 'Manager Choi' of Drafting. Another common form of address is to use a person's designated position or profession so a teacher may be referred to as 'Teacher Park'. This form of address also applies to government officials. As a title is a coveted reward and a badge of status and you are highly recommended to use their title to address your counterparts. 'Mr' and 'Mrs' may also be used but no 'Ms'. Korean wives generally retain their maiden names. If you are meeting a woman, ask her secretary if she prefers to be addressed as 'Mrs' or 'Miss'.

On many occasions a Korean will not introduce one person to another as we do. Instead, one person says to the other, 'I am seeing you for the first time' or 'I have never seen you before'. The other person repeats this. Only after determining who is superior and who is subordinate will the elder or senior of the two say, 'let us introduce ourselves'. Each person steps back and bows, stating their own name in a soft humble voice that cannot be heard. Westerners may be able to determine the relative status of Korean associates by observing the depth of their bows and who bows first. The subordinate bows first and lowest. Then they exchange cards. If you don't catch someone's name you can glean it from their card. Don't say 'sorry I didn't catch your name'.

Some nonverbal communication issues

Here are a few which are well worth observing so as not to offend in such a traditional society.

- Do not touch or pat a Korean, although two men may hold hands as they walk. This is merely a sign of friendship, nothing more.
- In public situations, personal space is very limited and you will be disconcerted by the closeness of others in buses, trains, markets and pavements etc.
- The Western version of gesturing 'come here' (waving the palm towards the face) is only used to call dogs. To beckon a Korean you should extend the arm, palm down and make a scratching motion.
- It is impolite to walk behind someone. As a result you will find as you are talking to another person a Korean will walk between you.

- When walking in public places it is conventional to keep to the left hand side.
- Don't eat while walking down the street nor blow your nose in public; wipe it with a tissue.
- Elderly people are much respected and you should stand if one enters the room.
- Always sit erect with good posture; slouching, feet on table, wearing sunglasses and hands in pocket at a meeting show a lack of respect.
- Koreans will smile not only when they are happy, but also to hide psychological discomfort as when sad, nervous or embarrassed. They will often cover their mouths when laughing. You need to look for other signs to determine which emotion is being expressed.
- Although Koreans are personally polite, crowds of Koreans are not. It's not impolite to push and shove your way onto a bus/train or to bump somebody off the pavement.

Privacy

Privacy is a luxury few can afford in such a crowded country. So Koreans have learned to put imaginary walls round themselves. If you visit your counterpart or representative on a hot day, you may find them in a vest, feet up on their desk fanning themselves. You should 'cough' to announce your arrival but do not knock. The person does not 'see' you until they have adjusted themselves. Then you 'see' each other and begin a formal greeting. To Western eyes the other person is in plain view, but to the Korean there is an invisible screen there and the cough is intended to indicate an impending interruption.

Getting down to business

Your first meeting

You first meeting is likely to be held in their office or a restaurant. You must be on time as punctuality is a very important cultural trait and expected of others. On being introduced you should shake hands with both men and women and accompany this with a slight nod of the head or a slight bow. The most senior person will offer to shake hands first and the most junior person bows first.

When entering a conference or dining room, wait to be shown to the seat designated to you. Even if you are a guest of honour, you should make a slight protest before going to the designated spot, as this demonstrates the trait of humility that is much appreciated by Koreans. As in other Asian countries, procedures commence by exchanging business cards, given and received with both hands, with the writing facing the receiver. Don't slip it into your wallet but show respect by reading the card with apparent care. Then place it on the table in front of you. If you place the cards in table order it will help you remember where Manager Kim is sitting.

Koreans feel more at ease once they are familiar with the company and the position of the person with whom they are meeting. If you can, have the message on your business card translated into Korean and printed on its reverse side. If you are representing a small or less well-known firm, be sure to give your counterpart some descriptive corporate literature as an introduction.

Your first meeting should be dominated by introductions, social niceties and casual conversation about your trip. It's getting to know you time—judging sincerity, commitment and building relationships. Your Korean counterpart will probably try to tease out of you who else you are meeting during your trip. If your counterpart feels that other Koreans are also interested in you and your proposal they will be more positive towards you, firstly because you must have something of value to offer, and secondly to make sure you deal with them and not the others. Take time in providing information at the first meeting as this is the period when Koreans need to feel you out and get a sense of your trustworthiness and objectives. The first meeting is therefore likely to accomplish little except create goodwill, friendship and trust. If you do that you will be achieving a great deal. Don't appear too pushy by trying to get down to business too soon, or the Koreans will assume that you are desperate. Public perception and image matter a great deal to Koreans.

You need to provide advance information about who will be attending from your side and their positions in the organisation, as the Koreans will seek to match you and your team up with those of similar rank. Koreans interpret status on the basis of age, level of education, current rank in a company, and previous professional associations. Koreans are really concerned about the status that an individual holds in a company or organisation. A delegation is not likely to succeed if the Koreans know that its head is not a senior executive and does not look senior in appearance. Keep this in mind when selecting your team or appointing a representative to work for you in South Korea. Familiarity with the country and its language are of secondary importance.

If you are a delegation or group, Koreans will assume the most senior person is the leader and that they speak for all members and the organisation. Individual or inconsistent messages are disconcerting to the South Koreans who then don't know who the leader is, whether the leader has any status, or whether the delegation has its act together.

While your hosts may have some familiarity with English, they are unlikely to be fluent so speak slowly and clearly and do not assume that they understand everything you said. Written English is often better understood than spoken English. So emphasise visual and graphical material rather than words and to repeat your key points. Have your basic materials translated into Korean. If your negotiations are technical or you are unsure of your counterpart's English ability, it is best to hire an interpreter to accompany you.

Don't ask negative questions as they reply in the converse way to Westerners. For example:

Question: Didn't Miss Lee call you yesterday?
Answer (Korean): Yes (she didn't)
Answer (Western): No (she didn't)
Solution: Always ask questions in the affirmative. 'Did Miss Lee call yesterday'?

Decision-making or passing the buck

The Korean decision-making process or *'pummi'* (proposal submitted for deliberation) parallels the Japanese *'ringi-sho'* system whereby a proposal circulates the organisation from bottom up so that by the time it reaches top management there is widespread consensus as to the desired course of action. Consensus is achieved by passing written suggestions around the office to receive approval from everyone. If something goes wrong later, no single person can be blamed for having made a poor plan/decision.

In many cases reality is different, as the *'pummi'* system has started to simply provide documentation for all company programs and ventures and to diffuse responsibility for decision implementation, while overall decision-making is highly centralised, particularly in those that are owner-managed. Thus decisions may be made quicker when the owner or founder is in charge than in China or Japan. This means that relationships with the Chairperson are pivotal in gaining positive decisions.

Overseas managers must obtain consensus when they want to implement new policies or management techniques. Circulate a new plan first as a suggestion and gain employee enthusiasm and support, taking on board well supported suggestions; then move the final plan down the hierarchy from top to bottom. Employees will feel involved in decision-making, yet will not be held responsible if things go wrong. Korean employees do not want to have any responsibility for any decision as individuals and attempts to do this will cause resistance.

Personal allegiances

You must not confuse the extraordinary work ethic of Korean workers with company loyalty. Their work relationship is conceived in personal terms with allegiance owed to the individual people who head the corporation or their particular unit, not the organisation as a whole.

This again brings personal relationships to the fore, as overseas managers must pay far closer attention to their personal relationships with employees than they would dream of doing in the West. Should the expatriate manager be changed, the bond is broken and employees may leave too or work ineffectively until a new relationship is in place. Overseas managers must operate in Korea over a long period if they want to achieve substantial business developments.

Negotiating

Once you have a trusting relationship with business partners negotiation can begin in earnest.

Negotiations can be difficult even when a relationship has been built up, as foreigners are considered fair game. The Korean approach to negotiations is that the end justifies any means necessary. The South Koreans will employ a range of strategies to get the best possible outcome for themselves. South Koreans feel justified in this as their perception is that they have been on the receiving end for too long at the hands of foreigners.

However, throughout the negotiations there will be a non-confrontational approach and any aggressive and adversarial behaviour on your part will be counterproductive, even though it appears they are rigid, hold their cards close to their chest, are non-specific and at times devious. For example, Koreans will often agree just to keep negotiations harmonious and report positive news, even if it is unwarranted, in order to maintain an optimistic and hopeful attitude that everything will turn out all right. Koreans regard saying 'no' directly as an affront and poor etiquette. They will skirt round the issue vaguely with 'we will consider it but I am not sure', 'we would like to', 'perhaps it may be possible'. Try to ease out the true meaning without causing a loss of face. A Korean 'yes' simply means 'I heard you' and not agreement. Koreans prefer to consider that they 'award' a contract rather than you the person or company 'winning' the contract, which smacks of them being beaten. Respond with similar terminology, stating 'you are very pleased that they have awarded (or given) you the contract'. The goal is to always keep harmony and allow everyone to 'maintain face'.

Just remain firm, calm and dignified in manner, and clear about your position in the face of their sometimes stubborn and unyielding approach. Koreans do not believe that logic and reasoning are the only elements to take into account in making a business decision and will consider personal relationships and your character because if difficulties should occur later the relationship will enable these to be ironed out between friends.

In Korean business flattery is a way of life. One must begin on the periphery of the business relationship, work one's way in and gradually zero in on the main business in ever decreasing circles. To go directly to discussion of the business dooms the project, as Koreans view impatience as a major personal fault. A skilled business person to them should move with dignity and deliberation, and study the senses, impressions and nuances being transmitted between the people present. Where relevant, items/projects are evaluated, this should be done first on a technical basis, and only then when satisfied, to a financial review.

Profit will often not be the only motivator or objective for a Korean business partner. Like the Japanese, the Korean is concerned with market share and growth. This has two implications:

- Firstly, an overseas company must be willing to wait for growth and market share to develop; making the quick buck and exiting is not an acceptable negotiating approach. The family-owned business can afford to take a long-term view, unlike a Western company with shareholders wanting their profit in the short term.
- Secondly, since money or profit is not the sole motivator, overseas companies should ensure other motivators relevant to the Korean culture are available for counterparts or potential employees such as position title, office size, company car, chauffeur, corporate credit card etc. In other words, ego fulfilment is important.

These are a few key points to remember when negotiating with Koreans:

- Never let the Korean side know your travel plans. Like the Chinese, Koreans will delay substantive negotiations until your taxi is at the door and then make an offer for an unreasonable agreement. Tell them from the start that you are willing to remain in the country as long as necessary.
- Be able to give in detail answers to all questions, especially those of a technical nature. Take a technical expert with you if necessary. If you show vagueness in your answers you will be seen as not having the expertise that evokes respect. If you have something that the Koreans want badly and that they cannot get elsewhere, you are in a position of strength. Let the Koreans know what you have to offer and present it as invaluable to their interests.
- Remain patient, relaxed and quietly insistent on your position. The Koreans will try to wear you down by long drawn-out team negotiations, waiting for you to give way.
- Let the Koreans know that you are willing to walk away empty handed; that no deal is more acceptable than a bad deal. If you show that you are anxious to make a deal, they will increase their demands.

- Don't make concessions unless both sides give way. If you give something away for nothing as a sign of good faith the Koreans will regard it as a sign of weakness.
- Contracts are not sacrosanct and Koreans are likely to delay signing and continue to manoeuvre for a better deal knowing they have hooked you. Alternatively, contracts can be signed with the Koreans knowing full well that they have no intention of honouring it. Further negotiations will probably be necessary.

The contract

As with many Asian countries, the Western concept of a legal contract that sets out duties and responsibilities for each side is not acceptable. In the Korean context, as with Japan and China, the contract is considered to be an organic document that changes as conditions change. They believe that contracts summarise a deal that has been negotiated, but allow for flexibility and adjustment as circumstances change. It is not uncommon for Koreans to change the 'rules' as the situation changes. This is why trusting relationships are essential, so that neither side feels the other is trying to do the other down and re-negotiation between friends is always possible.

Often, issues that have already been agreed upon are subject to future negotiations by the Koreans in order to extract additional advantages. Be sure to specify responsibilities and roles clearly. Should a signatory leave, the contract may be seen by the South Koreans as invalid, since the contract is part of the relationship with those who signed it.

The social context of business

Dining out

Business meetings over meals are very popular, but used mainly to develop and enhance relationships rather than for the actual conduct of business. You will either be guest or host; there is no sharing the bill in Korea. Overseas businesswomen should indicate their willingness to participate in business entertaining, as some Koreans may avoid inviting a woman out for a 'business' meal.

Apart from restaurants there are two main venues: the traditional *kisaeng* house (don't go in with your shoes on) and the more modern private room. Even when you are the guest of honour, make a slight protest before going to your designated spot, as this demonstrates humility, which is greatly appreciated by the Koreans. If you are hosting the meal, always direct your guest to a seat of honour. When drinking, be aware that tradition dictates that no glass should remain empty. South

Korean male colleagues will only be too pleased to introduce you to some drinking rituals. If you do not want to drink excessively, leave some alcohol in your glass. The local alcohol, *soju*, is very strong. The best option for a clear negotiating head next day of course is to give a firm 'no thank you I don't drink' and you will be served a soft drink or juice. Your host will pour for you and you should reciprocate by pouring for the host. Toasts are made by raising your glass with your right hand and saying *'gun-bei'*. Pass food and drinks using the right hand, with the left hand supporting the right forearm.

During dinner a small communal cup may be passed around; drink and pass on. Group sing-alongs (karaoke) are common, with each guest taking a turn to sing. Skill hardly matters but good-natured participation does. Be grateful that the government's curfew on entertainment establishments will terminate the carousing at midnight. Wives are seldom invited to these after work functions and many Koreans still feel ill at ease drinking with a woman present.

A home visit

Only after you establish a strong personal relationship will your Korean counterpart invite you to their home. Always remove your shoes before entering the house. Take an appropriate gift such as expensive cognacs, liquors, wines, champagne cake or fruit. The host takes on the attitudes of the servant. The hostess is likely to be in the lowest place, or may not even eat in the presence of the guest. Food is often served on small individual tables. Watch out for the very hot red pepper seasoning. To lay chopsticks or a spoon down on the table indicates you have finished eating. Laying them on the top of a dish or bowl indicates you are resting between mouthfuls. To leave nothing on your plate indicates that the host has not given you enough, so don't clean your plate.

Giving gifts

It has been claimed that the Asia-wide gift-giving tradition has been transformed in Korea into largescale bribery and corruption. According to some,
it is the only way of getting things done in Korea, and you have to play the game if you want to do business successfully there. While the standard operating practice of presenting a legitimate gift to a company occurs, you will need to provide substantial 'gifts' of money to individuals in the business and in government bureaucracy to grease the wheels for many contracts.

The need for a 'gift' will usually be inferred in conversation. Normally, overseas business people do not give the 'gift' directly, but rely instead on Korean intermediaries—such as the third party, local representative, consultants or joint venture partners—to carry out the delicate process at arm's length from you. If you are given a gift be wary about what might be wanted in return. Every gift given brings the expectation of something in return such as a favour, a business relationship, a reciprocal gift etc.

Small standard business gifts are not required for the early meetings. If you have developed a relationship with your Korean counterpart by letter or telephone prior to your visit, you may want to bring them a small token such as pen or a gift with your company logo. A gift of wine, whisky etc is also appropriate. If you meet with a group, you should have a gift for the senior person, as well as other gifts for all subordinates attending the meeting. The senior person's gift should be different and more expensive than the others. For example, you could give the senior person an expensive bottle of brandy, while the rest receive small gifts with the company logo.

New Year is the most usual time in Korea to exchange gifts, particularly with business associates in other firms. The government recognises the first three days of January as the New Year; however, most Koreans celebrate the new year according to the lunar calendar. Appropriate gifts include silk ties and scarves, leather goods, quality pens, and items with corporate logos. Korean business people will also appreciate an invitation for a fine meal and drinks. Never give money as a business gift. However, money is the common gift for weddings, funerals, and the first and sixtieth birthdays. Money should always be placed in an envelope.

When giving a gift to you, a Korean will try to minimise its value or importance by saying something humble like 'it is only a small gesture'. They may hesitate to take a gift from you but you should continue to offer it, as hesitation is an expected cultural behaviour. You should also show hesitation when receiving a gift. Do not open a gift in the presence of the giver; as it is considered quite rude, so wait until you can open it in private.

Other useful information

What to wear

Dignity and formality should be shown, so men should wear suits and ties and women should wear suits or dresses. Trousers for women are only appropriate for informal social occasions. Don't go overboard on flashy colours, male and female jewellery, and heavy perfumes, or you may be judged as not serious or professional. Dark suits and while shirts/blouses are expected. The winters are bitterly cold so a fur hat with ear flaps is essential, plus a warm overcoat. In contrast summers are hot, so tropical weight attire is necessary.

Language

In addition to Korean, some Chinese and Japanese is also spoken. English is not spoken widely except for younger business persons who have had some education overseas. Polite and honorific speech characterise the language.

Major holidays

As pageantry, merrymaking and colourful rites of traditional holiday festivals are important features of Korean life it is important that meetings/visits should be arranged to avoid any clashes.

January 1-3	New Year
January / February*	Lunar New Year
March 1	Independence Movement Day
March 10	Labour Day
April 5	Arbor Day
Early April*	Hansik Day
May*	Buddha's Birthday
May 5	Children's Day
June 6	Memorial Day
July 17	Constitution Day
August 15	Liberation Day
September / October*	Chusok (Korean Thanksgiving—Harvest Moon Festival)
October 1	Armed Forces Day
October 3	National Foundation Day
October 9*	Hangul Day
December 25	Christmas Day

*These holidays are based on the lunar calendar and vary from year to year.

Air raid drills and national security

There is always considerable concern over national security and infiltration of spies from North Korea. During drills everyone must get off the streets, leaving their cars parked at the side of the road and sheltering in an air raid shelter. There are sometimes blackout drills at night when all lights must be extinguished. There may be occasional roadblocks and restrictions on entry to certain parts of South Korea, especially in the north. Don't show irritation or indicate you feel they are being paranoid. The South Koreans take the drills and precautions seriously. So would you if the North Korean regime were on your doorstep.

Summary

- Korea's culture is strongly Confucian. That means face—courtesy, status, dignity, respect for authority. Western harsh directness, sarcasm, readiness to criticise, and impatience are counterproductive in the extreme.
- In general, Koreans are very conservative, intolerant of uncertainty and risk averse, and have a very strong work ethic.
- Business begins and ends on the strength of the relationship. Personal relationships are more important to Koreans than paper contracts or rational Western-style economic mutual interest.
- Koreans aim for group consensus, with the senior person issuing the final verdict. At each stage of a negotiation, all senior people are kept abreast of developments and related issues.
- Entertainment must be accepted when offered and reciprocated when possible.
- It is important to remember that although South Korea and its people appear to be Westernised they still adhere to Korean values.
- You must maintain your counterparts' kibun and face at all times.
- You'll need all the patience, flexibility, and respect you can muster to negotiate business deals.
- Koreans can be hard people to work with. But of the newly industrialised countries of the Far East, Korea has the cheapest wages, a well-educated workforce, and a burning national desire to progress. A well-prepared foreign business with open-minded personnel and high-demand products or services is likely to succeed in Korea.

Activities

Try working out the solutions to these two problems, then check your responses with those in Appendix B.

1   Bill Crosinzki was chosen to set up a branch office of his engineering consulting firm in Seoul. Although the six other ex-pats would eventually come over to act as managers/consultants, Bill was needed to hire local support staff. In particular, he required a local person with excellent accounting

skills and knowledge of Korean systems of accounting and reporting to handle the company's books. He was quite confident that he would be able to find the right person for the job because his company was prepared to offer an excellent salary and benefits package. After receiving what he considered to be several excellent leads from a friends at the Rotary Club and golf club, he was quite surprised to be turned down by all three prospective candidates. They were very appreciative of being considered for the position but all preferred to stay with their current employer. Bill just couldn't understand why all of these Koreans chose to pass up an increase in salary and fringe benefits.

How would you explain this situation to Bill?

2   Terry Yung, a senior publisher with an international book publishing house was sent to Korea to establish an Asian branch concerned with distributing their published titles throughout East Asia. The home immediately started routing their Asian order through Terry. However, his new staff were still learning their jobs and the demand became too heavy. Terry found that he was behind schedule in deliveries in a new and important likely best seller which was to have simultaneous publication throughout the world. The deadline was so critical that he had to work very closely with some of his staff to make sure that it was met. In the final hours Terry found himself in a hands-off effort helping secretaries and warehouse staff assemble and pack the required express deliveries. However, soon after pitching in to help he began to notice that his staff became very non-communicative and he seemed to be getting a lot of cold stares. Terry couldn't understand why his attempts to be helpful were so unappreciated.

What was the cross-cultural problem?

Further reading

De Menthe, B. (1988) *Korean Etiquette and Ethics in Business,* Lincolnwood, Ill., NTC Business Books.

Conducting Business in

Thailand

General background

Location

Thailand, formerly the Siam of *King and I* fame, runs south out of the Indo-Chinese lobe into the Malaysian Peninsula, where it borders Malaysia. Laos, Cambodia, and Myanmar (Burma) form its other land boundaries. Tropical rain forests dominate the southern peninsular region, with mountains in the north and plains in the central region. The capital, Bangkok (also known as Krung Thep), the largest city, is located in the central part, on the Gulf of Thailand. Chiang Mai, the second largest city, lies in the northern interior of the country.

History

The early Thai settlers migrated into the region from China around 700 AD. The area was already inhabited by the Mons and the Khmers, the ancestors of the modern Cambodians. The Mons were Buddhist and the Khmers were Hindu; both religions have had an influence on the Thai belief system. Modern Thailand began in the thirteenth century with the emergence of two principal Thai states: Sukhothai, founded in 1220, and Chiang Mai, founded in 1296.

Political system

Thailand is a parliamentary democracy with a monarchy. Democratic beliefs are strong in Thailand even though the military have interfered from time to time, while continuing corruption, political infighting and economic mismanagement have threatened to disrupt the fragile political stability. There have been a succession of coups and thirteen constitutions since 1932.

The National Assembly elect the prime minister, who then selects his cabinet and leads the government. The judiciary has been influenced by the British legal code. The king, who functions as the head of state, has provided a symbol of national unity, which has given stability even through an era of political instability. The king, who has been on the throne for fifty years, is respected, trusted and revered by his people and seen as the continuing ruler of the country, while successive governments have been overthrown. They are a flexible people, capable of adapting to change, with a strong attachment to democracy.

The Thais are very proud and protective of their independence, as they live in perhaps the sole Asian nation that developed independent of Western colonialism.

Economy

Since the mid-1970s the government has encouraged foreign investment, and the subsequent growth rate has been impressive. Government intervention in the economy has concentrated on improvements to the country's basic infrastructure, including port facilities, roads, communications networks, water treatment facilities, and power sources.

Agriculture has always been the mainstay of the economy, with the majority of workers employed in agriculturally-related activities. Manufacturing is moving to become the primary force behind the economy, but there is a shortage of skilled workers. A recent and fast growing development has been tourism, which brings in much needed foreign exchange.

Thailand is short of skilled technical persons since around 60 per cent of the children leave school at the end of primary education to work on farms with parents, or in factories to supplement the family income. This results in the lowest secondary education enrolment of major ASEAN countries. The government is trying to rectify the problem and strategies are being developed to improve the primary and secondary school retention rates.

Society and culture

With 82 per cent of the 58 million people in Thailand being ethnic Thais, the country is relatively racially homogeneous. Although there are several subgroups and dialects of Thai, they understand each other. Also present are small groups of Chinese, Malays, Mons, Khmers, Phuans, and recent refugees from Vietnam, Myanmar (Burma), Laos and Cambodia.

The Chinese form the largest minority with more than 12 per cent of the population. The strong work ethic, achievement orientation and ingroup support of the Chinese have ensured that they have flourished and now own many of Thailand's largest companies. The Chinese in Thailand have not become the target of racial discrimination and tension, as has happened in other parts of Asia like Malaysia and Indonesia, because there has been a considerable amount of inter-marriage. Sino-Thais often take Thai surnames and speak Thai rather than Chinese, making it difficult to distinguish them from 'pure' Thais. There are even some members of parliament and senior government officials who will admit to some Chinese ancestry. This increases the homogeneity of the country's culture and reduces possibilities of ethnic intolerance.

The Thais are a freedom loving people. and the country is often called the 'land of smiles' and 'the land of the free'. Thais emphasise the maintenance of the dignity of other people as well as of themselves. This focus on mutual respect facilitates harmony in relationships. Thai society is essentially a conflict avoidance society compared to Western conflict resolution approaches. Among the generally accepted Thai values and attitudes that defuse or avoid situations of potential personal or social conflict, are the concepts of *mai pen rai* and *chai yen yen*.

Mai pen rai means 'Never mind, it does not matter'. As a result there is a general mood not to overinflate problems and setbacks out of proportion. This attitude may lie behind the large number of bloodless military coups that have occurred rather politely without strife. Any displays of anger or rude behaviour are frowned upon. All differences are expected to be resolved without fuss. So *Mai pen rai*, in signifying a desire to keep relationships on an even keel and shrug off little frustrations to prevent anger being vented, becomes a way of reducing to a minimum difficulties that are bound to arise in human relationships and in society. Thus relationships are often kept at a superficial level so as not to become too involved with other people.

Chai yen yen characterises a person who avoids all direct displays of anger, hatred and aggression, etc.

Thais also adopt a social norm called *kreing chai*. This involves the desire to be self-effacing, humble and respectful, the wish to avoid embarrassing others or intruding on others. *Kreing chai* is used by Thais to rationalise personal weakness by claiming they avoided doing something not because they felt incompetent but because they did not want to show off.

As part of *kreing chai* there are rules relating to superior–inferior relationships as in Malaysia, including a special set of pronouns and language by which you address a superior. Thus there are clearly defined roles to play in relation to others. Social ranking itself is important in Thailand and is controlled by a combination of lineage, education and economic status. As part of this focus on status a Thai will refer to themselves in different ways depending on their status vis-a-vis the status of the listener.

The royal family as persons and as an institution are regarded with the greatest respect, and any slander or criticism of either is a legal offence. The popular Western film and play, *The King and I*, and the original book, *The English Governess at the Siamese Court*, have been banned in Thailand for this reason. The Thais employ a special honorific vocabulary when referring to the royal family or directly addressing them.

The family unit is central to Thai community life, with the extended family still common in rural areas. Traditionally, all daily endeavours focussed on food production, security and maintaining harmony between members. With the development of commerce, tourism, and the recent influx of foreigners, Thais have become more materialistic, downplaying the needs of family and community as wealth and making money become more salient personal goals.

While women are beginning to hold important professional and public service jobs, and have always managed the household with its finances, the Thai woman has generally been regarded as subservient to the Thai male. Many men still have a second, though unofficial wife.

Don't be misled by the smiles of the Thais. Their smiles can be deceptive and used to hide emotions, attitudes, and reactions to you. So do not assume that the situation is positive simply because a Thai smiles at you. It is very important that you also smile often and in every situation; a smile is the most useful nonverbal tool in this culture.

Religion

Over 90 per cent of the population practice Theravada Buddhism. The rest are mainly Muslims, generally Malay. Some of the hill tribes practice ancestor worship. The Buddhist approach to life, especially focussed on the understanding of human behaviour, has emphasised a contemplative and passive way of dealing with life. It focusses on self-realisation, knowing others, causality, knowing your potential, and knowing the appropriate time and place for dealing with things.

The King of Thailand, by constitution and tradition, is a Buddhist but also functions as the patron of all religious groups underpinning a broad-minded religious tolerance. The Thais are free in law to practice any religion. Their Buddhist faith leads Thais to value harmony and mutual respect, preserve the dignity of others, as well as their own, and to be rather tolerant.

Making contacts

While possessing a sound introduction or knowing an important go-between will greatly increase you and your companies credibility and acceptance, you are in order to write directly to Thai companies. It is better to write or fax rather than phone, since telephone conversations in English are more difficult to understand for the Thai, while a written communication can be translated at leisure if need be. As a result of the use of the concept of *sanuk* (is something pleasurable or not) by which to judge everything, there is a wide latitude of acceptance for spontaneity and a less formal approach. Impromptu meetings are therefore acceptable if all else fails but try to set up meetings in advance when on the first visit. The use of a local agent or representative who is conversant with ways of doing things and also fluent in both Thai and English is recommended if you intend to buy from or sell to Thailand. Embassies, chambers of commerce, or those with previous business experience in Thailand, are useful sources to tap for the names of reliable agents. It is essential that your agent has links with government officials, as the latter have considerable influence when dealing with larger projects.

Communication guidelines

Meeting people

New Year Festivals are not a time to schedule any business visits. In general, heavy traffic in major cities can mean that punctuality is a problem for both you and the Thais. So meetings often commence late as one party is held up. This has to be accepted with equanimity if you are the one kept waiting. You should not schedule any meeting for late afternoon since most Thais try to beat the traffic home by leaving early. They will appreciate your understanding of this. First meetings may be held in offices, restaurants, or hotel lobbies. Male visitors may be invited to clubs of which your host is a member. Some of these can be quite exclusive. You should stay in the most expensive hotel your company can afford, as this implies that your organisation is a very successful one. This will impress your Thai contacts.

The word *Khun* (pronounced coon) is used in place of 'Mr' or 'Mrs' and placed before the person's first name, i.e. the one which is listed first on their business card. For example, a Westerner with the name 'Peter Wright' would be called 'Khun Peter'. First names only are used among Thais and family names rarely. You should not refer to yourself with the word Khun; just say your first name. You are likely to be addressed by Thais by using 'Mr' or 'Mrs' and your first name, e.g. Mr Peter.

Until recently, Thais always greeted and said goodbye to each other with the traditional respectful greeting called the *wei*. This is a slightly forward bow, at the same time bringing their hands to a praying position in front of them between the chest and forehead. The exact location of the hands depends on the level of respect being offered. However, the fingertips should never go above the head. Among Thais, the height and depth of a person's *wei* indicates social status. If you want to *wei* back to your counterpart, don't worry about getting your hands at the correct height as the Thais are far more tolerant then the Japanese over their bow. The Thais will be delighted that you have used their greeting. If you don't know whether to shake hands or not, wait to see if your Thai counterpart extends a hand for a handshake. What to them is a foreign greeting—as the *wei* is to us—is only just catching on among the more educated and cosmopolitan Thais. You are not expected to *wei* secretaries and clerks. The *wei* can also be used when saying or 'Thank you' or apologising.

It is important to exchange business cards at introductions. Failure to offer a business card may make Thais suspicious of your position and authority. As Thais are impressed by status and position always have these included on your card.

Casual conversation at early meetings should include your travels, what you have seen of Thailand, your overseas experiences, your family, the plane trip etc. Thais are quite interested in what Westerners regard as more personal matters and you may well be on the receiving end of questions about your salary, the size of house you live in, the size of your car, your age, why you are not married etc. You should respond to these if they are too personal for you with vagueness. 'Like everyone else I could always do with more salary' or throw the question back at the Thai e.g., 'I drive a Ford. What are the popular makes of car here?' Avoid topics relating to politics, the royal family and religion. Be generous in your praise of the country and the Thai people and refrain from boasting about your country and yourself as this is seen as bad manners and lacking in modesty. Although gifts are not required for early meetings sample products or small souvenirs are always appreciated.

Some nonverbal behaviours to note

- Never place your feet up on a table or chair to reveal the sole of your foot to anyone, nor touch someone with your feet. As is common in Asia, the Thais regard feet as unclean.
- Don't stand over someone, especially if they are older or more superior, as it implies social superiority. This is difficult for Westerners who tend to dwarf some of the smaller Thais. You should try bending your stance a little rather than standing upright. This gesture will be appreciated even if to makes little difference to relative height.

- Always place your feet on the ground and don't cross your legs, as this is considered rude.
- Avoid physically touching a Thai or even the chair that they are sitting on; both gestures are considered rude.
- Don't point at someone with your finger. Angle your head or chin in their direction.
- Don't wag a forefinger to beckon someone. Use your whole hand with the palm facing down and the fingers pointing away from you, but moving toward you in a scratching motion.
- When passing an object, never toss it to a Thai. Always hand it over gently.
- Never criticise the monarchy or the government. It is illegal and the law is strictly enforced. Members of the royal family should always be publicly respected.

Getting down to business

Corporate structure

The typical business is headed by a senior member of a Chinese or Sino-Thai family who retains most authority and is involved on a day-to-day basis with a hands-on management style. The Thais have tended to avoid commerce due to the Buddhist preference for the priesthood, teaching and the public service. Other companies are owned by senior military leaders.

The manager's role is generally to maintain harmony and ensure there are no unpleasant situations. The fair and equal treatment of all employees is the aim. Harmony and fair treatment are seen as leading to the accomplishment of assigned tasks and achievement of the organisation's objectives. The Thai organisational environment is affected strongly by blood ties and bonds of friendship, plus the obligation to return personal favours.

Negotiation

Negotiation in Thailand takes time—lots of it. This stems from the Thai concept of time being somewhat elastic. There will be no rapid decision-making. This is where your agent can play their part. They must keep your interests alive in the minds of the Thais in-between your many visits. A Thai will promise to be in touch, but unless you keep pressing them there may be no follow-up. You will need to visit Thailand probably three times before your proposal will be seriously considered. However, the increasing international experience of some leading companies is turning them towards a more speedy process.

As the Thais are high power distance people, supportive of hierarchies and respect for all forms of authority, decisions are made by senior management with little consultation of lower staff. Rarely would there be any attempt made by less senior staff to influence or disagree with a decision since Thai society lives by the unspoken rule never to directly oppose or embarrass anyone.

In negotiation the aim is to maintain a calm professional polite manner as the Thais place a great importance on appearances and not losing one's temper. This composure is called *jai yen* (cool heart). Losing your temper brings loss of face for you and your counterpart who has behaved in some way as to cause you to behave like this. Try to smile through it all and remember that a smile can replace a cynical retort, a verbal 'no way' and an embarrassing error on the counterpart's side. The smile will probably be understood and accepted, whereas the verbal retort would not be. So in all your negotiations the main aim is to facilitate group harmony and avoid conflict. As criticism constitutes a personal attack in the Thai culture, you will receive minimal honest feedback about your business package, project proposals or products. You will have to pose indirect questions, particularly those that can be answered affirmatively but have a negative meaning, in order to determine what changes you need to make to your proposals.

The cultural propensity for spontaneity (*sanuk*) and *Mai pen rai* (it doesn't matter) intrude into the world of business. There is less concern about meeting deadlines and general productivity than most Westerners would want. Careful planning goes out of the window as Thais enjoy their spontaneity. To a Westerner this carelessness for detail, accountability and responsibility renders it hard to keep negotiations and ultimately business activity moving forward in a pre-arranged logical fashion.

Contracts are a sensitive issue in Thailand as they are likely to be offended by a demand for a detailed format. This implies they are not going to be honourable in their dealings. The Thais view contracts merely as an early step in developing a relationship. It is better to focus on your business objectives and include the appropriate level of details in order to avoid too many problems. Try to outline how disagreements should be handled.

The social context of business

Dining out

Business lunches and dinners are frequent, as Thais really enjoy dining out and combining business with pleasure. Business breakfasts are rare. The host pays for the meal and the entertainment. Splitting a bill is not done. If you are the only foreigner at the table it might be a good diplomatic gesture to accept the honour of paying; such generosity is appreciated. The Thais are likely to bring alcohol with them to a restaurant. Don't raise business issues until your Thai host does so.

Thais use chopsticks only for Chinese dishes. In all other situations they use a fork and spoon. The fork is used to push the food onto the spoon. When you are finished, place your fork and spoon together at the lower right side of the plate; otherwise, it will be assumed that you want more. Never pass food with just the left hand as it is considered unclean.

Despite the problem of AIDS, Thais are still very tolerant of prostitution and consider extramarital relations for men a normal activity. However, they will not take offence if you turn down an offer of a female 'escort,' or a visit to a 'massage parlour'. Discretion is viewed as a sign of maturity. The Thais are also inveterate gamblers.

A home visit

Home invitations are usually for an informal buffet for groups and not just for one or two special people. Shoes should be removed before entering a Thai home. Avoid stepping on the doorsill of a home (or temple), as it is believed that spirits and souls live there. Take a small gift with you such as sweets, handicrafts or souvenirs from home. Your gift should be wrapped in brightly coloured paper. Thais are very hospitable and if you praise some specific object in the home your host will feel obliged to give it to you, so make your compliments general about the house or children overall. Do not touch or photograph Buddhist shrines and other religious objects in the home.

Giving gifts

Some claim that there is corruption among the military and government officials who abuse their powers to enrich themselves and that many government coups have been prompted by corruption. Keep at arm's length from these activities and have your agent deal with such matters. The Thais are very discreet and the commissions required to undertake tasks are likely to be so subtle that you will miss the implications. In normal business activity it is acceptable to provide a small gift as a relationship develops. Thais usually focus on the thought behind the gift rather than its value. You can give souvenirs, alcohol, spirits, wine, chocolates or small gift sets. Flowers should not be offered as they are limited to funerals. Do not open any gifts in the presence of the giver.

Other useful information

What to wear

Men are expected to wear a suit and tie. Short sleeves are acceptable in the heat of summer, when ties and jackets can be dispensed with. For women a suit or dress is appropriate. Casual wear is not suitable for Thailand's better restaurants. Avoid purple as this is the royal colour.

Language

The Thai language is a tonal one so that the same word can be said in five different ways. Understanding the proper tone is vital. There are no plurals or tenses. Most Thais in the major cities speak some English but little is spoken in the rural areas. In Thai there is a polite ending for every sentence by adding *khrap* for men and *kha* for women. Men and women also use different versions of the same phrase when speaking.

Major holidays

January 1	New Year's Day
January/February*	Chinese New Year
February/March*	Makha Bucha Day
April 6	Chakri Day
mid-April	Song Kran Festival (Thai New Year)
May*	Royal Ploughing Day
May 1	National Labour Day
May 5	Coronation Day
May /June*	Wisakha Bucha Day
July /August*	Asalaha Bucha Day
July 12	Buddhist Lent Day
August 12	Queen's Birthday
October 23	Chulalongkorn Day
December 5	The King's Birthday
December 10	Constitution Day
December 31	New Year's Eve

*These are lunar-based holidays and change from year to year.

General facts

Tipping

Taxi drivers are rarely tipped. Hotel staff should be tipped. Carry loose change for tipping; however, never leave only 1 baht as that would be considered an insult.

Soi

In Bangkok, the Thais use the word *soi* and a *soi* number when giving addresses. *Soi* and a number refers to a secondary street that runs off a main road. The *soi* can have a number and a name. In identifying a building on a main road, Thais usually refer to its **closest** *soi* and number/name. For example, '*Sukhumvit, Soi 12,*' '*Soi 12 Sukhumvit,*' and '*Soi 12, Sukhumvit Road*' all refer to the same location, *Soi 12*, which is a secondary street off the main road, Sukhumvit. This method can make getting around Bangkok confusing. Thais are generally quite friendly and will assist you when you are lost if you ask politely and with a smile.

Transport

It usually takes about one hour to travel from the Don Muang Airport to Bangkok, but in the rainy season, this trip can take from one to two and a half hours. There are several ways to get into Bangkok from the airport including taxi, airport limousines, and hotel buses. For taxis, use the taxi reservations counter outside the customs areas; otherwise you are liable to be charged significantly more than the normal cost of the trip. Negotiate the price with the driver before getting into the taxi, for many cabs lack meters. Thai Airways has a minibus that runs from the airport to all major hotels. There is also a train service from the airport to the central station in Bangkok which takes only forty minutes. Inquire at the airport tourist office for details.

In Bangkok, rush hour seems to last all day. The alternative to taxis is to rent a car and driver. The cost is about the same for a rental car, although self-driving is not recommended due to traffic and driving conditions. A word of caution: if a foreigner is in a traffic accident, he or she will be judged at fault, not the Thai. Adjust your schedule to include traffic delays.

Ask a local before using a taxi for the appropriate price for the distance you expect to travel. Many drivers do not speak or understand English. Drivers usually inflate the fare 30–35 per cent. Offer to pay 75 per cent of the first stated price. Hotel taxis are usually more expensive, but the drivers often speak some English.

In summary

1　Thailand is ethnically and religiously very homogeneous, although the minority Chinese tend to have considerable influence in the business world.

2 Thai culture emphasises harmony, mutual respect, conflict avoidance, collectivism and high power distance.

3 In business, Thais are less formal and more spontaneous than other Asian cultures.

4 Time is a fluid concept in Thailand and negotiations are slow, with decisions emanating from the top.

5 Never lose your composure. Control your emotions and smile through it all.

6 Contracts indicate a lack of trust to a Thai, who view them only as an initial agreement to explore proposals.

7 Corruption is rife. Allow your agent to handle 'commissions'.

Activity

Try working out the solution to the following problem, then check your response with that in Appendix B.

1 Domenic Previn, a young sales manager for a small boat-building firm, decided to stop off in Bangkok to call on several potential clients after a business trip to Singapore and Brunei. Having set up three appointments in two days, he arrived for the first two scheduled meetings at the appointed times but was kept waiting for over a half hour in each instance. Based on these two experiences Domenic assumed that the Thais must be *'manyana'* oriented and not particularly concerned with the precise reckoning of time. With this in mind, he was not particularly concerned about being on time for his third appointment. Instead, he extended his visit to the local museum and arrived at his third appointment more than 40 minutes late. However, Domenic sensed that the Thai business people who were kept waiting were quite displeased with his tardiness.

How would you explain this reaction?

2 Ben Nguyen, production manager of a clothing manufacturer, was sent by his company to observe first-hand how operations were proceeding in their Thailand factory, and to help institute some new managerial procedures. Before any changes could be made, however, Ben wanted to learn as much as possible about the problems that existed at the plant. During his first week he was met with bows, polite smiles and the continual denial of any significant problems. But Ben was

enough of a realist to know that he had never heard of any manufacturing operation that didn't have some problems.

So after some creative research he uncovered a number of problems that the local manager and staff were not acknowledging. None of the problems were particularly unusual or difficult to solve. But Ben was frustrated that no one would admit that any problems existed. 'If you don't acknowledge the problems,' he complained to one of the managers, 'how do you expect to be able to solve them?' And then to further exasperate him, just today when a problem was finally brought to his attention, it was not mentioned until the end of the work day when there was no time left to solve it.

How could you help Ben better understand the dynamics of this situation?

Conducting Business in

Vietnam

'A tiger on a bicycle'

General background

Location

Vietnam forms a long narrow strip of land on the eastern side of the Indochinese peninsula with about 3 250 km of coastline. Its land borders are with China, Laos and Cambodia. There are three main regions: the Mekong Delta and coastal lowlands in the south; the mountainous region and Red River Delta in the north; and the central highlands in-between. The capital city is Hanoi; Ho Chi Minh City (Saigon) is the largest city and commercial centre.

Politics

The Socialist Republic of Vietnam (SRV) remains a communist state based on Chinese and Russian models, with local modifications to fit Vietnamese circumstances. The National Assembly is technically elected by the voters, but with a political system totally controlled by the Vietnamese Communist Party (VCP or Viet Nam Cong San Dang) democracy is but a dream. Carefully selected candidates are elected to the National Assembly with unbelievable majorities. The current legal system is still developing, applied inconsistently, constantly changing with little notification, and providing very little protection for foreign commercial interests. The rule of law applies to foreigners, while the spirit of the law is interpreted in favour of the locals. The Confucian aim for conciliation leads to compromise rather than legal remedies to resolve disputes.

Economy

Although North and South Vietnam were reunified over twenty years ago, Vietnam is still a poor country due to its isolation and the demise of the former Eastern European Soviet block and USSR which provided subsidised trade. The economy is characterised by soaring inflation rates, debt problems, difficulties and inefficiencies in production and distribution, and imbalances in supply and demand.

The new renewal policy (*doi moi*) has started a muted liberalisation of the economy, encouraging foreign investors to channel in more private investment, trade and multilateral aid in the pursuit of the increasing open business opportunities. This is despite the lack of proper commercial law and vacillating government policy which is trying to turn two ways at once like China—retaining the communist ethic but becoming modern. Restrictions on private companies have been reduced, while the heavy hand of the state has been lifted off state-owned enterprises which now have more managerial autonomy. Laws change with great regularity and without notice—sometimes back-dated—as the Vietnamese leadership attempt to balance the need for market reform and integration into the international economy without destroying too much of their puritanical socialist zeal. The attempt to develop commercial law and government policy on overseas involvement has been a flurry of knee jerk reactions that lacks overall synthesis and consistency.

Society and culture

Ethnicity

Vietnam is a densely populated rural country of 72 million people, most of whom are involved in agriculture or related jobs. Nearly 90 per cent are ethnic Vietnamese (Viets), with most of the remainder being ethnic Chinese (the Hoa). The majority of the population resides in the north.

Viets control the political and social life of the country and form a fairly close knit, nationalistic homogenous group. The Chinese community tend to live in and around Ho Chi Minh City and as usual have long dominated the commercial scene. Their business success was an anathema to the communist Viets after reunification and many Hoa fled to Cambodia and China to avoid persecution. Some are now returning, and together with those who stayed, are providing the major thrust behind the present economic developments in Vietnam. The Chinese maintain a tight network and sense of community through their family kinship groups.

Religion

Most Vietnamese would claim to be Buddhist, but Confucianism, Taoism and global Chinese beliefs in animism and ancestor worship have fused with Buddhism to form a common belief system (*Tam Giao*) that stresses the importance of maintaining harmony and balance within the typical Confucian pattern of a hierarchical, paternal and authoritarian society. Ancestors are believed to remain close to the living and can help or hurt the living. Roman Catholicism, a relic of French colonialism, remains the faith of about 10 per cent of the population.

Culture

The Vietnamese are fiercely protective of their independence and culture, with a deep sense of ethnic identity and national pride, based on their common language and the succession of long painful struggles for independence from the Chinese, French and Americans. Most Vietnamese consider themselves Vietnamese first and communists second. Positive comments about Vietnam and Vietnamese people are always welcome, but avoid any comment about communism, either for or against, since while some are fervent communists there are also many who privately oppose the ideology, and you will not know who is for and who is against.

Despite ancestor worship and a love of tradition, the Vietnamese also focus on the future. They find it difficult to understand why Americans are still soul searching over the Vietnam War, particularly since Vietnam has fought wars with Cambodia and China since then. For the Vietnamese the short war with the Americans was simply the final stage of a lengthy struggle for independence against colonial powers, and in any case has been overtaken by other events. Moreover, many of the rising generation of entrepreneurs were quite young during the American affair, with very little recollection of the fall of Saigon or even the war. The Vietnamese are far less xenophobic and more cosmopolitan than most other Asian cultures due to their long association with colonial powers. They have witnessed the success of overseas Vietnamese and been exposed to American capitalism. Another advantage is that their language is Romanised.

Thus there is a general feeling of friendship for Westerners, including Americans, as the Vietnamese traditionally welcome strangers as guests. As a rule they are gentle, friendly and hospitable people, although tenacious, and shrewd in negotiations. Added to this, the opening up of global communications is increasing awareness of what is going on in the rest of the world and the living standards there. There is a great desire for success nationally and among individuals, with the aim now to achieve parity, particularly with other Asian neighbours in terms of material wealth. They are very brand and fashion conscious, placing a high value on internationally known product names.

To achieve this goal, the Vietnamese are demonstrating a willingness to work hard and adopt an entrepreneurial spirit. To achieve personal financial status many hold two jobs. Everyone is trying to get into business and make money. As one business person said, 'if the Ho Chi Min trail was in operation today it would be a toll road'. This contrasts sharply with the more laid back manner of the Thais, Filipinos and Malays. However, the downside of running two jobs often means that state employees will put their more lucrative private interests ahead of their official jobs, reducing the efficiency of the public service tremendously. However, even in the south Vietnam is still an unattractive destination for those used to comfort and luxury.

The Confucian ethic still dominates family and social values, despite considerable pressures from the communist party to place its needs first. There is a strong sense of community and collective responsibility, exemplified by an emphasis on the family, on obligation, loyalty and honour, on education, learning, respect to elders, tradition, and politeness. The extended family is still very important in rural areas, with members supporting and contributing to the financial, social and everyday needs of the group. A person's identity is derived from their position within the family group and is reflected in the constellation of honorifics and titles employed to address persons of varying degrees of blood relationship. When doing business there, it is essential to ask about their family, talk about yours, and give small gifts to their children. In other words, show that you have a genuine concern for family. However, the nuclear family is becoming obvious in urban areas as the government has been promoting quite vigorously a policy of family planning to temper population increases, coupled with an inevitable migration from rural areas to a potentially better lifestyle in major centres.

Although women have full equal rights with males in law, in reality Vietnam is a typical high power distance patriarchal society and most organisations are dominated by men. Women are regarded as vital resources in the industrial and business world and an increasing number are achieving high occupational or political status and accorded much respect. However, many women are still the workhorses, strong and resilient, primarily in low paid agricultural and light industry work.

Education

As in all Confucian countries, there is a strong respect and demand for education. With a literacy rate approaching 90 per cent, thinkers are more revered than doers, with the result that until now business persons have not earned as much respect as the scholar or bureaucrat. However the education system is suffering as fees are now payable above the third year of primary school, causing many people to take their children away from school to work. The local graduate is becoming a rare bird, yet paradoxically there are many Vietnamese sporting degrees and academic titles.

Don't take the qualifications at face value unless they come from a university you recognise as reputable. Many hold low class degrees from some sympathetic but hardly acceptable third world or former Eastern European communist establishments. Many of these 'friendship' degrees were awarded on the basis of time spent in the institution rather than on academic attainment. The academic titles 'engineer' and 'doctor' are used as general titles with the former rarely having any real connection with a Western concept of what the possessor would be capable of doing. Such titles can be held by those with qualifications in any field including journalism, economics and foreign languages! There is a generous embellishment of academic titles for anyone who has managed a three-year degree program, many of which were 'on the job' programs providing maximum credit for work experience, coupled with very minimal course attendance. Western university accreditation committees generally regard most Vietnamese PhDs as equivalent to Masters level. You should not select staff on the basis of qualifications without first determining where and how the qualification was obtained.

The north and south divide

There is a north–south divide in Vietnam stemming from old rivalries and political systems. Apart from the intense nationalism and Confucian philosophy that pervades the whole country, there is a noticeable dichotomy between the attitudes and personalities of those living in the north from those in the south. While southerners tend to be individualistic, commercial in approach, and worldly, the northerners are more group-oriented, reserved, conservative and austere. This may stem from the southerners' greater exposure to Western influences when it was an independent state. Life was easier in the south, leading to less xenophobia, more openness and greater tolerance of individuality. Southern Vietnam has more businesses and investment currently than the northern part of the country. This is a historical legacy of the pre-unification days, and the location of the commercially minded Chinese. There is therefore possibly more future potential to tap into in the north as it develops.

Making contacts

As usual in Asia, connections and introductions will advance your business interests in Vietnam. It will take a lot of effort to obtain a positive response without a written introduction or a meeting arranged by an acceptable third party. Cold calling via formal letters or phone may only work if you represent a large, well-known international company. Using your introduction you should write to a named person in the organisation with which you want to do business before you attempt to call for a visit. Provide details about the purpose of your visit, your business proposal, your company and its products/services and any references you can provide. Have important parts translated if possible. Send multiple copies of essential documents, as decisions to see you will be group decisions. Avoid jargon and colloquialisms; write plain English in short sentences.

The aim is an invitation for further discussion. You must be specific about what you seek; there can be no 'fishing' expeditions. The Vietnamese will not waste their time—or yours. You should gain introductions to several companies as well, so that you build up contacts and don't forget to make yourself known to government officials and Local People's Committees, all of whom influence most final outcomes where permissions and permits are required.

The information provided enables the Vietnamese to decide whether they wish to see you and prevents them being surprised by any proposals you make later. If there is to be a response it will be fairly quick, although likely to arrive by a letter rather than fax or telephone, as both are inordinately expensive. Therefore in your planning leave a good time gap to enable letters to pass both ways. Use the time wisely and conduct as much background research—through the Vietnamese Embassy at home, your Embassy in Vietnam and any other person/ organisation with contacts there—on such matters as the condition of the marketplace, competition, and who could function as a local representative and interpreter.

When you visit, take a high powered delegation with top technical experts if necessary who can answer in detail and confidently all the tricky technical/scientific questions which will inevitably be posed. This shows the value you place on the possible business activity and the competence and expertise your company possesses. Punctuality is not a virtue and you must not be surprised if your Vietnamese counterpart turns up late or sends a replacement. Even talking to a stand-in is important, as decision-making processes are spread broadly in Vietnamese organisations and it is another contact who might prove a conduit to further contacts or who can bring influence to bear.

Use the services of some well-established consulting firms that are intimately familiar with the Vietnamese market, as it is difficult to find a reliable and credible local representative with valid claims to have the right connections and to know the market. Obtain references and verify for yourself the quality and range of the representative's/consultant's previous work in Vietnam. Review a prospective representative's client list and referrals as well the extent of their connections because a Vietnamese firm's contacts are important. Make sure that you personally develop strong positive relationships with government officials and leaders of community committees that matter, as your local representatives can cease to be the flavour of the month for quite trivial reasons and take you with them. So don't depend solely on your representative. Many overseas organisations have started to use experienced firms, agents and consultants based in Singapore or Hong Kong to sell their products and services, or transact other business with the Vietnamese, as it can take many months to obtain permission to open a local office. But in Vietnam, the cliché 'out-of-sight, out-of-mind' runs true. You need some ongoing presence. Referrals and suggestions are available from the embassies and chamber of commerce offices in your home country.

If your business can stand the cost, or the project is substantial, you may wish to base an employee in Vietnam to supplement the local representative, however as yet offices of overseas organisations are only allowed to perform research or support services. It can take up to eighteen months to process the application to establish a local office. For any business endeavour to be consummated, you must be perceived as willing to make a long-term commitment to the country, as a trusted friend/organisation for the country and have a presence there either through a local representative or an expatriate from your organisation.

Ho Chi Minh City (Saigon) is the most efficient place to do business, but as everyone wants to place their business there, it is quicker to set up in Hanoi to avoid the application queue. But wherever you decide to do business in Vietnam you will not escape the standard business practice of corruption.

Networking is an essential part of doing business in Vietnam. The Vietnamese are usually quite friendly and enjoy widening your circle of acquaintances, as they are part of the camaraderie too. Receptions and conferences at home and overseas are also useful ways of meeting influential and knowledgeable third parties or even possible partners, since only the best Vietnamese are chosen to represent the country overseas on these occasions. Make sure business cards are exchanged, as these contain contact information. Going with a trade delegation is a cost effective way to make relevant contacts and open doors. Indepth business negotiations will not be done, but the start can be made on exploring possibilities and commencing the buildup of relationships needed prior to business. Be careful with your use of expatriate Vietnamese (*Viet Kieu*) to assist with setting up your operation or interpretation as they are not readily accepted by local Vietnamese who may resent them as traitors who fled and gained a better life for themselves by their selfish desertion of the mother country.

Communication guidelines

Greeting and meeting people

While most Vietnamese are early risers, with businesses and shops opening early, the best times to schedule an appointment are between 9.00 am and 11.00 am, and from 3.00 pm to 5.00 pm. Avoid scheduling meetings for Saturday afternoons, although Saturday mornings are quite acceptable.

As your appointment will have been made well in advance, possibly by letter, you should always confirm it as soon as you arrive in the country, as other issues may have occurred in the meantime which could prevent the Vietnamese person from attending. Meetings are less formal than in other Asian countries, with ritual not highly in evidence and less strict adherence to protocol. The Vietnamese accept that foreigners do not know all the nuances of their culture and do not expect it, though the fewer errors you make the better.

On first meeting smile, shake hands and make sure you address them by their correct name and title. The Vietnamese will often give a slight bow to indicate respect. Business cards, presented and received with both hands, are always exchanged at the first meeting. It is sensible to have some of your cards printed in Vietnamese on the reverse. You must not write on someone's business card, as this is regarded as a sign of disrespect. While you don't need to demonstrate feigned awe at the card as in Japan, it is still expected that you read it and not simply put it straight into your pocket. While most Vietnamese will shake hands with both men and women at both the beginning and the end of a meeting, some Vietnamese males from rural areas meeting with an overseas woman may not do so. In these circumstances, a slight bow of the head will suffice. In introducing yourself, speak your name slowly and distinctly, as many Vietnamese are unfamiliar with foreign names.

Vietnamese names follow the sequence of Chinese names with family name first, then middle name, and finally given name. Unlike many Asian cultures, most Vietnamese use their given names. So it is quite acceptable and even expected for you to address a Vietnamese by their given name with the appropriate title, such as 'Mr', 'Madame', 'Miss', 'Director' or 'Dr'. For example, 'Nguyen Duc Thac' should be addressed as 'Dr Thac'. In writing formally, the letter would commence 'Dear Dr Nguyen'.

Many Vietnamese who know each other call to each other by the name of the relationship. These gender specific titles are tacked onto the given name. This is to indicate respect. A general polite hello and goodbye is to use the appropriate title, the given name of the person, and the words *xin chao* (pronounced 'seen chow'). Vietnamese are very appreciative when foreigners try to use their language. If you wish to be really formal, the greeting must be qualified by a pronoun that indicates the relationship between the two people. Examples of different greetings include,

'chao ong' = formal hello to a man your age or older
'chao ba' = formal hello to a woman
'chao anh' = greeting a man you know well
'chao chi' = greeting a woman you know well
'chao em' = greeting a male or female child

plus many more depending on age, gender and relationship. Do not use 'chao' alone as this is impolite.

As you can see, this plethora of greetings means that you should not try too many honorific titles in Vietnamese unless you are really sure of your ground. Another alternative is simply use the internationally accepted 'hello'. Another confusion is that *'chao'* also means 'goodbye'. Therefore many Vietnamese will greet you with other expressions like 'What are you doing?' *(Anh dang lam gi do?)* or 'where are you going?' *(ahn dang di dau do?).*

Start your meeting with some casual talk on topics like the weather, your recent travels, previous visits to Vietnam, interesting things you have seen in Vietnam, and your interests. Don't forget to ask about their family. The Vietnamese are very proud of their history and culture—not in the sense of boasting about their victories over colonialism, but they genuinely enjoy talking about their cultural heritage. Your interest in their culture and history will be extremely well appreciated, particularly if you focus on pre-twentieth century. The Vietnamese interest in their history enables them to draw parallels between current activities and occurrences in the past. If you can try your hand at this and draw realistic parallels that support your position, you will be on strong ground. Viewing things in the context of tradition is hard, but you should do some homework on Vietnamese history and culture before your visit.

The Vietnamese appear to possess inordinate curiosity and will ask quite personal questions sometimes about age, earnings, marital situation etc. These are common between Vietnamese but they do not realise that Westerners are a little more reluctant to self-disclose. Try to deflect the questions with a light hearted reply. In terms of income you can always say that you could always do with more, and as for age, that you are well under 75 years old. Turn the questions back at the Vietnamese too. Knowledge of your married status, occupational position and status help the Vietnamese to determine their status relative to yours. Don't tell any jokes—even inoffensive ones—as their sense of humour is very different from a Western one.

Vietnamese are very self-effacing and will not boast or indicate their real potential and skills to you. In fact they may deny their competence. To them politeness involves rejecting compliments and remaining self-effacing. Don't boast about your accomplishments either—let the third party do that for you.

At the conclusion of a meeting you should express your appreciation that your counterpart/government bureaucrat has been so generous in making time to see you in their busy schedule. Thank them for enabling this opportunity to meet. Your manner and speech should demonstrate a discreet and sincere humility and politeness, but don't overdo it.

You will find that the Vietnamese exude friendliness and will smile at you throughout the meeting. You must sample the food and tea served to you as it is impolite not to taste even a small amount. Although it is not necessary, you can give your host a small gift at the end of the first and subsequent meetings.

Before meeting with a senior minister or company official it is advisable to meet with middle level officers to do some fact finding and conduct additional research, so that you will be well prepared to conduct business and perhaps conclude a preliminary understanding and/or agreement. Only arrange a meeting with a senior official when you have a specific proposal to offer. If you are still trying to sort out options or are hazy about some points, a senior Vietnamese official is unlikely to invite you back for future meetings. In any case, you will only have a short meeting on one or two occasions so you must be ready to begin discussing business soon after the commencement of the meeting. With middle- and junior-level people you should not discuss much business during the first meeting but should attend to relationship building. It is appropriate to state your company's general objectives in the country.

Few Vietnamese have a strong enough grasp of English to use it for the medium of discussion. You will need to use a translator. Always hire your own or take one with you from home. Never rely on your counterpart's translator. The Vietnamese tend to speak at a lower sound level than that in the West. If your interpreter is speaking softly, that is perfectly normal. Do not ask them to speak louder. The use of an interpreter will at least double the length of the meeting. Add to this the more leisurely pace of Vietnamese business meetings and you soon realise that one meeting per day is all that can be managed.

Always be polite and maintain your composure, even in difficult circumstances. While it is very unlikely that you would get into any kind of trouble, your business reputation could become tainted if you appear to be loud, rude, and generally negative, as this type of information is often shared between ministries and senior officials.

Some nonverbal behaviours to note

- Vietnamese avoid intense eye contact. In fact it is respectful and deferential not to engage in eye contact. It is essential that you only maintain limited eye contact when talking with Vietnamese persons.
- Don't place your hands on your hips as this indicates aggression; folded arms are a sign that you reject the other person or do not believe what they have said.
- The Vietnamese will smile in what appears to be inappropriate contexts. Smiling can indicate a wide range of emotions such as sadness, embarrassment, scepticism, and avoidance of conflict. In the last situation the wry smile replaces a retort.
- Pass things from one person to the next with both hands.
- Do not touch a person's head, as it is considered the spiritual centre of the individual.
- Do not cross your legs at a meetings nor allow the sole of your foot show; both are regarded as rude and disrespectful.
- Never point at someone or summon them with the index finger. To beckon a person, use your whole hand with the palm facing down and your fingers pointing away from you but waving toward you.
- Some Vietnamese males do not traditionally shake hands with females, so an overseas business woman will have to initiate the handshake by holding her hand out.
- Vietnamese males are uncomfortable kissing the cheek of a woman, patting shoulders or arm grasping.
- The Vietnamese feel uncomfortable with open shows of affection between males and females but you will find people of the same sex will walk hand in hand. This has no implication of sexual preference. It indicates that they have a good relationship with you and trust you so don't recoil in horror, as that would signal rejection of a friendship.
- It is expected that Vietnamese women will not travel alone. An overseas business woman should therefore have a travelling companion to avoid unwanted comments from men.
- A blank face on a Vietnamese is a certain sign of difficulty with you or your proposal. You may unwittingly have annoyed the Vietnamese person or caused a loss of face.
- The Vietnamese use nonverbal cues to judge status. If your demeanour exudes calmness and moderation then you will be evaluated positively. Speak quietly at a volume level that is just loud enough for your audience to hear. Loudness is interpreted as aggressive.
- Never sit with your back to an alter in a house.
- Never praise a baby too openly as this is considered an ill omen.
- In general the Vietnamese are more subdued in their cultural protocol, and are not as tied to maintaining honour and face as the Japanese and

Chinese. They are a little more individualistic, don't have great rituals at introductions like bowing, or the *wai*, and they are less formal over dress and dining rules. **The major objective that you must achieve is to give them respect without patronising them and to command respect for yourself without being domineering.**

Getting down to business

The business environment

The combination of a Soviet style command economy and Confucianism has led to a hierarchical and authoritative culture, with crippling effects on the economy. The invasive effects of government in all aspects of business still leads to a proliferation of permissions, permits and approvals to do anything, even though the general policy is to develop the economy through a more open approach. The dominant group politically and socially is still the ruling party officials. However, new entrepreneurs and business people are quickly setting up a rival elite in the economic field. This latter group is becoming more and more influential on the political elite as they recognise that the future development of the country depends on their skills and success.

In Vietnam business companies are owned by three groups: by the central government; by the Local People's Committees in the fifty-four Vietnamese provinces; and by private enterprise. The central government-owned and operated companies are usually large national businesses but vary widely in the quality of their management. There is a fairly low level of management quality in companies run by Local People's Committees. As expected when a Vietnamese has a personal interest in the survival of their own business it is run reasonably efficiently, in an entrepreneurial manner and generally well-managed. Those companies established during the last decade tend to be patriarchal family affairs with centralised but reasonably quick decision-making. Foreign trading companies are not at present allowed to operate in Vietnam.

In each ministry, while the minister is usually a political appointee, the deputy minister is likely to be a technocrat. Each ministry also has an international relations directorate, through which all contacts and approvals must go. It can be very helpful to cultivate ministry contacts, as they may be able to help you deal with any obstacles in other ministries.

Local People's Committees (*Uy Ban Nhan Dan*) have their tentacles into everything they possibly can and you cannot avoid having to do business with them, particularly in the way of 'sweeteners'. These committees oversee local city and district investments and projects, and operate like the local Mafia, running independent kingdoms. The Vietnamese call them 'big men in little provinces'. This can lead to conflict between the Local People's Committee and the relevant state ministry with you as piggy in the middle. Approvals by Hanoi ministries can be impeded and thwarted by dominant persons on these committees. Therefore you must develop a strategic alliance with the local committee, meeting them even before going to national government level so that what is being presented there already has some acceptability locally. Keep the committee regularly appraised of progress and developments. They don't take kindly to surprises and will kill a project without hesitation. There are no short cuts and an irritated Local People's Committee is to be avoided at all costs (and some of the costs may literally be bribes!!)

If different ministries are involved there can be many delays since they do not share information willingly, and prefer to operate independently, creating a lack of co-ordination, overlap and contradiction. Each ministry will promulgate their own regulations and circulars to govern the current operation of the law. These can be changed without notice and you can be left guessing as to what today's interpretation is. You will be on the receiving end of different messages about what forms must be filled, which ministry must be visited next, how the particular regulation is being interpreted today in contrast to yesterday or even tomorrow. All you can surmise is that it may be different from yesterday's and no doubt will have changed again by the time you reach a critical day for finalising a deal or establishing a project. Some laws and regulations are enforced even before they are published and may even be applied retrospectively, drastically altering the conditions and parameters under which you were originally operating. A major task in doing business in Vietnam is maintaining sound contacts to keep you abreast of such changes.

Approvals can take between one to three years, depending on the size of the project. A good local representative or staff appointee who knows influential people in the relevant ministries and local people's committees is vitally essential to manage this business aspect for you. This person must also provide for you accurate translations of the new laws and regulations as they appear in the official government newspaper and official gazette. While the Vietnamese are practical, flexible, and prepared to take more calculated risks than other Asian neighbours, patience and flexibility are essential when dealing with the bureaucracy.

Another problem in doing business in Vietnam is the ideological commitment of many bureaucrats, particularly those who are older and who come from the north. Business common sense and entrepreneurial strategies come a poor second to rigid communist thinking about a socialist style of business. Finally, as public servants are poorly paid (the reason why many have second jobs), the greasing of palms is the only way much business progress will be attained. Leave this sordid aspect to your representative who will know how much, when and to whom to provide the required 'incentive' for an essential permit stamp. Officials at ports and customs offices are skilled exponents of extracting some bribe, otherwise much needed equipment and perishable materials will rust and rot respectively in the customs warehouse. Your representative should not be overly generous in the hope of covering long-term obligations, as officials are moved around a lot and the person expected to provide your ease of passage will not be there next time. A more acceptable form of bribe and one which the Vietnamese find very acceptable is the offer to train a family member for a position in your company in Vietnam, or educate them overseas to make them more marketable back home etc.

Employees have limited loyalty to the organisation but considerable loyalty to the individuals for whom they work. This even extends to public servants who are processing your applications and permits, who will offer to provide 'extra services' (for a retainer of course) to ensure you get the assistance you need. In dealing with other businesses you will come across their employees who will offer to work directly with you, cutting out their employer. While this behaviour is unethical from our standards, it does imply that generally if you can build up a positive relationship with Vietnamese whom you engage locally, they will exhibit a personal loyalty to you which indirectly will benefit your business. Demonstrate a paternalistic bent by showing interest in their families and their events such as accepting wedding invitations, employing family members, paying for medicines and visiting their sick parents/children, and taking them out for a meal.

In dealing with or managing Vietnamese, you will find that individually you can work on the same wavelength, but get them in a group and you will have to cope with inert socialism, enjoying one another's company in a family atmosphere, but little being achieved. It is necessary to train the individual supervisor very delicately and then the supervisor will train individual workers. Group training is not possible as they will reject ideas and be stubborn, finding change difficult to accept. At an individual level, let the counterpart or employee tell you that they know what to do, and let them do it. But tell them that if things go wrong to come and see you and you will help. You cannot push; a soft touch is required to transform the individual and make them feel they still have your respect and support. If errors are made by the Vietnamese person never shout but try to rectify it in a gentle way.

Negotiation

Business meetings are usually conducted at long tables with each party facing each other. With senior government you may find settee type chairs arranged in a U shape round three sides of the room. The two principals sit at the bottom of the U and talk across a tea table. Each delegation sits on opposite sides of the room in order of precedence. Do not sit down until the senior Vietnamese person present is seated. Allow your hosts to show you where you are to sit. Sit with your feet firmly planted on the floor and do not cross your legs. There is the usual discussion of pleasantries to create a sense of familiarity and harmony, and to establish the status of the various participants. Even though communist, Vietnamese society has a strong focus on status and rank. They feel uncomfortable dealing with someone whose rank and status they do not know.

Remember to take your own interpreter in order to obtain a truthful account. Your interpreter can also fill you in on the side conversations, which often reveal more than the conversation directed at you.

The senior member of each team will make an opening statement. Other members of the delegation/team should not join in unless invited to do so. The team leader should introduce members during the introduction, indicating their expertise and reasons for their presence there. Team members will be called on to answer specific questions by the leader.

You will learn little about your counterparts. Negotiation will be slow as the Vietnamese are overly concerned with building up the relationship first. Another reason for slowness is reluctance to make decisions that could be costly if a mistake were made. They have little experience in international business and are tentative until they are really certain a good business relationship is possible. They may agree to do things they don't want to do simply to get a contract signed. This becomes the jumping off point for further detailed discussion that may even negate the terms of the initial contract. The emphasis is on relationships, with rules of business taking a bad second place. They seek flexibility and freedom to adapt to particular and ever changing scenarios.

Thus a contract provides no real protection and is used by the Vietnamese simply to get a relationship started. The real negotiations start then and the terms of the contract will change as circumstances change. Moreover, should the original signers change the contract loses its validity, as personal relationships are regarded as being central to the deal. The central government will also step in to nullify a contract or some of the terms that it does not like. Vietnamese bureaucrats like meddling in this way as it provides a demonstration of their personal power and patriotic diligence. Vietnam does not have a commercial court system. However, an arbitration system is being developed. Verbal agreements are usually honoured if a relationship is already strong, but in a new relationship a verbal agreement carries little weight. Whenever possible, incorporate a foreign jurisdiction into your legal documents and clearly explain how disputes will be resolved.

The main criteria by which the Vietnamese will judge you and any proposal you have, will include evaluation of your long-term commitment to their country, the extent of technology transfer and amount of local employee training. Technology transfer and human resource development are vital issues for the Vietnamese in attempting to develop their economic and business life, and so they can become critical factors in determining your success. While some of the aspects of technical transfer and human resource development may on the face of it appear to have minimal payback for the overseas organisation, the benefits are in reality considerable to the overseas organisation. Not only is a deal successfully concluded, but the chances of success once the project is up and running is maximised, for few Vietnamese have specialised knowledge or training for manufacturing or management functions. The Vietnamese love multimedia and high tech presentations, possibly because of language difficulties.

Officials at senior levels have the authority to make decisions and will often do so quickly. Middle and junior officials are not too keen to make decisions until they know the opinion of their seniors. They are also dealing with many new capitalistic concepts and working out how they fit into their political and cultural milieu. However if they perceive the benefits they will rationalise their views and become very quick and eager learners of new ideas. As the Vietnamese have few resources to check technical issues out, or any other matters concerning your proposal, they will generally accept whatever information you provide. Consensus building and harmony are the key aspects of decision-making, and the process remains very bureaucratic, with most decisions made by committee. When negotiating with government enterprise, the decision maker is likely to be the senior party official present, who may not be the spokesperson. That is the person with whom you must get onside. As in China there is an aversion to perceiving the foreigner making too much money out of Vietnam. The foreigner should be helping Vietnam and its people develop, not treating it solely as an investment, however risky.

Vietnam is a high context culture full of circuitous approaches and much being left unsaid. Their verbal messages disguise and hide the true meanings and intentions. They believe that indirectness indicates respect for the other person's intelligence and insight. The Vietnamese use silence to express feelings of being uncomfortable. Do not feel obliged to fill the silence, particularly by offering more information or concessions. The silence is sometimes used for this very reason, as the Vietnamese know that overseas people are uncomfortable with silence.

The Confucian belief in harmony also flows into business relationships. The Vietnamese are very concerned about the feelings of others. They will say 'yes' when it is really 'maybe'. They will offer 'perhaps' when 'no' is nearer the mark. Rejection will be contained in phrases such as 'it is difficult', or 'it will need approval from the People's

Committee'. Lying is morally acceptable in order to maintain a harmonious relationship and avoid conflict. Vietnamese try to avoid saying 'no' and go to great lengths to maintain harmony. The word '*da*' actually means 'I understand' rather than 'yes'. So don't make erroneous assumptions. Check out the responses by asking indirect questions. If there is a problem the Vietnamese will probably not tell you until it becomes severe. On the other hand the Vietnamese will also often solve problems themselves without telling you.

Do not display your annoyance by raising your voice, nor be too forthright in your opinion. While the Vietnamese can be frank and open, they value modesty and politeness in self and others, and will hide their anger. Be willing to retreat a little if, as you slowly focus on your target issue, you feel the climate of the meeting change. Don't keep poking into a sensitive spot. You will not accomplish your aims quickly and the Vietnamese will always keep you wondering what their real opinion and viewpoints are on your proposals. Never become angry at the slowness and demand action or show irritation if something goes wrong. This only indicates to the Vietnamese that you lack self control and may not be good news to do business with. Frankness and criticism are regarded as extremely discourteous. Their reaction to displays of emotion is to smile quietly, a smile that hides their loss of respect for you. For the Vietnamese a calm unruffled personality is a great positive.

The Vietnamese want to beat the overseas person in negotiation; it is a little like winning another war against the foreigner. You will need to stand your ground, in a composed and respectful way, and explain why you hold a particular position and why you cannot change it. Once they understand that you are not being simply obstructive but following international business practice of which they may be unaware, your position will be received well and attempts will be made to accommodate it. Don't reveal upfront what you want, or what your bottom line is. The Vietnamese will always try to gain further concessions. Make your sacrifice at the end to conclude the deal. They believe they have won and you have lost something you were prepared to offer anyway.

The Vietnamese will say yes to anything even though they know they cannot achieve the request, so rather than ask the Vietnamese business person if can they deliver your shipment by a particular date, for which the answer will always be yes, rephrase and ask when will the shipment be delivered. Do not cause any Vietnamese to lose face by embarrassing them or drawing attention to their mistakes. Criticism of your competitors is not acceptable either, as the concept of competition is very young and undeveloped. It is better to emphasise the quality of your product/service, rather than focus on the shortcomings of the competition. The Vietnamese will negotiate simultaneously with a number of companies for the same supplies or project, selecting the best deal they can obtain. Letters of understanding and preliminary agreements are not worth the paper they are written on in many cases as every competitor has been issued with them.

There are times when disagreement is necessary, even in a culture that promotes harmony and face. The key is to honour the face of your counterparts by agreeing initially. Disagreement may then be voiced privately and in circuitous ways, sometimes through a third party. The aim is a message with vague innuendoes in the hope that the other party receive the message without losing face. In Vietnam, agreeing to disagree is not an option. You will never impose your opinion, nor make the Vietnamese retract openly. Your project will be sabotaged by a deliberate go slow or ignoring of your proposals.

The only ritual you will face at a meeting is drinking tea. Don't take a sip until the senior Vietnamese person has raised their cup to their lips. You don't have to drink it all but take a few sips. Fruit, usually oranges and grapes, will also be placed on the middle of the table or between armchairs. Don't dig in until your hosts starts or invites you to eat.

The cost of faxing and telephoning is so high in Vietnam compared to other living costs and earnings that the Vietnamese appear not to keep in touch with you when you are in your home base as you would like. If you want to ensure continuing and regular communication, it is in your interest to offer to reimburse your counterpart for their communication expenses. So that you do not make them feel a loss of face, explain that you are deeply committed to developing a strong relationship and that you would be pleased to pay for all documented telephone and fax communications for a stated period so that this relationship can be strengthened even further by enabling them to communicate with you as often as necessary.

The social context of business

Dining out

The Vietnamese enjoy dining out and will take every opportunity available to set up a business lunch or dinner. Eating with potential business partners is a normal way of establishing a business relationship and promoting contacts. The aim of the dining out is not to negotiate but to get to know each other. If possible you should pay, as they have difficulty affording it and your visit is a not to be missed chance to enjoy a night out for them. At a large traditional buffet or banquet, everyone eats off the same plates together, sampling portions of each dish, so don't pick up a plate to make it your own. Since everyone shares, don't take too much off any one dish. Eating is performed slowly.

Rice, rice noodles and wheat are the mainstay of most Vietnamese meals. A paste made of fermented fish juices, called *nuoc mam*, which has a very distinctive odour, is used to flavour most dishes. Chicken and beef (including steaks) will also be served, as well as many exotic seafood delicacies. If you are guest of honour you will have the dubious offering from the host of the chicken's head. Don't refuse it. The rice bowl containing the mix of rice and morsels of food you have taken from the central plates is held with your right hand close to your mouth. Your left hand is used to hold the spoon to feed yourself irrespective of your right hand being the preferred hand. Rest your chopsticks horizontally across the rice bowl when not using them. Unlike China and Japan, you are expected to pour your beer and mineral water yourself, and you should not bother pouring for anyone else. The table setting will often be Western style with knives and forks as well as chopsticks. The table is likely to be rectangular rather then round as in other Asian countries. In some outdoor restaurants, you may find a small gas-stove at the side of your table on which your raw food choice will be cooked.

Punctuality is expected for arrival at dinners/banquets. Senior and elderly guests should be greeted first and never leave until the most senior person has departed. There is much drinking and toasting. Vietnamese seem able to drink most people under the table. The Vietnamese toast of *tram phan tram* means empty the glass 100 per cent. If you can't cope with that much alcohol, make it known in advance to your host that you have stomach problems, are taking medicines, or are teetotal. It is quite acceptable to sip soft drinks or tea. You may be 'challenged' by your Vietnamese counterparts to try some exotic delicacies such as dog in the north or cobra in the south. This is a traditional male activity and is not mandatory. If you can rise to the occasion, (few can!!!), you will enhance your business relationship no end. As Vietnamese men may feel uncomfortable socialising with foreign women, it is better to check with your hosts whether a spouse is invited.

The Vietnamese all enjoy karaoke, discos and night clubs. It is likely that as your personal and business relationship flourishes you will be invited to this more informal gathering, particularly if you join in, as karaoke is an enhancer of rapport and camaraderie. It is also appropriate for you to invite your counterparts to such an event once your business relationship is going well.

A home visit

You are unlikely to be invited to a home as the Vietnamese regard their homes as small and shoddy, and they have meagre resources to provide entertainment with. You should only go therefore when invited as they like to be well prepared. If you are invited never refuse, as it will sour a relationship. Gifts such as flowers, tea, coffee, incense or a small craft token from your native country for the adults and/or the children are always well received.

If you are invited over the Tet New Year you are honoured and may be asked to be the first person to enter the house in the new year. This person is always seen as an auspicious person who brings luck. Take presents of alcohol for adults and red envelopes of new money notes for the children.

Giving gifts

Some claim that corruption and bribery is endemic at most levels to fast-track permits and applications etc, but leave your representative to deal with these matters at arm's length and do not give money yourself. It is little wonder that commisions are common when middle-ranked bureaucrats earning less than $100 per month have to make decisions about contracts worth tens of millions of dollars. The situation can often also be managed by providing a consultant with a fee heavily weighted to cover all expected payments. The provision of a department store credit card valid for a few thousand dollars, coupled with a paid vacation or business trip to a major city overseas where it can be used, will also work wonders. Back home all are kept happy as all that is visible at audit are fees for consultants and representatives.

Gift giving is not perceived as a bribe when given as a token of appreciation at the end of meetings and on signing a deal, rather it is regarded as part of the reciprocity and obligation of friendship. Gifts should vary in value so that the senior Vietnamese person receives a high value gift with the value getting lower down the line. Even most junior members of the counterparts side receive a small gift. The ideal gifts for such occasions are corporate logo gifts, gifts (such as pictorial calendars, handicrafts and cultural items) from your home country or city, expensive pens for senior officials, moderately priced pens for middle-level officers, and expensive chocolates for female executives. Alcohol and liquors are gratefully received at senior levels, as imported alcohol costs too much for most people to buy. Make-up for wives and female executives is very much appreciated. Technical or specialised professional books that are unobtainable in Vietnam are also welcome as Vietnam struggles to develop its skills and knowledge.

Don't give gifts that depict figures, or designs on textiles etc. that represent monkeys, pigs or cows. However, gifts that depict or represent the crane (longevity), turtles (endurance), and the buffalo (loyalty) are well appreciated. The gifts should be wrapped neatly. Use red paper, as red is a lucky colour. Avoid white (death) and black (sorrow). Gifts will not be opened in your presence as that is considered rude. You should do the same and contain your curiosity. It is sensible to take extra gifts with you as it is impossible to know how many people you may have to provide for. Give the cheaper gifts in the early stages of negotiations or at first meetings. Retain the more expensive ones for more important events, such as when a transaction is signed, when eventually meeting a most senior person, or to enhance a developing relationship with a person who has influence.

The best gift for your business counterpart is a trip overseas (ostensibly for 'training'), or a company sponsored scholarship overseas for their children, particularly if it is close to your headquarters, so that visits can be made regularly to meet with you and their children. The training trip can also be a useful fact finding mission for government officials or private companies as they can tour your and other business/ government organisations. Such trips should also include time out for the Vietnamese to take the chance for the first time to enjoy the sights, experiences and culture of other countries. It pays dividends, as they come to understand how the rest of the world operates.

Other useful information

What to wear

The dress code is less formal than Japan or Korea, but err on the side of overdressing if in doubt for any function. Don't wear anything too garish or extravagant. Men usually wear business suits or shirts and ties. For factory and site tours, men should wear shirts and slacks. For women, dresses, suits and troursers are appropriate. Most Vietnamese women wear trousers with a cotton blouse. Many companies require their staff to wear the company uniform to create a sense of group togetherness. Winters in northern Vietnam can be quite cold and sweaters worn under a jacket are commonplace. Don't wear shorts (except at the beach) or revealing clothing.

Language

Vietnamese is the official language, but each region has its own dialect. The written language, *quoc ngu*, is based on a Latin phonetic alphabet. The Vietnamese language is based on syllables, with accent marks used to denote tone. French is spoken by older persons who in pre-revolutionary days were of high status. Some English (in the south from the war time), Russian, and Chinese are also spoken in major cities.

The language is very formal and Vietnamese add 'Mr,' 'Mrs,' or 'Miss' to every sentence to enhance respect. For example, the Vietnamese don't simply say ' I am sorry,' they will say 'I am sorry to you'.

Major holidays

	January 1	New Year's Day
	February 3	Founding of the Communist Party of Vietnam
	January/February*	Vietnamese Lunar New Year (*Tet*—the most important holiday of the year—everything comes to a standstill for five days. It is important that all employees get home to spend several days with their families. It symbolises the threshhold to a new part of each person's life)
	April 30	Liberation of Saigon/Victory of North Vietnam in 1975
	May 1	International Labour Day/Workers' Day
	May 19	Ho Chi Minh's Birthday
	June*	Buddha's Birthday (*Dan Sinh*)
	September 2	National Day of the Socialist Republic of Vietnam
	September 3	Anniversary of Ho Chi Minh's death
	December 25	Christmas

*These holidays are based on the lunar calendar and differ from year to year.

A few other matters

You are being watched!!!

There is still constant surveillance by security organisations. Each street is controlled by an informal chief who reports every change. The information function of street vendors needs to be taken account of too. Whether in villages, towns or large cities, life is organised in small 'hamlets' where everyone knows everyone else. The concept of privacy is vastly different than what which Westerners are used to and though expatriates may enjoy the solidarity of this neighbourliness it becomes intrusive and oppressive at times. House personnel also form part of the dense information web and will regularly provide detailed reports about an expatriate's activities.

The government also monitors faxes, e-mail correspondence and telephones, so be discreet in transmitting sensitive business information or comments about the country, its policies, or particular senior persons. You may even be monitored in your hotel room, meeting rooms, and in the car provided for you. Your friendly Vietnamese maid, driver, counterpart, and even translator may be passing on information about you to the government. This is done for reasons of both security and business competitiveness. So be careful and discreet at all times.

Prices

There is a three-tier goods and services pricing system with overseas persons charged the most (how did you guess!!), overseas Vietnamese charged a little less and locals getting the cheapest deal. The argument that in a socialist country all people should be treated equally is ingeniously altered into another logical argument that foreigners can afford more and should therefore pay more to help the local economy. However, higher prices for electricity, water, land leases etc, for overseas businesses rebounds on the Vietnamese as it consumes scarce resources that could be better used for building up their international and local business enterprises.

Lucky days

Like the Koreans and Thais, the Vietnamese are strongly affected by beliefs in luck and superstition, and still visit fortune tellers. Your Vietnamese counterparts may want to sign documents, start projects, hold an opening ceremony only on certain days as some days are supposed to be more auspicious than others. The Vietnamese also prefer not to start a trip on the 7th, 17th and 27th of a lunar month just as the 3rd, 13th and 23rd are not days on which to return from a trip. Always ask your counterparts when they would like to conduct major events.

Currency

You can bring in hard currency without much restriction. Getting it out is another matter. You cannot take more out than you took in. It is a wise move to declare more money on entry than you are actually taking in. This leaves you able to exit with that larger amount if necessary.

Transport

Most of the country's roads are war-damaged and neglected with only around 10 per cent paved. There is one expressway in the north nine miles (15 kilometres) long, linking Hanoi with Noi Bai International Airport, making travel more efficient. With driving on the right-hand side of the road, congested and poor road conditions, it is safer and more inexpensive to hire a car and driver. Road and traffic conditions make self-driving very dangerous.

Communications

Do not phone or fax from your hotel as the bill for these can exceed the room bill by a large measure. Many telephone numbers may be incorrect because the telephone system is being updated.

Health

There are no Western standard hospitals in Vietnam. You would need to get out to Hong Kong or Singapore if something serious occurred. Some business people carry some of their own frozen blood just in case.

Summary

- Overseas business persons must overcome problems of changing laws, bureaucratic procedures and communist ideology by appointing a representative or staff member who is fluent in Vietnamese and who has high level contacts.
- Maintain close and amicable relationships with the relevant Local People's Committees.
- Some claim bribery is endemic but leave it to your representative.
- There are a variety of power networks to circumvent.
- Communist ideology and Confucian philosophy combine to create a highly rigid, structured, authoritarian society.
- Business ventures in Vietnam must be regarded as high risk and long term, serviced by a consistent staff who deal with the business activities there.
- Respect is the key to successful business activity. You must show respect to the Vietnamese and by your demeanour earn their respect.
- Politeness and the avoidance of confrontation is essential. Little white lies are preferable to being offensive.

Activity

Try working out the solution to the following problem, then check the response in Appendix B.

1 A Western fertiliser manufacturer decided to venture into the vast potential of Third World markets. The company sent a team of agricultural researchers into northern areas of Vietnam country to test soils, weather conditions, and topographical conditions in order to develop locally effective fertilisers. Once the research and manufacturing of these fertiliser products had been completed, one of the initial marketing strategies was to distribute, free of charge, 10 kg bags of the fertiliser to selected areas of rural farmers. It was thought that those using the free fertiliser would be so impressed with the

a

dramatic increase in crop productivity that they would spread the word around their villages to their friends, relatives, and neighbours.

A small team of salespeople went from hut to hut in those designated areas offering each male head of household a free bag of fertiliser along with an explanation of its capacity to increase crop output. Although each head of household was very polite, they all turned down the offer of free fertiliser. The marketing staff concluded that these local people were either disinterested in helping themselves grow more food and eat better, or so ignorant that they couldn't understand the benefits of the new product.

Why was this an ethnocentric conclusion?

12

Overseas assignments: Expatriate selection, problems and training

Introduction

Success and failure in expatriate postings

This chapter attempts to identify: (1) the major difficulties that expatriates face in the international assignment, and (2) the specific human resource management practices that may be employed in order to help individual managers and their families deal effectively with the challenges of expatriation.

The past few years have witnessed a marked upsurge of interest in the problems of staff sent on assignments overseas. This increase is partly the direct result of a rapid increase in both the number and size of multinational corporations and small to medium businesses involved in global business, plus government bodies offering services to developing countries. In particular, organisations have developed a heightened sensitivity to the business, financial and emotional costs associated with expatriate failure.

In today's global context, the problems faced by those undertaking expatriate assignments and training for such assignments should be treated seriously, both by organisations and business courses. In the current environment of international trade and development it is vital that those representing business and government endeavours overseas appreciate and respect cultural differences, not just in management and business techniques, but in everyday behaviour, verbal and nonverbal interaction, values, and underlying philosophy of life.

Completing an international assignment presents expatriates and their families with a variety of difficulties and challenges which are compounded by little or no preparation at all for dealing with different cultural approaches to business and to the personal difficulties of settling into a new job and country. During the past two decades organisations of all sorts and sizes have been plagued by a persistent, recurring problem: significant rates of the premature return of expatriate staff. This is costly in terms of management performance, productivity in the overseas operation, client relations, and operations efficiency. The average cost per failure to the parent organisation ranges between $50 000 and $100 000.

In addition to the financial losses from an aborted assignment, there are also psychological costs for the staff member. An expatriate who 'fails' may suffer loss of self-esteem, a severe career setback, and the loss of prestige among peers. Thus a great deal is at risk, and it is clear that preventing selection mistakes must be a priority for any organisation sending people overseas.

Despite the clear need for effective selection and training policies and programs for expatriates, few organisations have employed more than simplistic methods in selecting and training expatriates.

While statistics on the premature rate of return of expatriates are difficult to determine, attrition rates quoted for Americans returning home prematurely vary between 18 per cent (from UK where one would expect easy adjustment), to 36 per cent in Japan and 68 per cent in Saudi Arabia (Caudran 1992). Figures for Australians sent on overseas assignments are likely to be similar. This represents an enormous financial loss as it can cost up to five times the employee's base salary to maintain the employee and family on an overseas assignment. Some of those who soldier through are often operating at lower efficiency levels than they should be, costing losses in time, absences through health/stress, and damaging the reputation of the organisation.

Why are so many assignments unsuccessful? Managerial and technical competence does not appear to be the major issue. Cultural adaptation processes rather than technical/work related competence have mainly determined the expatriate's success or failure. The major causes of expatriate failure appear to be, in descending order of importance:

1 inability of the manager's spouse to adjust to a different physical or cultural environment;
2 the manager's inability to adapt to a different physical or cultural environment;
3 other family-related problems;
4 the manager's personality or emotional immaturity;
5 the manager's inability to cope with the responsibilities posed by overseas work;
6 the manager's lack of technical competence;
7 the manager's lack of motivation to work overseas.

These factors show obvious weaknesses in selection procedures and in preparation for an overseas assignment. The point that leaps out is the spouse's failure to adjust. This has most influence upon the expatriate's own adjustment and performance. This issue of spouse adjustment will be considered in greater detail below. Another factor is the shortness of assignment for Western managers, which limits their time to adapt and get to know the culture. One explanation is that, given the nature of their control mechanisms, many Western companies perceive greater value in rotating between a series of overseas posts, rather than keeping people in a single post. The longer the assignment, it is feared, the greater the risk of 'going native', and 'in the eyes of the parent' identifying too strongly with local norms. But this policy has a negative side: the short-term manager has little time to learn how the behaviour of local business persons is determined by their culture, and to make predictions based on such experience.

When it comes to international assignments few companies give candidate selection the attention it deserves. In 98 per cent of the companies responding to Selection Research International's *1995 Survey of International Sourcing and Selection Practices*, it was shown that line managers interview candidates for international assignments using 'technical skills' and the 'willingness to relocate' as their chief criteria. However, when asked to determine the principal factors contributing to failed assignments and ineffective performance, these same companies pointed to 'personality characteristics' and 'interpersonal style' as the culprits.

The survey also reveals that line managers have minimal training to interview for international positions, that fewer than 10 per cent test to screen candidates and that only slightly more than 50 per cent provide any cultural briefing. None of the companies responding to the survey had a competency-driven system in place to integrate selection, training and development, and performance management. The hard truth is that without the necessary employee selection processes in place no organisation stands much chance of competing successfully in the global market.

Problems in expatriate selection and training

An ingrained practice when selecting potential expatriates is the use of the 'domestic equals overseas performance' equation. The assumption behind this formula is that 'managing a company is a scientific art. The executive accomplishing the task in Sydney, New York, or London can surely perform as adequately in Seoul, Beijing or Jakarta'. 'Technical expertise' or 'having a successful track record' is overwhelmingly the primary selection criterion.

As the result of such beliefs, most organisations send the expatriate and family members abroad soon after selection without any acculturation training whatsoever. When acculturation training is administered, it often is too general or is not followed up with an evaluation of its effectiveness. A variety of reasons are given by organisations for not investing in pre-departure training:

- a feeling that such training programs are generally ineffective;
- past dissatisfaction with the training program on the part of expatriate trainees;
- the time between selection and departure is short, and there is not enough time to expose the expatriate to in-depth acculturation training;
- the view that because the expatriate's assignment is temporary, it does not warrant training expenditures.

There has been a low priority in Australian education for international competency. Not only have most current managers and potential managers never received any training on cross-cultural issues, most did not have to study any foreign language as part of their qualifications. Many business courses at tertiary level do not contain material on the psychological, sociological and cultural aspects of working in another country. It is only recently that many universities have realised, from a reverse situation, that the overseas student who is proving to be a lucrative source of income, needs considerable help to settle into a different type of academic style and set of cultural practices. If the overseas student finds Australian life bewildering, then so too must expatriate managers as they try to function in the home culture of the overseas student.

Most organisations prefer to staff key positions overseas with home-country nationals because they believe that these persons possess qualities and characteristics which are not possessed by host-country nationals, such as familiarity with corporate objectives, loyalty to the company, adherence to its style of management or, when the company is in the process of establishing new activities in a country, a shortage of persons with the required skills/knowledge. Additional reasons include the desire to provide the organisation's more promising staff with international experience to equip them better for more responsible positions in a global economy; the need to maintain and facilitate organisational co-ordination and control; and the organisation's conviction that it must maintain an image and presence in the host country.

Personal factors associated with successful expatriation

These factors can be organised into two categories: (1) personal characteristics of the expatriate manager; and (2) characteristics of the expatriate's family.

Personal characteristics

Studies on the personal characteristics of successful business expatriates suggest that they have superior intelligence, self-confidence and a strong drive for responsibility and task completion. Ideally, it seems, they should have the stamina of an Olympic swimmer, the mental agility of an Einstein, the conversational skill of a professor of languages, the detachment of a judge, the tact of a diplomat, and the perseverance of an Egyptian pyramid builder. Additionally, they should also have a feeling for culture; moral judgments should not be too rigid; they should be able to merge with the local environment with chameleon-like ease; and should show no signs of prejudice.

The research to date indicates the following personal characteristics as potentially critical for successful performance in a foreign environment:

1 **Technical ability.** Obviously the expatriate must have the necessary technical knowledge and skills to do the job. Confidence in one's ability to accomplish the purpose of the overseas assignment seems to be an important part of expatriate adjustment.

2 **Adaptability to cultural change.** Business persons working overseas must be able to adapt to change. Research shows that many are exhilarated at the beginning of their overseas assignment. However, after a few months a form of culture shock creeps in, and they begin to encounter frustration and feel confused in their new environment. One analysis noted that many of the most effective international business persons suffer this cultural shock. This may be a good sign, because it shows that the expatriate is becoming involved in the new culture and is not isolating themselves from the environment.

As this initial and trying period comes to an end, an expatriate's satisfaction with conditions tends to increase. In fact, after the first two years, most people become more satisfied with their overseas assignment than when they first arrived. Research also shows that men tend to adjust a little faster than women, although both sexes exhibit a great deal of similarity in terms of degree of satisfaction with overseas assignments. In addition, people over 35 years of age tend to have slightly higher levels of satisfaction after the first year, but those under 35 years of age have higher satisfaction during the next three to four years. However, none of these differences are statistically significant.

Other elements of adaptability include emotional maturity to deal with the new situation, toleration of ambiguity and uncertainty; work experiences with cultures other than one's own, previous overseas travel, a knowledge of foreign languages (fluency is not generally necessary), experience of integrating with different people, cultures, and types of business organisations; the ability to solve problems within different frameworks and from different perspectives; and flexibility in managing operations on a continuous basis, despite lack of assistance and gaps in information.

There is evidence that expatriates who are able to find substitutes for their interests and activities at home, are more likely to be successful in adjusting to the new culture. Examples of replacing activities are learning to value raw fish and *yakisoba* rather than hamburgers and french-fries, discovering new hobbies such as scuba diving in the South China Sea, collecting butterflies in Malaysia, or appreciating indigenous music in Korea. They replace activities that bring pleasure in the home culture with similar, yet different activities in order to help themselves enjoy more fully their experience in the host culture.

3 **Independence and self-reliance.** In many overseas assignments, staff must carry out responsibilities and functions at levels higher than those to which they are accustomed. At the same time they have fewer people to call on for assistance and guidance, and must often be more self-reliant. One analysis reports that some of the determinants of independence and self-reliance include prior field experience (domestic or foreign), special project or task force experience, a hobby or interest that requires a high degree of self-reliance, and a record of extracurricular college activities or community service activities.

4 **Cultural empathy.** Clearly, the ability to understand why foreigners behave the way they do is important in adjusting to a new cultural environment. All too often adaptation problems arise because expatriates are unable to face a new world of cultural patterns that are potentially at odds with their own value systems and living habits. For example, expatriates sometimes fail to learn when 'yes' means 'yes', when it means 'maybe' and when it means 'no'; what to focus on and what to ignore. As a result, when they face host-country nationals and their different behavioural assumptions and expectations, tensions rise.

Even performing the simplest of actions may produce unexpected and seemingly unintelligible responses from the new cultural environment. The most successful expatriates constantly recognise that they may not fully understand the situation and that they must find ways to get reliable information and expertise. They 'know that they do not know'. They also recognise that they are in a difficult situation and that they will not act as effectively overseas as they did at home—especially in the initial stages. Other expatriates and host nationals who have previously faced and dealt effectively with the same or similar problems can often best empathise with the newcomer's difficulties. This heightened individual awareness and enhanced knowledge of the local scene may give the expatriate the ability to understand local behaviour better and to be more objective in his or her views of local life.

5 **Leadership ability.** The ability to influence people—leadership—is another important criterion in selection. However, determining whether a person who is an effective leader in the home country will be equally effective in an overseas environment can be difficult. In determining whether an applicant has the desired leadership ability, many organisations look for specific characteristics, such as maturity, emotional stability, the ability to communicate well, independence, initiative, and creativity, as well as good health. If these characteristics are present and the person has been an effective leader in the home country, then the assumption is that the individual will also do well overseas.

6 **Stress tolerance.** Expatriates and their families frequently operate in an environment that is personally highly stressful. Separation from friends, leaving one's home country, and drastic changes in one's cultural environment generally create an experience of stress or emotional disturbance. As a result, many expatriates develop symptoms of transfer anxiety, culture shock, social dislocation, exile complex (feeling abandoned by headquarters), frustration and disappointment. Recent studies indicate that experienced expatriates have found many highly effective and creative mechanisms for coping with the stress of intercultural adaptation. For example, one expatriate family made a rule forbidding complaints during meals; they only allowed positive statements about the new physical environment, culture or other conditions that might cause stress and frustration.

In addition, many of the most effective expatriates create 'stability zones' for coping with the problems of cultural adaptation. That is, when conditions in the host culture become overly stressful, they briefly retreat into an environment that closely recreates home. Examples of successful stability zones are playing a musical instrument, keeping a diary, watching video-movies in one's native language, or going to an international club, associating with other compatriots, and celebrating one's own national events. For example, Melbourne Cup Day is celebrated by Australians shivering in the Antarctic and sweating in the jungles of Borneo. Such temporary withdrawals produce a rhythm of engagement and withdrawal in the manager's involvement with unfamiliar environment.

7 **Physical and emotional health.** It is essential that overseas staff have good physical and emotional health. Some examples are fairly obvious. An employee with a heart condition would be rejected for an overseas assignment. Likewise, an individual with a nervous disorder would not be considered. The psychological ability of

individuals to cope with culture shock would also be considered, as would the current marital status, as it affects the individual's ability to cope in a foreign environment.

8 **Motivation for a foreign assignment.** Although individuals being sent overseas should have a desire to work abroad, this is usually not sufficient motivation. They must also believe in the importance of the job and even have something of an element of idealism or a sense of mission. Applicants who are unhappy with their current situation at home and who are looking to get away seldom make effective overseas managers. A desire for adventure or a pioneering spirit is a must, particularly for an assignment in a developing country. Other motivators often cited include chances for promotion and the opportunities for travel and to improve one's economic status.

9 **Age and experience.** Most organisations strive for a balance between age and experience. There is evidence that younger persons are more eager for international assignments as they tend to be more 'worldly' and have a greater appreciation of other cultures than do older staff. But, young people are often the least developed in terms of management experience and technical skills. They lack real-world experience. To gain the desired balance, many firms send both young and seasoned personnel to the same overseas post. Ideally, the team should be selected for both its youth and its experience.

10 **Communication and language skills.** One recognised weakness of many organisations is that they do not give sufficient attention to the importance of language training. English is the primary language of international business, and most expatriates from all countries can converse in English. However, those who can speak only English are at a distinct disadvantage when doing business in non-English-speaking countries. Traditionally, Australians, Americans and British have done very poorly in the language area.

Adaptability of the spouse and other family members

Although personal characteristics of the staff members are important, a variety of studies suggest that adaptability and effectiveness of the staff member depends to a large extent upon how happy the expatriate's spouse and children are in the foreign environment.

Most organisations do not seek the spouse's opinion concerning the international assignment, nor do they offer any pre-departure training for spouses. A major source of spouse discontent is that organisations do not offer job finding assistance for spouses, even though approximately 50 per cent of them worked prior to the international assignment. Certainly, many wives are bored and have no meaningful role to fulfil. This leads to discontent.

The organisation must determine whether the family is united in its desire to make the move. Or, at the least, open minded about the prospect. The company should conduct a 'family screening process' investigating such factors as: marital stability, responsibilities for aged parents, the presence of learning disabilities in a child, behavioural problems in teenagers, and the strength of family's ties to the community, friends, other family members. A wife who always expects to visit her mother every Sunday afternoon or a husband who is totally wrapped up in his local football or basketball team are not good bets for an expatriate assignment. Neither is a spouse who would prefer to maintain their own employment career. Even older children need consideration in terms of education, career prospects, peer group, extended family relations etc.

The more the spouse is in early agreement with the assignment, the more they engage in self-initiated departure culture preparation and training, and this seems to increase the desire to succeed. The factors that influence the spouse's ease of adjustment are:

- the size of the expatriate national community, which affects opportunities for cultural and social support;
- relationships between the local community and the expatriate community;
- distance between the home and host country economies;
- opportunities to work. A spouse who has qualifications and wishes to work is frustrated when circumstances in the new setting prevent this;
- availability of international schooling at post for children;
- lack of dependent relatives back home.

If the family is not happy the expatriate often performs poorly. In a recent survey of eighty US companies assessing the reasons for expatriate failure, the number one reason was the inability of the manager's spouse to adjust to a different physical or cultural environment. This is because the spouse is often more immersed in the day-to-day culture than the employee, and therefore the challenge for successful adjustment is different and greater.

For example, the spouse may have to find out all the essential elements of running a household, the arrangements for servants, the best places to go for groceries, whether to beat down the price or not, where to purchase products on the black market, where to pay the electricity, how to access money at the bank, how to purchase a bus ticket or negotiate with taxi driver etc. The spouse must deal with the foreign culture in a most immediate, everyday basis. The constant frustration of not understanding and not being able to get simple things done isn't easy to deal with; all expatriates have to cope regularly with a phone that doesn't work, electric power that cuts off, and, filling water containers at 4 a just to be sure that there is some water.

Experience indicates that most people get used to these irritations and work round them in various ways. However, loneliness and isolation are more difficult to cope with. Most expatriate wives leave their family and friends at home in order to follow their partner. This separation causes a spouse to want more time, attention and companionship. However, this is exactly the time when the expatriate often works long hours to deal with the unfamiliar working conditions of the new assignment, unable to spend as much time as is necessary to reduce family anxiety and dissatisfaction.

Day-to-day details

Upon arrival in the new country, ex-pats should be briefed about details that go beyond basic housing and schooling arrangements. The local support staff (usually someone in the company's local personnel department) or better, if the organisation already has ex-pats onsite, a willing sponsor in the country who is matched with the newcomer who can help convey this information on a one-to-one basis.

Some things I wish I had been told, either by a professional or a volunteer, include:

- the meaning of the abbreviations in host persons' titles;
- where to pay bills such as phone, electricity etc;
- how to set up a bank account in less than three months;
- where the nearest ATMs are located;
- the penalties for making mistakes on all of the above;
- where appropriate health care arrangements can be made and where to find emergency phone numbers;
- how to get a house phone in less than six months;
- how to arrange for a driver's license—and where to find a *translated* book of driving rules;
- where to find information on local social and religious groups that welcome and support ex-pats (the International Newcomers Club, University Women, Rotary, Lions etc);
- where the best and cheapest shops are;
- where to eat out without fear of typhoid, severe gastro enteritis etc.;
- particular closing times for banks, post offices, shops, especially as affected by religious observances.

Most expatriates find that immediately becoming affiliated with the overseas branch or group of one's social (e.g. Rotary), sporting (tennis/ bridge) or religious group fosters a healthy resettlement. These are the people who can most likely fill the void created by the loss of family and friends back home, and provide sympathetic informal counselling if needed. Eventually, the ex-pat becomes part of the network to aid others, and just the feeling of being needed contributes significantly to their own emotional health and wellbeing.

Questions you need to ask when considering a post overseas:

What are the culture patterns that impact in the everyday living and business world of country X?

- What is a typical workday? Do people tend to work 9 to 5? Are you expected to work late?
- Preferred interpersonal style: how assertive or deferential should you be? How much initiative should you take? Should you make suggestions on how to improve things?
- What is the social distance between boss and subordinate? How is respect shown? Are you expected to 'roll up your shirtsleeves' and join workers who need help? Is there antagonism between workers and management?
- Do people socialise after work? Who can you or should you invite to dinner? What are the cultural structures that surround entertaining?
- What is considered effective leadership? What leadership styles are admired and respected? Do people like authoritarian leadership? Should leaders be 'visible'? How are promotions made?
- How are decisions made—by the most senior person or by group? What is role of individuals?
- Are organisations 'bureaucratic', informal? How are people addressed?
- What are attitudes about touching, hugging, etc? How do people greet each other? In the West shows of affection can be considered (and sometimes are) sexual harassment, is it the same in this country?
- How should you dress for work? Is this an important issue?
- How are people rewarded at work? Is there 'merit' pay? Is the possibility of promotion important to people? How important is 'getting ahead'?
- Is 'loyalty' highly valued and expected?
- What do you need to know about communication styles? Is rationality stressed over emotional? Should you be aggressive, deferential? does 'yes' mean 'yes' and 'no' mean 'no'?
- Does the culture stress individualism over social groups? Are people out for themselves or for the common good? Is teamwork stressed?
- What is the role of gift giving? When, where, and how much? Is gift giving an element of corruption; an expected necessity to obtain business?

- Is a third party introduction necessary to obtain entree to those I wish to do business with? How can the third party help when contentious issues arise?
- Is maintaining face important?
- How are strangers treated? What are attitudes and stereotypes about your nationality?
- What are attitudes about women in business, the workplace, the social setting? Will you be an 'ethnic/religious minority' in that country? Will that be an issue?
- How is ambition viewed? Are people entrepreneurial?
- Are concepts about space (privacy) different than yours?
- Time—does '10.00 am, mean exactly 10.00 am? What does 'soon' or 'tomorrow' mean?
- How do people tend to negotiate—formal, informal? How much reliance is there on trusting relationships? Is it essential that relationships come first before business—how important is 'small talk'? What do you talk about before getting into business?
- What are typical career patterns? Do people stay at one company all of their working life? Is ambition viewed positively?
- What kind of government is there—e.g. socialist, dictatorship, constitutional monarchy etc?
- What is the dominant religion and what effect will this have on you, your business activities and social life?
- Are there regulations that a foreigner would find unusual? Are there laws against discrimination—race, sex, religion?

Conclusion: Could (or would) you be comfortable doing business or working there? why? or why not?

Culture shock

Culture shock may seriously unsettle most people assigned overseas, but it is a natural and healthy way of reacting to a new set of cultural perceptions. It may be defined as a sense of psychological disorientation that most people suffer when they move into a culture that is different from their own.

The expatriate cannot resort to cues that are automatically employed when creating relationships, reacting to other people's behaviour, and deciding how to behave in his/her own culture. Insiders' perceptions of reality and their priorities differ from his/her own. The outsider cannot assume a body of shared experience, and if not given training does not know basic daily behaviours such as how to:

- greet people;
- converse appropriately with superiors, peers and subordinates;

- offer, receive or refuse invitations;
- give and ask for opinions;
- express agreement and disagreement; etc.

This sense of disorientation may not be any less when the new culture is superficially like your own. Slight differences are profoundly shocking when you expect everything to be the same. You become aware of cultural dislocation when first encountering behaviour that does not occur in your culture, or behaviour that occurs, but with some other meaning in your culture. You may be equally shaken by the non-occurrence of expected behaviour. Culture shock is cumulative, and arises from a series of small incidents, but the awareness of shock may hit suddenly. It is usually associated with unpleasant effects such as:

- *Tension and frustration.* Energy levels seem low and decisions are not made as quickly as usual;
- *Alienation.* Homesickness and antagonism towards locals and their culture develop, mixing socially only with members of your own culture;
- *A need to be alone.* Resorting to solitary activities, including drinking.
- *Depression and anxiety.* Homesickness, worry about health, and an increasing tendency to emotional outbursts suggest an unhappy, tense person.

Overcoming culture shock

How do you avoid it? How can you ensure the family surfs the wave of change without a bump? Let's not kid ourselves, it's tough out there. Try moving *your* family to Beijing, Bombay or Brunei—and these aren't the most difficult locations, according to hardship allowance statistics.

There is a cycle of adjustment that most people on overseas assignment pass through. This is illustrated in Figure 12.1. The timespan of various parts of the cycle and the depth of feeling at each differs between individuals, but it is a common series of emotional experiences.

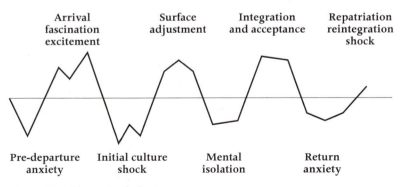

Arrival fascination excitement	Surface adjustment	Integration and acceptance	Repatriation reintegration shock
Pre-departure anxiety	Initial culture shock	Mental isolation	Return anxiety

Figure 12.1 The cycle of adjustment

It is difficult to avoid some culture shock, but to overcome the worst effects:

- expect to experience culture shock. It is a natural reaction to novelty among emotionally mature people. Treating culture shock as a pathology or sign of mental imbalance is likely to create far worse problems;
- learn the symptoms;
- accept your need to learn about living in the new culture. Cultural adjustment is best seen as being a learning process;
- discover as much as you can about the new country, its culture and history. Start this learning before you arrive;
- do not restrict yourself to members of your own culture. The cultural insulation that they provide may be comforting in the first days, but merely delays the adaptation that sooner or later you will have to make;
- break into the local culture by using its members as informants. Find members who are happy to answer your questions about their culture;
- keep an open mind on the new culture. Neither condemn it out of hand (and certainly not on the basis of your experiences in the airport), nor praise it excessively. What seems rational and irrational? Look for evidence that shows why apparently irrational behaviour may be only non-rational in your terms, and try to think yourself into the local culture so that the non-rational appears rational;
- check what communicative forms are appropriate. Ask informants from the local culture and experienced outsiders from your own culture. Who should be addressed by first name? or by title? How are invitations made, accepted, and refused? How are opinions expressed? agreement and disagreement? What do members of the culture mean when they say 'yes, maybe'? 'tomorrow'?

Many immigrant communities cope with culture shock by recreating aspects of their home cultures. This creates a sense of home and community and is a way to defeat loneliness, but only as long as it does not prevent some contacts with the local community. This sort of 'coping' response may be sufficient for the expatriate who is sufficiently protected by members of his/her own culture, or spends only a short time in the new culture. But it does not resolve adjustment problems for the long-term expatriate who has personal and professional needs to become involved in the host society. The expatriate who finds themselves the sole representative of their country, or among a small group only, cannot depend on cultural supports. Unless prepared to accommodate the host culture, learn about it and make friends of its members, they are condemned to loneliness.

Table 12.1 Rating scale on successful expatriate qualities

Directions:
The following list of qualities have been identified in the management literature as being associated with success in an overseas environment. Consider the list and rate the degree to which you possess each quality on a scale of 1 (low), 3 (moderate), or 5 (high). Also ask a colleague to rate you. This will give you an overview of some of your strengths and liabilities and your likelihood of success.

Qualities	Self rating	Colleague rating
Technical skill/competence for assignment		
Resourcefulness/resilience		
Comprehension of complex relationships		
Adaptability/flexibility		
Emotional stability		
Ability to deal with ambiguity/uncertainty/differences		
Desire to work overseas and with people who are different		
Adaptability of your spouse and family		
Willingness of your spouse to live abroad		
Stability of marriage and family life		
Management skills applicable to another culture		
Administrative skills suitable for another culture		
Communication skills		
Successful domestic career performance		
Language ability for host culture		
Cultural empathy/sensitivity		
Cultural specific knowledge		
Interest in host culture		
Ability to get along with host nationals		
Tolerance of others' views, especially when they differ from your own		
Sensitivity to attitudes and feelings of others		
Good health and wellness		

Making an effective selection decision for an overseas assignment can prove to be a major problem. Sometimes as many as a dozen criteria are used. Table 12.2 reports the importance of some of these criteria as ranked by Australian, expatriate, and Asian managers from sixty leading

Australian, New Zealand, British, and US MNCs with operations in South Asia. There was considerable agreement on the rankings of the criteria by the various groups.

Table 12.2 Rank of criteria in expatriate selection

	Australian managers $n = 47$	Expatriate managers* $n = 52$	Asian managers $n = 15$
1 Ability to adapt	1	1	2
2 Technical competence	2	3	1
3 Spouse and family adaptability	3	2	4
4 Human relations skills	4	4	3
5 Desire to serve overseas	5	5	5
6 Previous overseas experience	6	7	7
7 Understanding of host country culture	7	6	5
8 Academic qualifications	8	8	8
9 Knowledge of language of country	9	9	9
10 Understanding of home country culture	10	10	10

* American, British, Canadian, French, or New Zealand managers working for an MNC outside their home countries.
Source: Stone, R. J. (1991) ,'Expatriate Selection and Failure,' *Human Resource Planning,* vol. 14, no. 1, p. 10.

The balance in the weighting of the criteria should vary depending on the level and type of personnel sent overseas. Chief executive officers have to be good communicators, display management talent, maturity, emotional stability, and manifest the ability to adapt to new environmental settings. Functional heads need to be mature, have emotional stability and technical knowledge about their job. Troubleshooters should have technical knowledge of their business and be able to exercise initiative and creativity. Salespersons have to understand the local negotiating techniques, be good at relationships, emotionally stable, and respectful of the laws and people in the host country etc. In short, the nature of the job should determine the relative importance of selection factors.

There can be problems in some overseas countries, particularly Islamic ones, for women on international assignments. Clients may refuse to do business with female representatives. One organisation explained: 'The desired expatriate is a thirtyish married man with preschool-age children. This is to project our image as a conservative institution with good moral fibre. . . . Many of our potential female expatriates are single, and a swinging single is not the right image'.

International personnel selection procedures

All staff being considered for overseas assignments must be subjected to formal screening procedures that help ensure careful selection of personnel for international jobs including an interview, and written personality tests, using qualified psychologists to assist in this screening process.

Testing procedures

Some evidence suggests that although psychological testing is appropriate, it is not commonly used. This contrasts with the more widespread testing used by organisations when selecting domestic staff. The reasons given for not testing include:

- Tests are too expensive and you have to be a mathematical and psychological wizard to construct and interpret them.
- What you get for your money and effort is not worth it.
- Current tests have low validity for selection on expatriate assignments.
- We have used tests in the past and found that they did not improve the selection process. We now use the candidate's domestic record and our personal opinions about his adaptability potential. We think that our overseas experience enables us to be excellent judges about a candidate's probability of succeeding abroad.

Interviewing procedures

Most organisations usually screen people for overseas assignments by one or more interviews. This sometimes includes spouses too. This lends support to the contention that organisations are becoming increasingly cognisant of the importance of the adaptability of the spouse to living in a foreign environment for successful performance abroad.

Some of the interview questions should be designed to help the candidates and their spouses carefully consider what they will be getting into. Examples include:

- Can you imagine living without television? your regular daily newspaper?
- What is your tolerance for waiting for repairs?
- How important is it for you to spend significant amounts of time with people of your own ethnic, racial, religious and national background?
- As you look at your personal history, can you isolate any episodes that indicate a real interest in learning about other people and cultures?

- Will your spouse be interrupting a career to accompany you on an international assignment? If so, how do you think this will affect your relationship with each other?
- Would you be happy with the children in boarding school back home, seeing them only in the long vacations?
- Are you prepared for major adjustments in your home and work life?
- Are you prepared to be separated from your family, loved ones, friends?
- Are you prepared to live in another country where you may not understand the language?
- Are you prepared to give up all the services and facilities you take for granted here—medical, legal, financial?
- Are you willing to try new foods?
- Are you prepared to live with new security considerations? possible political instability? crime? corruption? major class differences?
- Are you prepared to live in a different climate with perhaps hot, humid temperatures or torrential rainfall?
- Are you prepared for living in a culture very different from your own, with customs and attitudes you have never encountered before?
- Are you prepared to be patient in a way you probably never had to be here at home?
- Are you prepared to frequently misunderstand and be misunderstood?
- Are you prepared to put in storage or divest yourself of most of your belongings for a period of one year or more?
- Are you capable of dealing with the tremendous contrast of poverty and wealth existing side by side in some parts of the world?

Answers to the above questions should give not only the organisation but the interviewee some idea of suitability for an overseas career. After facing the reality of such questions, some individuals remove their names from consideration for overseas transfer.

Candidate motivations

Why do individuals accept foreign assignments? One answer is that there is a greater demand for their talents abroad than at home. One study administered an opinion questionnaire to 13 000 employees of a large electrical equipment manufacturing firm with operations in forty-six countries. There were 200 multiple-choice items in the questionnaire, and the instrument was translated into twelve foreign languages to accommodate all groups of people. Fourteen goals were found to be of varying degrees of importance. These extended from a desire for training to the need to work for a successful company. Table 12.3 presents a brief description of the ten most important goals.

Table 12.3 Goal ranking among overseas personnel seeking foreign assignment

Rank	Goal	Questionnaire wording
1	Training	Have training opportunities to improve present skills or learn new skills
2	Challenge	Have challenging work to do—work that gives you a personal sense of accomplishment
3	Autonomy	Have considerable freedom to adopt your own approach to the job
4	Earnings	Have opportunity for high earnings
5	Advancement	Have an opportunity for advancement to higher-level jobs
6	Recognition	Get the recognition you deserve for doing a good job
7	Security	Have job security (steady work)
8	Friendly department	Work in a department where the people are congenial and friendly to one another
9	Personal time	Have a job which leaves you sufficient time for your personal and/or family life
10	Company contribution	Have a job which allows you to make a real contribution to your company's success

Source: Sirota, D. & Greenwood, J.M. (1971), 'Understand your overseas work force', *Harvard Business Review*, Jan.–Feb., p. 55.

This study found that the importance of each goal was somewhat influenced by the individual's occupation. The most important objectives related to achievement. The least important related to what the organisation gives to its employees.

In drawing together their findings the researchers grouped the participating countries into clusters: Anglo (Australia, Austria, Canada, India, New Zealand, South Africa, Switzerland, United Kingdom and United States); Northern European (Denmark, Finland, Norway); French (Belgium and France); northern South American (Colombia, Mexico and Peru); southern South American (Argentina and Chile); and Independent (Brazil, Germany, Israel, Japan, Sweden and Venezuela). On the basis of these groupings they were able to identify major motivational differences. Some of their findings included the following:

1 The Anglo cluster was more interested in individual achievement and less interested in the desire for security than any other cluster.
2 The French cluster was similar to the Anglo cluster except that less importance was given to individual achievement and more was given to security.

3   Countries in the Northern European cluster were more oriented to job accomplishment and less to getting ahead; considerable importance was assigned to jobs not interfering with personal lives.

4   In South American clusters, individual achievement goals were less important than in most other clusters. Fringe benefits were particularly important to South American groups.

5   Germans were similar to those in the South American clusters except that they placed a great emphasis on advancement and earnings.

6   Japanese were unique in their mix of desires. They placed high value on earning opportunities but low value on advancement. They were high on challenge but low on autonomy. At the same time, they placed strong emphasis on working in a friendly, efficient department and having good physical working conditions.

A more recent study found three major reasons why personnel accepted overseas positions. The most important reason was the enhancement of one's business career locally and internationally. This included such things as increased promotion potential, the opportunity to improve career mobility, and the opportunity for greater responsibility. Some candidates felt that all managers who wanted to reach the upper ranks had to have international experience and/or these jobs were necessary in gathering knowledge and experience for future assignments. The second most important reason was the attraction to overseas assignments. This included the opportunity to go overseas, the desire to live in a particular locale, and encouragement from one's family to take the assignment. The third most important reason was technical competence. The individual had knowledge of the particular job to be done and/or had proven performance or capability in this area of work.

Support during the assignment

To minimise the risk of expatriate failure, organisations should allow expatriates sufficient time to adapt to the foreign environment. The pressure to produce immediately in an overseas assignment compounds the demands imposed on the expatriate and may negatively affect performance on the job. As business follows the development of relationships, their performance should be assessed on the basis of long-term profitability, rather than in the short term.

Organisations should also establish and co-ordinate a support system that attends specifically to the needs and aspirations of expatriate employees. This 'social network' helps to reduce the 'out of sight, out of mind' dilemma by providing organisational information on the politics and day-to-day activities of the headquarters.

The support system should also monitor the training and development needs of expatriates. By providing continuous management training, companies ensure that expatriates improve their technical knowledge or capacity to manage others in cross-cultural work settings.

Repatriation of expatriates

For most overseas managers *repatriation*—the return to one's home country—occurs within five years of the time they leave. When they return, these expatriates often find themselves facing readjustment problems.

Reasons for returning

The most common reason for expatriates returning home from overseas assignments is that their formally agreed-on tour of duty is up. A second important cause is that expatriates want their children educated in a home country school, and the longer they are away, the less likely this will happen. A third reason for return is because of unhappiness in their overseas assignment. Those with families who return home early often do so because the spouse or children do not want to stay, and the company feels that the loss in efficiency/productivity is too great to be offset by short-term personal unhappiness. Of course some are recalled for failure to do a good job.

Readjustment problems

Returnees are frequently surprised and many are highly disappointed by what they experience at home and develop reverse culture shock. They feel strangers in their own work place and that their experience is not valued. The family as a whole may consider themselves worse off financially. Although they do not expect anything unfamiliar when returning, they often find that the country and the organisation have changed considerably. Re-entry shock may occur for six months or more, as readjustment to the lifestyle and tempo of the changed home and organisational cultures occurs.

Here is a summary of the major reasons for re-entry shock:

1 The 'out of sight, out of mind' syndrome is common, so the returnee has a lack of information on organisational changes.
2 Organisational changes made during the time the individual was abroad may make their position in parent headquarters redundant or peripheral.
3 Technological advances in the parent headquarters may render the individual's existing skills and knowledge obsolete, leading to job alienation—a sense of being out of touch with technological innovations and organisational changes, including personnel moves. One international manager complained, 'When I walked into the

office the first day back, I couldn't see anyone I knew. All the old faces had gone. It was like starting out again'.

4 *Reduced financial benefits.* Expatriate inducements including cost-of living allowances are no longer forthcoming. This may represent a decline in living standards. In addition, those who sold their houses and must now buy new ones find that the monthly cost is often much higher than when they left a few years earlier.

5 Expectations that the international assignment would help career prospects are rarely met. Few expatriates are promoted upon their return.

6 Having less autonomy than in the overseas position. Many expatriates found their overseas jobs more challenging: they miss the greater responsibility, the authority and the professional freedom in decision-making; The entrepreneurial individual who has enjoyed seniority in a small joint venture project or a foreign subsidiary finds it difficult to fit back into a headquarters post which is more routine and offers fewer opportunities for initiative.

7 Not receiving any career counselling from the company.

8 The children re-enter public schools where the classes are much larger than they were in the overseas private schools. They leave the friends they have made in their expatriate schools and have to fit back into home schools where they may know no one.

9 Less domestic help. Domestic help is easily hired and relatively cheap in many less developed countries.

10 A different pace of social life. In countries where expatriates are few, expatriates and their families often lead intense social lives, mixing with the same small group of fellow nationals and locals who speak their language. At home, social activity may be less focussed and more limited.

It sometimes takes from 6 months to one year before operating at full effectiveness.

Transition strategies

To help smooth the adjustment, some organisations have developed *transition strategies.* One is the use of *repatriation agreements,* whereby the organisation tells the individual how long they will be posted overseas and promises to give the individual, upon return, a job that is mutually acceptable. This agreement typically does not promise a specific position or salary, but the agreement may state that the person will be given a job that is equal to, if not better than, the one held before leaving.

Another strategy is to use senior executives as mentors or sponsors of staff abroad. The mentor maintains contact and prepares the career development of the expatriate on return and is responsible for:

- protecting the expatriate's professional/career interests in headquarters;
- keeping the expatriate up-to-date with headquarters changes and developments, including policy changes;
- ensuring that all agreements reached between the expatriate and headquarters are honoured; ensuring that repatriation training is provided, as agreed; reintroducing him/her to the headquarters on repatriation.

The role of the sponsor is to stay in touch and let the expatriate know that they are not being forgotten by the company.

A third approach is to keep expatriate staff appraised of what is going on at headquarters and to plug these managers into projects at the home office whenever they are on leave in the home country. This helps maintain the person's visibility and ensures the individual is looked on as a regular member of staff.

Debriefing

A sympathetic debriefing helps the returned expatriate and spouse overcome the worst effects of reverse culture shock on re-entry to the home culture. The manager who expects to be debriefed on home leave and repatriation, and who knows that the debriefing output will serve useful functions, is made aware that his/her experiences are valued. This manager is more likely to be motivated while at post.

Debriefing serves organisational interests in other respects. Many companies possess potentially invaluable sources of information in the form of their members' expatriate experiences, but rarely use them.

In the final analysis, a proactive strategy that provides an effective support system to allay expatriate concerns about career issues while serving abroad may work best. Tung found that successful Australian, US and European organisations that she studied had (1) mentor programs; (2) a separate organisation unit with primary responsibility for the specific needs of expatriates; and/or (3) maintenance of constant contacts between the home office and the expatriates. To the extent that the organisation can address these types of problems, the transition will be smooth and the expatriate's performance effectiveness once home will increase quickly. Organisations could use the following survey (Table 12.4 on pages 272–3) to assess the repatriation experiences of their staff.

Cross-cultural training needs and approaches

Only 32 per cent of a recent survey indicated that the companies had formalised training programs to prepare candidates for expatriate assignments. In general the study showed that the more rigorous the

Table 12.4 Assessment of repatriate experience

Rate each item on a score of 1 = strongly disagree to 7 = strongly agree. The higher the overall score the more favourable the repatriation experience.

Cultural re-entry	Score
1 The transition back to the home lifestyle was very easy	____
2 I do not miss the people I worked with in the overseas assignment	____
3 I felt comfortable giving up the friendships that I had developed overseas	____
4 The transition of my spouse and/or children back to their normal lifestyle was very easy	____
5 My family and friends back home were interested in hearing about my experiences living overseas	____
6 Life back home seems exciting in comparison with the cultural experience I had during my overseas assignment	____
7 My company provided me with help regarding relocation problems like housing and transportation	____

Financial implications	
1 The total financial package that I received in my new local job assignment was better than my total financial package overseas	____
2 The salary offer in the local job assignment was better than my salary overseas	____
3 The fringe benefits in the new local job assignment were better than when I was working overseas	____
4 The cost of buying a house upon returning from overseas was very reasonable	____
5 My personal finances since returning from overseas are in better shape than before I left for the overseas assignment	____
6 My company provided me with interim financial assistance when I returned from overseas	____
7 My company provided me with considerable accounting advice/financial planning upon my return from overseas	____

Nature of job assignment	
1 It was clear to me what permanent job I would have when I first returned from overseas	____
2 I experienced more autonomy in my new job than had been the case in my overseas assignment	____
3 My job status is less in my new job than had been the case in my overseas assignment	____
4 A mentor was appointed to help me appraise company developments when I first returned from overseas	____
5 A mentor helped in finding a good job assignment for me when I returned from overseas	____
6 The present job is less challenging than the one I held overseas	____

Table 12.4 Assessment of repatriate experience *(continued)*

7 I consider that the company was fair with me in terms of identifying a suitable job assignment for me when I returned from overseas _____

8 I view my present job assignment as very permanent _____

9 I feel a high sense of job (employment) security with my present company _____

10 Looking back at it, I consider that the overseas assignment benefited me in terms of career opportunities in the company _____

11 Overall, the managerial skills I gained overseas are being utilised by my employer now that I am working back home _____

12 I was placed in a 'holding pattern' when I first returned from the overseas assignment _____

13 My company was helpful in providing me with career counselling when I returned from overseas _____

14 My company provided my spouse with considerable help with career counselling when I returned from overseas _____

Source: Napier N.K. & Peterson, R.B. (1991), 'Expatriate re-entry: What do expatriates have to say?' *Human Resource Planning,* vol. 14, no. 1, pp. 26–7.

Table 12.5 Your organisation's policies

Review the policies followed by your organisation in making expatriate postings, and their outcomes.

1 What are the attributes of success and failure in expatriate postings?
   • How does the organisation measure success and failure?—what criteria are set for success?
   • How does headquarters explain success and failure?
   • How do successful and unsuccessful expatriates explain their performance?
2 Are the organisation's criteria appropriate? If not, how might they be revised? Given existing criteria, what personality and professional types are most likely to succeed in expatriate postings for your organisation?
3 How important is the failure of the spouse to adjust as a cause of any failure?
4 How does the organisation involve the spouse in the decision to take the assignment?
   • What briefing and training does the spouse receive before departure?
   • How could the organisation play a greater part in:
      (a) finding employment for the spouse?
      (b) supporting the spouse at post?
5 How often are women selected for expatriate postings?
   • What risks are associated with sending women on expatriate postings in your particular organisation?
   • Given changes within the environments of international business, are these assumptions of risk still realistic?
6 What support does the organisation give expatriates in planning their career paths?
   • How might this career pathing be improved?
   • How would improved career pathing affect:
      (a) the individual ?
      (b) the dependents?
      (c) the subsidiary?
      (d) headquarters?

Table 12.5 Your organisation's policies *(continued)*

---

7 What cultural and other support does the organisation give expatriates, their spouses and other dependents at post?
   • Is welfare assistance given?
   • What cultural support is given?
   • How does the organisation help the expatriate and their dependants overcome the effects of culture shock?
   • How might this support be improved?
8 How are expatriates and spouses debriefed on their return to headquarters?
   • What functions are debriefing outputs currently serving?
   • How might debriefing processes be improved?
   • What other functions might debriefing outputs serve?
9 What problems do expatriates and spouses typically experience on repatriation and when returning to headquarters
   • What support does headquarters give to repatriated staff and spouses?
   • How might this support be improved?

---

training, the greater the likelihood of success. The notion that employees should be trained to meet the specific problems posed by an expatriate assignment has been late in developing. Most surveys show that:

• many of the programs offered lasted five days or less;
• less than half of the respondents' top managements believed that language facility was important.

It suggests that headquarters are not learning from the experience of returning repatriates in developing relevant orientation programs.

Why training is ignored

Why do headquarters staff so often omit to properly train their staff before sending them on expatriate assignments? The most common reason is that management does not believe cross-cultural training is necessary. A good domestic track record is used as the criterion, while ignoring cross-cultural-related skills in selecting expatriate candidates. But a good domestic track record is not a good predictor of overseas success. Other reasons for not training include:

• *the temporary nature of the assignments*. Assignment length is always likely to influence the length and composition of the training program. But every assignment, no matter how short, can benefit from some training. Even if the assignment lasts for only a few days there will be considerable benefits for any negotiations and needed relationship formation.
• *doubts as to its effectiveness*. Some training is almost always better than none. When some training has been attempted, doubts as to its effectiveness might reflect a failure to evaluate it rigorously.

- *lack of time.* Appointment should be early enough to provide sufficient lead time for adequate training before relocating. The organisation that has a history of persistently giving its managers only a few weeks' warning before transferring them needs to review its expatriate staffing policies.

In sum, the failure to train tends to reflect a lack of a clear-cut expatriation policy, and failure to understand what training can—and cannot—achieve.

The training needed by the expatriate manager and spouse

Appropriate training for the expatriate manager and spouse falls into two broad areas:

- training to work in the new culture;
- training to live in the new culture.

The expatriate manager who adjusts in one area does not necessarily adjust in the other. Training should take into account both sets of needs. As the spouse's difficulty in adjusting to the new situation is a common cause of the manager's failure, both should be trained together wherever appropriate.

Training and briefing may be needed in the six categories below. Categories (a) and (b) below relate only to working in the new culture; (c)–(f) relate to both working and living.

(a) technical training;
(b) management training;
(c) domestic information;
(d) counteracting culture shock;
(e) cross-cultural training;
(f) language training.

(a) Technical training

The expatriate must be briefed on:

- technologies used by the foreign organisation with which they are unfamiliar, including alternative technologies;
- local attitudes towards and opportunities/constraints for technology transfer and innovation;

(b) Management training specific to the post

The expatriate must be trained in and understand:

- the local organisational structure; strategies and opportunities for change; structures for control and communication; structures for planning, motivation, and conflict resolution; organisational climate; informal structures;

- investment and treasury factors, including accounting and auditing procedures, relations with financial sources, protection of assets in the local country, procedures for repatriating capital and earnings;
- the company's relations with public-sector bodies;
- the business environment; local and international markets, competitors, distributors; relations with other subsidiaries; tariff and other barriers; economic indicators, political and governmental influences, political risk;
- cultural marketing issues and strategy; product characteristics, channels of distribution; advertising and promotional strategies; market research;
- human resource issues; training resources and policies;
- policies regarding ethical issues.

Exactly how much the spouse needs to know about the organisation's scope of operations is influenced by the degree of business entertainment that they have to undertake.

(c) Domestic information

The expatriate and spouse must be given practical and current briefing on such issues as:

- accommodation;
- details of schools, hospitals, medical issues, social services, etc.;
- shopping facilities and availability of domestic goods and services including power and water;
- customs regulations and procedures;
- import regulations; insurance, banking; transfer of finance home.

Spouses may have greater need for briefing on these topics than the employee as they live more of their life among the daily activities of the culture. The information given must be practical and up-to-date. Ideally, the couple should be sent on information trips to the host country before the assignment. These give them opportunities not only to inspect the local organisation but also to review their domestic information needs.

(d) Overcoming culture shock

Culture shock is never entirely overcome, but the worst effects can be mitigated by adequate preparation/training of appropriately selected persons and following some of the suggestions given above (see pp. 260–4).

(e) Cross-cultural training

Cross-cultural training aims at achieving three related outcomes. It teaches:

(a) *about the other culture*; values within the other culture; how the manager and/or spouse can generalise beyond the models used in the training to other and new situations; how the culture is reflected in significant historical, political and economic data.

(b) *how to adjust to the other culture*; develops non-evaluative attitudes towards the culture; demonstrates how cultural values are expressed in behaviour; develops a capacity for weighing the significance of culture as against other factors in determining behaviour.

(c) *how the culture affects attitudes towards work*; e.g. performance standards, degree of personal involvement, motivation, concepts of responsibility and authority, conflict and its resolution, organisational climate; how the culture influences formal interactions, e.g. organisational structures and systems, roles and relationships, planning needs and procedures, communication systems; how culture influences relations between organisations, e.g. development of commercial and professional associations, negotiation practice, ethical norms.

(f) Language skills

The degree of proficiency required depends on the country in which the assignment is to be conducted as this affects the quality of English spoken. It also depends on the degree of contact with host country nationals. However in all countries it is useful to have a basic ability to greet people, make simple requests, purchase goods, etc. in the local language.

Training design and implementation

In general, the criterion for all materials and techniques, and so for all training, is that it should:

- teach real skills, which the trainee can use in real situations;
- teach skills that cannot be otherwise acquired as economically;
- generate meaningful changes in behaviour;
- be motivating: the trainee perceives intrinsic rewards in training which answer the question 'What's in it for me?'

Long term assignments

There are six major types of cross-cultural training programs.

1 Environmental briefings

These provide information about such things as geography, climate, housing and schools. Simple and easy to prepare, this method fails to meet the needs of people crossing cultures.

2 Cultural orientation

This is designed to familiarise the individual with cultural institutions and value systems of the host country. This is the *intellectual or university model* consisting of lectures, videos and reading about the host culture. It is assumed that simply gaining information about another culture is effective preparation for living or working in that culture. This sort of program is often only a few days long and can range from superficiality to some depth. This is perhaps the most economical and simplest of all methods as it follows the approach to teaching and learning found in tertiary education. Typically, a trainer lectures to a group of trainees about different aspects of another culture. This method can provide an intellectual understanding of different aspects of cross-cultural interaction. The disadvantage is that it transfers knowledge on the cognitive level, which does not necessarily help sojourners in their interactions with the hosts. The following are the five major arguments against this model.

- **Source of information**. In the university model, the trainees receive all the information from the experts or from printed materials. In real-life situations, one has to develop one's own network for collecting information.
- **Problem solving**. In the classroom situation the emphasis is on solving well-defined problems using well-developed methods. In real-life situations, the trainee has to define a problem and then find ways to solve it. The emphasis is not on finding the optimum solution but on finding a workable solution that is acceptable to the hosts.
- **'Emotional muscle'**. In the classroom people are trained to look at issues rationally, giving a backseat to emotions. In effect, trainees do not learn to handle emotions well, in other words, they do not develop 'emotional muscle'. In cross-cultural interactions, people need a lot of emotional resilience because personally held values are challenged and one often needs to behave in ways that can be disruptive to one's personal value systems.
- **'Paper versus people'**. Trainees are evaluated on the basis of their written reports in the classroom situation, whereas in the actual encounter success is measured in terms of the effectiveness of the relationships that are established with the hosts.
- **Communication**. The classroom situation demands mastery of written and, to a lesser extent, oral communication. In cross-cultural interaction, one needs mastery of oral communication along with a good sense of nonverbal communication and active listening.

3   The area simulation model

This is a culture-specific training program. It is based on the belief that an individual must be prepared and trained to enter a specific culture. It involves simulation of future experiences and practice in functioning in the new culture through modelling, role play and cultural assimilators. One particular technique—the cultural assimilator—is so useful that it is detailed below. Programs in this model must be tailor-made to suit the location and sometimes the work role of the person.

For example, Jim is a human resource expert, sent out from Australia to develop and implement a new performance management system at his company's subsidiary in Japan. When conducting similar operations back home he uses techniques such as brainstorming, encouraging individual participation, holding individual consultations and encouraging innovative ideas. If he doesn't hear that there is a problem with the content, and receives adequate nonverbal feedback at group and individual meetings (head nodding, eye contact, etc.), he assumes everyone agrees with him.

However, based on the cultural differences between the two countries, Jim is likely to meet problems if he does not adjust his approach to ensure it is consonant with cultural expectations in Japan. Three areas that will create problems include:

Work style. Japanese employees prefer to work in groups, sharing the task/exercise with others;

Feedback process. Due to their low-risk nature, issues of hierarchy, and the need to 'save face', Japanese participants are unlikely to offer Jim their opinions, particularly if their supervisor also happens to be in the room with them;

Communication style. In Japan, it is rude to maintain eye contact with a superior (in this case, Jim), who is 'deserving of respect'. In fact, if participants were to look Jim steadily in the eye, they would be conveying in their culture the message that they considered themselves his equal.

The area simulation model must address these cultural differences, so that Jim understands why and how to redesign his approach so he can achieve the same bottom-line goals as at home.

The strengths of this method include the following:

- Affective learning is emphasised, as well as factual cognitive learning.
- Doing is emphasised as opposed to intellectualising. The problem has to be discovered and then solved.
- The attitude of accepting the cultural barriers with understanding and then learning to work with the barriers is encouraged.
- Above all, the trainees are not allowed to depend on the trainers. The ability to handle problems independently is crucial. Dependence on the trainer is an unwanted outcome that many orientation programs produce. This method avoids this problem.

- This method provides the participants with the opportunity of testing themselves during the training. The trainees can drop out if they discover that they cannot handle the overseas assignment.
- This method also provides feedback to the trainees as to how they should change their behaviour. Hence it is possible for the trainees to learn new behaviours.

The criticism of the cultural assimilator is that it is not possible to create another culture in full as it can only cover what are deemed to be the most salient issues on a one-by-one basis.

Another variation of this model is the simulation game, which provides structured exercises. The games divide the participants into two groups and requires each group to learn the behaviours of a hypothetical culture. Once the trainees have learned their roles, they interact with one another. The interaction involves the trainees on the affective and behavioural levels. In many ways the trainees experience the feelings they will have in another culture and emotions often run high. At the end the trainer debriefs the trainees and a discussion of 'what happened' and 'why' follows. Typically, cognition follows effect. One advantage is that there is no way the trainees could build negative stereotypes about any real culture. Another advantage is time. The game takes from two to four hours depending on the number of trainees. One of the popular simulations are BAFA–BAFA which is detailed below.

4   The cultural awareness model

This assumes that for an individual to function successfully in another culture they must learn the principles of behaviour that exist across cultures. The cultural self-awareness approach to cross-cultural training is based on the assumption that an individual's effectiveness in intercultural communication can be improved by developing the individual's cultural self-awareness—the ability to recognise cultural influences in personal values, behaviours and cognitions. This ability has several beneficial results: (a) it should enhance a person's skill at diagnosing difficulties in intercultural communication; (b) it should be easier to suspend judgments when confronted with behaviour that appears odd; and (c) it should make individuals aware of their ignorance of the other culture and correspondingly, increase their motivation to learn about it. These programs are often generic with specific emphasis on a particular culture only as required.

5   The self-awareness model

This is based on the assumption that understanding and accepting oneself is critical to understanding a person from another culture. Sensitivity training is a main component of this method. This method involves considerable expenditure of time and commitment.

6   Field experience

Here the participant is sent to the country of assignment to experience some of the emotional stresses of living and working with people from a different culture. Few organisations have time to do this before the assignment commences.

Apart from the self-awareness model, input for these offerings can be obtained from those who currently are working (or have worked) in the country to which the participants will be sent, from local managers and personnel who are citizens of that country, and with guidance from psychologists and sociologists.

Short-term assignments

For those visiting another country on a one-off or occasional basis to work with clients on projects, and for staff members who deal extensively with clients from that country at home, short one-week in-house training programs can be very effective. Such programs can be designed around a series of mini-lectures, videos, case studies, cultural assimilators and role plays that cover topics ranging from how to handle introductions and the proper way to exchange gifts, to the correct way of interpreting business behaviour. At the end of such a program participants have a basic understanding of how to interact with and conduct business with members of that culture. More importantly, they know the types of information they lack and how to go about learning more about becoming more effective intercultural communicators.

The cultural assimilator

The cultural assimilator was introduced above as a culture specific simulation program. It has become one of the most effective approaches in cultural training. It is a programmed learning technique that exposes members of one culture to some of the concepts, attitudes, role perceptions, customs, and values of another. These assimilators can be developed for any culture.

In most cases these assimilators require the trainee to read a short episode of a cultural encounter and choose an interpretation of what has happened and why. If the trainee's choice is correct, they go on to the next episode. If the response is incorrect, the trainee is asked to reread the episode and choose another response. To develop assimilators it is necessary to determine the major dimensions of social perception and cognition that are used in each culture, and the extent to which these dimensions influence responses. Themes, or culturally-determined viewpoints, are then isolated as representative generalisations about that culture. The end product is a culture training manual of about 100 critical incidents for one particular culture that the learner interprets, responds to and assimilates immediate feedback. Because the assimilator uses short incidents describing intercultural encounters, it can be used in a number of ways such as role play, group discussion or with individuals, using written or video presentation modes.

The program explains why an answer is correct or incorrect. If incorrect, the learner reviews the episode and reinterprets. Feedback exposes the learner to major themes characterising the two cultures, home and host. The cultural assimilator can be validated by asking persons of the host culture to respond to the interaction incidents without seeing prepared alternatives. This method is superior to the university model or lecture method. It has been well researched and validated, with positive research findings supporting its use.

A major way to collect incidents for the assimilator is to interview returning expatriates and host nationals to obtain specific intercultural occurrences or events that address common problems, or conflicting or puzzling situations that are critical for success in the host culture. These incidents can be pleasant, unpleasant, or simply non-understandable occurrences. To be classified as a critical incident, a situation must meet at least one of the following conditions:

1 An expatriate and a host national interact in the situation.
2 The situation is puzzling or likely to be misinterpreted by the expatriate.
3 The situation can be accurately interpreted if sufficient knowledge about the culture is available.
4 The situation is relevant to the expatriate's task or mission requirements.

Here is an incident from a Malay cultural assimilator to illustrate how critical incidents are used:

Example from a Malay cultural assimilator

'Mary Field went on an exchange to an overseas branch of the international bank she worked for. She was amazed at the questions that were asked her by Malays whom she considered to be no more than colleagues, customers or casual acquaintances. When she entered or left her apartment, or at lunch break people would ask her where she was going or where she had been. If she stopped to talk she was asked questions like, "how much do you make a month?", "how many children do you have?" "are you married", "have you eaten?" or "where did you get that dress you are wearing?" She thought the Malays were very rude.'

Why did the Malays ask such 'personal' questions?

1 The Malays were uncomfortable about the way in which she lived and they were trying to get Mary to change her habits.
2 The Malays like to pry into other people's business.
3 The colleagues and casual acquaintances were acting like friends do in Malaysia, although Mary did not realise it.
4 In Malaysia such questions are perfectly proper when asked of women, but improper when asked of men.

Participants read the incidents or role play them and then select the response they think is the best. Explanations to each answer are then provided.

1 You selected one. Incorrect. There was no information given to lead you to believe that the Malays were unhappy with Mary's way of living.
2 You selected two. Incorrect. This is not why the Malays ask such questions. They were not prying. Whether or not some information is personal depends upon the culture. In this case, the Malays did not consider these questions too personal. Can you think why? Try again.
3 You selected three. Correct. It is not improper for in-group members or even casual friends to ask these questions of one another. Furthermore, these questions reflect the fact that friendships (even casual ones) tend to be more intimate in Malaysia than in the West. As a result, colleagues and casual acquaintances are generally free to ask questions which would seem too personal in the West.
4 You selected four. Incorrect. Such questions are indeed proper under certain situations. However, sex has nothing to do with it. When are these questions proper? Try to apply what you have learned about proper behaviour between friends in Malaysia. Was Mary regarded as a friend by these Malays?

Example from a Thai cultural assimilator

'One day a Thai administrator of senior rank kept two of his assistants accompanying an expatriate business person waiting about an hour for an appointment. The assistants, although very angry, did not show it while they waited and urged the expatriate to ignore the delay. When the administrator walked in, he acted as if he were not late. He offered no apology or explanation. After he was settled in his office, he called the waiting group in. The assistants began working on the business for which the administrator had set the meeting just as though there had been no delay.'

Which one of the following best describes the chief significance of the behaviour of the Thais involved?

1 The Thai assistants were extremely skilful at concealing their true feelings.

2 The Thai administrator obviously was unaware of the fact that he was an hour late for the appointment.

3 In Thailand subordinates are required to be polite to their superiors, no matter what happens, nor what their rank may be.

4 Since no one commented on it, the behaviour indicated nothing of unusual significance to the Thais.

Answers:

1 Option one is not entirely true, although it is characteristic of Thais to try to appear reserved under any circumstance. If the assistants were skilful at concealing their true feelings, there would be no doubt about their feelings.

2 Number two is a very poor choice. While the administrator behaved as if he were unaware of his tardiness after observing the hour's wait, it is more than likely he was aware of his lateness.

3 The third choice is the correct one. The information in the episode is fully used. This 'deference to the boss' may be observed anywhere in the world, but it is likely to be carried to a higher degree in Thailand and other Asian countries than in Western ones. Certain clues support number three—the assistants' concealed feelings; the administrator failed to apologise; no one mentioned the tardiness subsequently; the appointment was kept.

4 Number four is completely wrong. While the behaviour reported in the passage does not seem as significant to the Thais as it might to Westerners, why was nothing said about the tardiness? And why were the assistants 'very angry' although they 'did not show it?' Is there a more significant level of meaning for this behaviour?

When trainees use the assimilator as a programmed learning tool, they go on selecting until they find the correct response. In a classroom situation, the incidents can be role-played and the responses discussed. Incidents are extremely useful for generating group discussions and trainees can also share their own related experience to make the discussion more interesting. Another format provides incidents in videotaped form.

These critical incidents make participants more aware of their own values and behaviours. By knowing this, the trainees can program themselves to suspend judgment when interacting with hosts. Family members, especially children who will be accompanying the parents, need to be included in the cultural assimilator training.

The assimilator approach to training is not expensive. A typical 75 to 100 incident program often requires approximately 200 hours to develop. Assuming that development of the assimilator by a training specialist is costing the company $50 an hour, the cost is around $10 000 per assimilator. However, this cost can be spread over many trainees, and the program should not need to be changed. Most importantly, research shows that these assimilators improve the effectiveness and satisfaction of those being trained as compared with other training methods.

Self-confrontation training techniques

Using videotape in therapeutic and educational situations is becoming widespread and its success is well-documented. In this approach a trainee plays a role with a person from another culture in a simulated cross-cultural encounter and the situation is videotaped. Following the inter-action, the encounter is played for the trainee and trainer to point out strengths and weaknesses in both the verbal and nonverbal behaviour of the trainee. The trainee can observe responses and evaluate behaviour for improved performance in future role-play situations and for actual performance in a different culture. This is a culture general approach, although the situations can also be specific to a particular culture.

This technique uses a psychological principle of stimulated recall that is useful in rapid learning. After replaying the behavioural situation on videotape, trainees are able to relive the scene and recall their thoughts at the moment, thus permitting complete use of the psychological impact of self-confrontation.

Simulation

This is a form of inductive learning that creates a situation in a classroom that is similar to the real life experience. It recreates a work, family, or social environment in a controllable form. Observers then evaluate the interpersonal factors during the process and report back their findings after the exercise. The real learning occurs when the total group analyses what happened in terms of participation, co-operation and communication during the game, and how much such behaviour is found on the job.

BAFA–BAFA is a simulation in which participants are divided into two cultures, Alpha and Beta. After learning the 'rules' of their culture they are required to interact with members of the other culture. The

Alpha culture is a warm, friendly, and patriarchal society which speaks English. The Beta culture does not use English and are hard working, and their task is to accumulate as many points as possible. Once the participants in the two cultures learn the rules and the language, they are to interact with each other. Visitors to the other culture are often confused (as they are in an actual cross-cultural situation) by the strangeness of the foreign culture. This confusion often becomes frustration and hostility. In the debriefing of the simulation, participants come to realise the rationale behind the behaviour they had observed during the activities. A discussion of their reactions and the specific skills that are associated with effective interactions are also discussed.

This simulation has been used in academic and business settings and in other programs in which it is important for the participants to have an experiential understanding of the meaning of culture. After playing BAFA–BAFA participants report they have learned the following:

- What seems logical, sensible, important and reasonable to a person in one culture may seem irrational, stupid, and unimportant to an outsider.
- Feelings of apprehension, loneliness, lack of confidence are common when visiting another culture.
- When people talk about other cultures, they tend to describe the differences and not the similarities.
- Differences between cultures are generally seen as threatening and described in negative terms.
- Personal observations and reports of other cultures should be regarded with a great deal of scepticism.
- One should make up one's own mind about another culture and not rely on the reports and experience of others.
- It requires experience as well as study to understand the many subtleties of another culture.
- Understanding another culture is a continuous and not a discrete process.
- Stereotyping is probably inevitable in the absence of frequent contact or study.
- People often feel their own language is far superior to other languages.
- It is probably necessary to know the language of a foreign culture to understand the culture in any depth.

Evaluation of training and the overseas deployment processes

Evaluation is important because it tells the organisation whether or not its cross-cultural training resources and overseas deployment processes are operating to optimal advantage.

Expatriates returning from an overseas assignment are a valuable resource. Much can be learned from their cross-cultural experience. The information can be used to improve the whole deployment process. Some possibilities to consider are:

- Data gathering from all employees who return from either temporary or longer relocations abroad. A standardised questionnaire or interview procedure can be developed and the results stored in a computer for future use. Separate records can be kept on those in the premature return group. Interviews with high performers abroad might be videotaped.

- Findings should be studied for ways to improve recruitment and selection of personnel for overseas assignment; employee training programs for foreign deployment; management policies and practices at foreign sites; consumer, customer, public and employee relations in target countries; and relocation assistance for the returning expatriate employees.

Preparing in advance if you are a small business organisation

In this size of business you will be unable to afford a comprehensive program of the sort suggested above. You may have little choice over which member of staff goes overseas to negotiate a contract or manage a contract you have obtained. However, there are still a number of steps you can take in order to learn about the region's history, culture and people as well as determine the cultural suitability and overall business prospects for your product or service.

The following is a brief series of steps you should consider taking.

- Contact the Asian country's commercial office within its embassy or consulate. Even tourist offices can provide you with general information about a country. Contact the Australian government supported interest group for that country if there is one, e.g. Australia–China Council; Australia–Japan Council.
- Make use of the general information on Pacific Rim countries that can be obtained by fax through the USA's PacRim Hotline (Tel. 202-482-3875), which provides trade and economic statistics, as well as summaries of other business related issues.
- Contact export promotion agencies such as Austrade.
- Find out if your state, city, or community has a 'sister' state/city relationship with specific places in Asia.
- If possible, conduct a fact-finding trip to your country of interest. Participate in any delegations/trade missions/trade shows that your local business chamber, or other trade organisations sponsor.

- Develop a relationship with your country's embassy/high commission in the Asian country.
- Utilise the expatriate community located within that country, as well as those who have recently returned home as sources for valuable information about the country and its business and social climate and practices.
- Contact immigrants from that country to discuss social and cultural issues that might impact on doing business there. Seek contacts from them back home as such contacts are very useful in developing business ties in Asian countries. .
- Be creative. Find common connections with companies in the country or with those individuals who have experience doing business in the country or with the specific company with which you are dealing. For example, perhaps a supplier or client company or individual who you interact with also does business in the Asian country.

Building relationships with government officials and private businesspeople from each country takes time. Do not wait until you are ready to enter a country or are bidding for a contract before you visit the country or join the local chamber of commerce and other trade groups. To promote your interests, develop relationships with as many people as possible and learn as much as you can about local procedures and policies. Be ready to demonstrate how your project and company can benefit the local country. Offers of assistance for local companies and worker training are generally well received by the governments and private industry.

If you are dealing with government officials, take the time to research their political priorities and objectives before you seek a face-to-face meeting. The more you are able to address their objectives and concerns verbally or in the terms of a proposal, the easier it will be for you to gain approvals and contracts. Remember to be discreet and tactful in any verbal discussions, particularly with government officials. In Asia people must like and trust you if you are to succeed. How often have you given business to people who were arrogant or condescending?

In some countries it can be almost impossible to get through the right doors without some sort of introduction. If you do not know someone who knows the company with which you would like to do business, consider indirect sources. Trade organisations, lawyers, bankers and financiers, common suppliers and buyers, consultants and advertising agencies are just a few potential introducers.

The future of cross-cultural orientation

The inevitability of cross-cultural interaction and the importance of orientation has now been accepted. However, cross-cultural orientation has yet to reach all who need it, not just in business, but in education, nursing, tourism etc. Cross-cultural orientation could well become a part of the school curriculum in the future so that students are prepared to interact effectively in multicultural settings whether overseas or more importantly in the home country.

Summary

Selection

Companies should select effective, rather than marginal employees for overseas assignments. A well thought out selection system which assesses personal qualities such as adaptability, ability to communicate, emotional stability, willingness to learn from experience and adaptability to change, ability to integrate with others, confidence, flexibility, sensitivity to differences in culture and possession of relational skills, as well as technical competence, increases the likelihood of selecting the best candidate for the job.

An underutilised criterion for the selection of expatriates is the adaptability potential of the spouse and other family members. Few companies interview the spouse of the candidate. Companies can go some way to resolving potential family-related problems by involving the spouse in the proposal for overseas assignment as early as possible. This means, first, securing their opinion concerning the planned assignment. And second, providing training that builds up interest in the assignment and new environment, and giving preparation for living there.

The important factors for success in an expatriate assignment which must be considered in the selection process are:

- adaptability and stress tolerance
- technical competence
- spouse and family adaptability
- human relations skill
- understanding of host country culture
- knowledge of language
- desire to serve overseas
- previous overseas experience.

Training

Organisations should offer formal training programs to prepare expatriates and their families for their overseas assignments. Even the most careful selection does not eliminate the need for training. Programs such as cultural assimilator training, critical incidents, simulation, sensitivity training, field experiences, in addition to informational discussions are needed.

Repatriation

Re-entry shock should be minimised by using mentors who can help with the development of career plans before returning home and making sure that information about the organisation and changes at home are fed overseas.

References

Caudron, S. (1992), 'Preparing managers for overseas assignments', *World Executive Digest*, Nov., pp. 72–3.

Some guidelines in the use of English and interpreters

The art of communicating through an interpreter

If you are not fluent in the language of your customer, client, or counterpart you will have to depend on an interpreter, whether negotiating or socialising. Even if you are fluent you may find that your clients and counterparts disguise what they want to say amongst themselves by speaking in their own language. For example, both Taiwanese and Mandarin are spoken during business discussions in Taiwan, depending on which you don't understand.

Your interpreter acts as a transmitter of your words, ideas, humour, intelligence and personality. What I have said about building strong business relationships in virtually every chapter may have sounded relatively easy to do; accomplished while communicating solely through an interpreter, it is hardly a simple proposition. Few overseas business people understand how to be interpreted well, and this is unfortunate, since to be clearly understood you must know how to get your message clearly interpreted. Most people who have problems communicating their facts and arguments to the overseas party blame their interpreters. A better approach is to take *responsibility* for getting your message better interpreted.

What are the secrets of being interpreted well?

* First, limit your sentences to 7 to 15 words, maximum. This may seem like a lot of words, but it's not. Write your script out and you'll see what a challenge it is to speak in short sentences, getting your points across clearly and succinctly. (Use the sample script below as a model.) The shorter your sentences, the less likely that your audience will lose your train of thought and become fatigued.

- Use short, simple sentences. Avoid use of slang, clichés, analogies, or idiomatic expressions that are specific to your language or culture. Avoid sports analogies, as not all Western sports are popular in Asian countries. Even with baseball, a popular sport in East Asia, analogies can be misinterpreted by your listeners and should be avoided, e.g. ballpark figures; on the ball; good batting average; going in to bat first etc.
- Pause after each sentence and allow the interpreter to translate it; otherwise, they may try to summarise groups of sentences. Speak about only one concept at a time.
- Avoid buzzwords and explain concepts thoroughly. For example, words like 'empowerment' may not have a direct translation, and therefore the interpreter may translate parts of the word separately and most likely incorrectly. Instead of saying 'MBO' or 'management by objectives', explain exactly what you mean. This does not imply that your counterpart does not understand terms and concepts, but rather that these concepts may have different names in their culture. More importantly, the interpreter may not understand the intention or concept and may incorrectly translate the words.
- Be redundant. Given that much of your message fails to pass through your interpreter to your audience, and that much of that will be comprehended only hazily because your words have been denuded of their emotionally and culturally conditioned content in the process of translation, it doesn't hurt for you to reiterate important points to check for nods of comprehension.
- Be prepared to explain and/or present each major point in two or three different ways, as the point may be lost if discussed only once. In the West if you repeat yourself, everybody falls asleep. In Asia, repetition means that you're really serious; repetition is good in there. It is incredible how much you need to repeat yourself to be effective. Observe strictly the golden rule for good speaking and presenting in the West: First tell your audience what you're going to tell them; then tell them; and lastly, tell them what you've told them.
- Find and train a good interpreter. If you cannot take one with you, such as a well, qualified person from that country who has migrated to yours, the best way to find an interpreter is through referral. Call your business colleagues and ask if they know of an interpreter they have used before. If you are considering a long-term and intensive business connection with a particular country it would be worthwhile engaging the interpreter on contract, one able to cover immediately all those tasks that need effecting such as translating incoming faxes, writing outgoing faxes, making overseas telephone calls and accompanying you on your trips. Providing most of your

communications in Mandarin, Japanese, Malay or Thai will certainly make your counterparts believe you are serious and well set up to do business with them.

- When I say 'train' your interpreter, I mean to rehearse your presentation with them several times. No interpreter will be able to translate all of your technical terms without opening a dictionary; this should be done at home and not in front of your audience. Whenever possible, educate your interpreter beforehand about the intricacies of your product and/or service. The interpreter's accuracy in translating may depend on the product/service knowledge that you provide them with beforehand. If you travel to a country frequently you may want to hire the same person each time, so that over time they will become more knowledgable about the technicalities of your business. In essence, your interpreter will be your most valuable marketing and presentation tool. Moreover, if there is *any* humour, irony, or special verbal twist in your presentation, make sure the interpreter has rehearsed it, found just the right nuance to translate it, and knows the body and facial language in which to deliver it, so that you audience gets your message clearly and responds favourably.

- Always use your own interpreter. Never rely on one provided by your counterpart, because that interpreter works for your counterpart and is more likely to protect the latter's business interests. It is common and preferable to have a different interpreter represent each side during negotiations and meetings.

- Do not speak until your interpreter has finished, as interruptions may cause them to lose the thread of what they were saying. We often forget, especially when things get heated during a negotiation, that anything we say that is not heard by their interpreter will not be understood at all on the other side. We can get angry and cut in before the interpreter has finished the last sentence. Of course, the person across the table senses that the foreigner is angry about something from his or her gestures and expression, but much of the message is coming across garbled. Remember that in many countries it is not a good indication of your character to lose control. Permit the interpreter to spend as much time as needed in clarifying points whose meanings are obscure. Don't be concerned if a speaker talks for five minutes and the interpreter covers it in half a minute. Ask the interpreter for advice if there are problems.

- When speaking through an interpreter, always face your business counterpart, not your interpreter. The interpreter is only there to facilitate your business interests. Your goal is to develop a business relationship and personal rapport with the local business person, despite your language differences. I agree it is uncomfortable looking at a listener who cannot understand your language. A formal

Japanese, Korean or Chinese senior person will believe you are not giving them the attention they deserve if you do not face your counterpart throughout the tedious process and will take it as a sign of disrespect. Rehearse doing this as part of your pre-trip training.

- You can expect your counterpart not to trust your interpreter. Don't trust their's either. Suggest to your interpreter that they break into the conversation to retranslate what a Chinese negotiator has said if *their* interpreter fails to translate something, or if the tone of their statement has been modified by their interpreter in any way. Note also that the oldest trick in the book is for someone to *pretend* that they don't understand your language, when in fact, they can comprehend conversations amongst your team. So make sure you're out of earshot before discussing sensitive topics amongst your colleagues. The trick works both ways, of course. Lastly, have your interpreter debrief you after each meeting. They often overhear utterances on the other side that you should know about. An interpreter from an achieving country will usually behave professionally in giving an unbiased account of what was said. An interpreter from an ascriptive culture is also there to support their own team, interpreting gesture and meaning and advising on how to counter the confrontational conduct. The answer is always to take your own interpreter. This also stops any conferring in the local language in your presence.

- Some Asians will always bring an interpreter to negotiations—although they speak English fluently. When the Westerner addresses the interpreter, and when the interpreter translates into their language, the Asian has twice the time to plan an answer, a second bite of the apple. Of course this can work both ways too. Even if you know the language, it is always advisable to hire a interpreter. In addition to minimising misunderstandings, an interpreter provides you with additional time to prepare a response while the discussion is being translated.

- Recognise that the speech sound level in some of the Asian countries is lower than in Western conversations. If your interpreter is speaking softly, it may be considered normal. Do not ask them to speak louder, unless necessary. Similarly, make sure to speak at the same sound level as the others in a discussion. Often people speak very loudly when interacting with people who communicate in another language, forgetting that it is a language barrier, and not a hearing one.

- Ask direct questions and avoid double negatives to minimise confusion. It may be valuable to verify the cultural suitability of certain direct questions with your interpreter before the encounter. You may simply need to reword a question. The key to success is making sure that your interpreter understands the intention behind your questions.

- Don't expect an interpreter to work for over two hours without a rest period. Consider using two interpreters if interpreting is to last a whole day or into the evening, so that when one tires the other can take over.
- After meetings, confirm in writing what has been agreed using two copies for each party, one in English the other in the local language prepared by the interpreters.

Treat your interpreter with respect, particularly if they are a local person. An interpreter who is reprimanded in front of his/her fellow nationals loses face, and is alienated. And an alienated interpreter is more likely to constitute a security risk.

However, mistakes do happen. One interpreter translated 'it goes without saying' as equivalent to 'it walks without talking'; 'the spirit's willing but the flesh is weak' as equivalent to 'the alcohol is strong but the meat is undercooked'. When President Carter visited Poland in 1977, he used a Polish-speaking American who rephrased Carter's 'when I left the United States' as 'when I abandoned the United States'. Such gaffes occur when the interpreter has a less than intimate knowledge of the other language.

Sample presentation script

Read each sentence out loud and then pause as if you were speaking through an interpreter. Notice that each sentence takes 4–7 seconds to say and expresses only one idea at a time. Having your opening presentation scripted in this fashion will get any negotiation in Asia off to a good start.

- I want to thank you for inviting me to meet you today.
- I am going to tell you about a new technology my company has developed.
- It is part of the global war against international terrorism.
- In 1997 the world's terrorists attacked 4 400 times.
- That is twelve incidents every day on average.
- Most of these violent attacks involved the use of bombs and explosives.
- Terrorism is world wide and Asia cannot avoid such incidents.
- The name of the new technology is *Bio-cryotic Displacement Analysis*.
- I have a video to show you.
- I have also a display of the equipment for you to see.

Language style

When writing letters and faxes to persons whose English is not totally fluent, use dot points, just like the sample script above. This forces you to write in simple, clear and concise one item sentences, differentiating between different items covered. Keep your material free from slang and jargon. Asians in particular do not understand metaphors and allusions to sports, such as ' throwing someone a curly one', ' batting on a difficult wicket', 'skating on thin ice'.

If you have no native speaking inhouse translator who can translate the documents perfectly, the golden rule is to communicate by letter and fax in English if at all possible. It is better to say it in English than provide badly translated business correspondence and advertising material. It may be misinterpreted and also misconstrued as evidence that your company is sloppy in its business approach. After having material on your products/services etc. translated, have it retranslated back by another independent translator just to check it still means the same.

Much of the world's international business is conducted in English, because the British Commonwealth and North America, which participate in a large percentage of world trade, speak a common language. This tendency will only increase as the role of Internet for communication, information, and advertising increases. But the level of understanding is still limited and the vocabulary size of many Asians is small. So use the following suggestions to help you use a style of English suitable for those who are attempting to converse with you in their second language.

1 Try to limit your vocabulary to the most common 2 000 words in English, that is, those words typically learned in the first two years of language study by a someone learning English as a second language. Be particularly careful to avoid uncommon or esoteric words; for example, use 'fat' rather than 'obese', 'effective' rather than 'efficacious', 'helpful' rather than 'facilitating', 'a large number' rather than 'a plethora', etc. Remember if you have a penchant for using erudite words often derived from Latin and Greek, that you may sound learned at a management conference in the UK, but your message will be lost in Asia.

2 Restrict your use of English words to their most common meaning. Many words have multiple meanings, and non-native speakers are most likely to know the first or second most common meanings. For example, use 'force' to mean 'power' or 'impetus' rather than 'basic point'. Other examples include using 'to address' to mean 'to send' (rather than 'to consider'), or using 'impact' to mean 'the force of a collision' (rather than 'effect').

3 Whenever possible, select an action-specific verb (e.g., 'ride the bus') rather than a general action verb (e.g., 'take the bus'). Verbs to avoid include 'do', 'make', 'get', 'have', 'be', and 'go'. For example, the verb 'get' can have at least five meanings (buy, borrow, steal, rent, retrieve) in, 'I'll get a car and meet you in an hour'.

4   In general, select a word with few alternate meanings (e.g., 'accurate'—1 meaning) rather than a word with many alternate meanings (e.g., 'right'– many meanings).

5   In choosing among alternate words, select a word with similar alternate meanings rather than a word with dissimilar alternate meanings. For example, 'reprove' means to rebuke or to censure— both similar enough that a non-native speaker can guess the meaning accurately. In contrast, 'correct' can mean either to make conform to a standard, to scold, or to cure, leaving room for ambiguity in interpretation by a non-native speaker.

6   Avoid long sentences, double negatives, or the use of negative wordings of a sentence when a positive form could be used.

7   Become aware of words whose primary meaning is restricted in some cultures. For example, outside of the United States 'check' most commonly means a financial instrument and is frequently spelled 'cheque'. The Australian word 'rort', meaning to take advantage of the system by corrupt means is not known in Asia.

Finally:
There is a joke that goes,

Q: 'What do you call a person who can speak two languages?'
A: 'Bilingual'.
Q: 'How about three?'
A: 'Trilingual'.
Q: 'Good, how about one?'
A: 'Hmmm . . . British/Australian/American' (depending on your nationality).

The importance of an interpreter in business negotiations cannot be over-stressed. It is the interpreter who can assist with the accurate communication of ideas between the two teams.

B

Sample answers to activities

Chapter 2

1 Although Phil thought he was giving a straightforward answer to a rather mundane question about his father's health, his response, from Mr Chang's perspective, made Phil appear to be a very undesirable business partner. Coming from a society that places a very high value on family relationships, Mr Chang thought it quite inhumane to leave one's aging father at a nursing home in the care of total strangers. If Phil couldn't meet his primary obligations to his own family members, Chang reasoned, how could he be trusted to meet his obligations to his business partners?

2 Marina had forgotten all about *feng shui*. Most Chinese are still concerned that the orientation of buildings and their internal layouts are consonant with creating 'good' flows of *chi*. In designing any building or office layout etc, it is wise to bring in a *feng shui* expert in the early stages so that those who will own, live or work in it feel that it is blessed with positive energy.

Chapter 3

1 In any society gifts are given as a way of symbolising certain thoughts. Yet like other aspects of culture, certain gifts symbolise different thoughts in different cultures. In the West, chrysanthemums are given for a number of general purposes. But in some Asian countries, including Taiwan, white chrysanthemums are used traditionally as funeral flowers. Also Colin's flowers sent another unintended message. Although it is appropriate to take flowers as a gift when invited to someone's home for dinner, to present flowers

at other times to the mother of an unmarried woman could be interpreted as an expression of a man's serious intentions toward the daughter.

2   This scenario illustrates the high value Westerners place on science, logic, and rational thought. Since there were no logical links between any of these unfortunate happenings at the plant, Frank and his fellow ex-pats concluded that they were just an unfortunate, yet unrelated, series of accidents. The local workforce, on the other hand, believed that there were some sinister forces at work that required the services of a religious specialist. And it was these beliefs that were the direct cause of Frank's two managerial problems—morale and absenteeism. Unfortunately, by getting caught up in their own value system Frank and his colleagues missed the major point: It makes little difference whether or not the belief in evil spirits is true or false. Frank was no more capable of proving that evil spirits did not in fact cause this series of events than the local workers could prove that they did. What he failed to understand was that (1) the workers did believe that evil spirits were at work, and (2) this belief, whether true or false, was causing a major problem for the company. The only reasonable way to solve that problem is take an action that will enable the workers to perceive that the power of evil spirits has been neutralised and that their safe work environment has been restored.

3   The demise of these joint venture negotiations cannot be explained solely by the fact that contemporary Taiwanese firms are inextricably wedded to traditional practices. In fact, many Taiwanese firms have shown an enormous willingness to adopt innovative policies and strategies, yet equally high on the Taiwanese list of cultural priorities is the value placed on respect for elders and saving face. Even though Mr Laing may have disagreed with his grandfather's position, it would have been totally inappropriate for him to have disagreed with his grandfather in a *public* meeting. The Taiwanese way would have involved private discussions between Mr Liang and his grandfather to gently try to convince the former president of the need for these innovative policies. Chris's forceful arguments to effect a change in the old man's mind in front of more junior staff was seen as a serious breech of etiquette, which caused the old man to lose face.

Chapter 4

1   Malays do not budget their time in the same way that Western persons do. Time is considered to be a much more flexible commodity. The best piece of advice we might give Nathan is to be patient and allow

more time when conducting business affairs in Asia than would be normal in the West. Moreover, what Nathan considered to be 'small talk' is a very important part of the process of doing business in Asia. Trust is an important ingredient in business affairs. Before engaging in meaningful business relations most Malays need time to get to know those with whom they are about to do business. They feel that there is no better way to do this than to discuss a wide variety of non-business topics. And finally, Malays define private and public space somewhat differently than they do in Noosa, New York or Nottingham. They can be quite open in those things they consider to be public, and much of what we would regard as personal matters and business is thought to fall into the public domain.

2 Just as in Western society, it is customary in Malaysia to shake hands as a gesture of friendship. When communicating extreme friendliness, a Western male may grasp his friend's right hand with both of his hands. If, however, such an emphatic handshake is given to a Malaysian male you be sending an extremely offensive message. Generally throughout the Muslim world, where the right hand is sacred and the left hand is profane, touching someone with the left hand is highly offensive. Additionally a Malay handshake is often light and sometimes no more than a touch.

3 Herb had not realised that Brunei is an Islamic country. He made two major errors. First he had pictures of pigs in his presentation. Pigs and pork products are *haram* (forbidden) in the Islamic religion. Herb was being very insensitive in showing these pictures. Second, he did not show any understanding that his company needed to engage Islamic persons to slaughter and prepare the meats products for Brunei should they obtain the contract. Animals must be slaughtered in a particular way and food products be prepared by Islamic persons if the food is to be regarded as halal. Otherwise Moslems are not supposed to eat it.

Chapter 5

1 Although cameras can be valuable for documenting a foreign culture, they must be used with care. There is the simple matter of violating one's privacy, a notion that most of us can relate to. How would a typical middle-class Westerner, for example, feel if someone dressed in foreign clothing started taking his picture while he was cutting his front lawn or cleaning the car? But for a number of other cultural reasons many rural Indonesians would be reluctant to have their picture taken. First, a sizeable number of them are Muslims, and as such resist being photographed because of the Koranic prohibition

of depicting the human form. Second, whereas the Westerner looks for 'picturesque' scenes of people doing traditional things, the local people themselves may feel that the foreign photographer is documenting their 'backwardness', or lack of modernisation. And third, some of the more primitive Malay groups in the more remote areas of Indonesia (e.g., Kalimantan), who may not fully understand the technology of the camera, believe that having their pictures taken is tantamount to having their soul entrapped in the camera. In a society where witchcraft and superstition still exist, the thought of anyone, capturing one's soul can be terrifying.

2 Public humiliation is one of a number of techniques that can be used quite effectively in the West to change people's behaviour. In the world of Islam, however, where the preservation of dignity and self-respect is absolutely essential, public reprimand will be totally counterproductive. If the Indonesians feel that they have suffered a loss of personal dignity because they have been criticised in public, they take it as a dishonour to both themselves and their families. And when Marc insisted on using this 'motivational' technique, he was alienating not only the individual to whom the reprimand was directed, but also all of his fellow workers, who felt hurt on his behalf. When this happens, the person giving the reprimand loses the respect of those witnessing it.

Chapter 6

1 Here is an example of how certain nonverbal actions—in this case the pounding of one's fist into one's palm—have very different meanings across cultures. In Singapore, as well as in several other Southeast Asian countries, such a gesture is a sexual insult, comparable in the West to extending the middle finger.

Chapter 7

1 Robert had the typical Western concept of time and operated under the assumption that since time is money, there is no reason to waste it. Such a definition of time assumes that the end product of negotiations between two companies is more important than the process that brings it about. But in the Philippines, as in many other Asian cultures, the *process* is also vital. It is not enough just to make a decision on the merits of the product, but important that those entering into a business relationship enjoy one another's company and build a strong foundation of mutual trust. To the Filipinos, Robert's insistence on getting down to business as quickly as possible was bypassing some very important components of the negotiation process.

2   Western culture is basically monochromic, emphasising promptness and schedules. Keeping to an agreed-upon schedule takes priority, even when confronted with unanticipated contingencies. If need be, personal pleasure, or sometimes even quality, will take second place to meeting the deadline. The Filipinos are interested in efficiency and meeting schedules, but they don't give deadlines the same top priority as we do. The work will be done but the Filipinos do not work well to deadlines.

Chapter 8

1   Sam's problem stemmed from making the unwarranted assumption that informality at the party could carry over into a business context. In fact, Japanese make a very real distinction between these two social situations. Japanese senior executives can be informal and playful at parties, but it is not the environment in which to discuss business matters. The two realms are kept quite distinct in Japan.

2   Even though Japanese women receive considerable education, they have not been fully accepted into the higher echelons of the corporate world. The Japanese negotiators simply were not very subtle in their efforts to disguise their displeasure or discomfort with having to negotiate with a woman.

3   The Japanese have great difficulty saying 'no'. Instead of saying 'no' in a direct, unequivocal way, the Japanese are more likely to give a conditional response, an irrelevant tangential response, ask a counterquestion, change the subject, leave the room, or say nothing at all. Of all the indirect ways that the Japanese say 'no', silence is the most difficult for Westerners to handle gracefully. We place such importance on words that the absence of them becomes very disorienting. We feel that silence is inherently unnatural, and frequently say things to fill the silence. Unfortunately, we may say things to break the silence that should not have been said. Tom would have been better off to have waited out the silence and then come back with another proposal or a question that would have kept the discussions on track.

4   The employee–employer relationship in Japan is very different than in the West. When a Japanese firm hires an employee, they become part of the corporate family. Whereas labour and management in the West operate largely from an adversarial and contractual perspective, the relationship between the Japanese worker and the company is based on loyalty and a long-term commitment to one another. Not only do most employees expect to stay with the firm for the duration of their careers, but also the firm takes an active role

in the personal lives of its employees and their families. Housing, recreation, and schooling for the children are just some of the areas arranged by the employers for their workers. Moreover, there is far less separation of business and personal matters between Japanese employees and their supervisors. Thus, it is little wonder that the Japanese thought that Ken was not acting like a responsible manager when he showed unwillingness to become involved in their personal lives.

Chapter 9

1   The unwillingness of these three Korean accountants to leave their current employer stems from a sense of loyalty felt by many Korean workers that is not shared by their Western counterparts. Koreans— unlike the Japanese who are extremely loyal to the *company* they work for—have relatively little loyalty to their companies, *per se*, but the do have a strong sense of loyalty to their *bosses* within the company. When Korean employees do change companies, they frequently are following bosses who take them along when they move. Even though it may be every bit as difficult for foreign firms to recruit Koreans away from their current jobs as it would be to recruit Japanese, the nature of the workers' loyalty is different in these two countries.

2   In Korea, as in many other parts of the Asian world, status and rank are important elements of social and business relationships. In the West, particularly Australia and the USA, where people have a tendency to play down status differences, it is not unusual for the boss 'to roll up their sleeves' and start working alongside those of lower rank and position. In fact, the boss is likely to become more popular by working alongside the workers, particularly when there is a problem, for its shows a spirit of empathy and democracy. In Korea, however, a senior executive or owner boss doing manual labour, or even working with lower level staff, is seen as a deliberate rejection of self-respect. And if those in high positions are not willing to maintain their high status and self-respect, it is unlikely that they will continue to receive the respect of their employees. To the Korean employees it would have been far preferable to have missed the deadline than to have their boss lose his self-respect by engaging in manual labour.

Chapter 10

1   The meaning of time and punctuality varies not only from culture to culture, but also within any culture, depending on the *social context*.

In Thailand, a person of high status should never be kept waiting by a person of lesser status; an older person can be late for an appointment with a younger person, but the reverse is not true. Although punctuality for its own sake is not valued in the same absolute sense as it is in the West, there are some social situations that demand punctuality and others that do not. The Thai managers/ business owners who were older than Domenic could certainly keep him waiting, but the reverse was not appropriate. This example should remind us that when in Thailand, and most other Asian cultures as well, it is important to understand the nuances of values, attitudes and behaviours.

2 Asians in general, and Thais in particular, place a high value on harmonious personal relationships. Conflicts are avoided at all costs and every effort is made to be polite and non-confrontational. Also, Thais have great difficulty in admitting failure, for to do so is to be humiliated or shamed, that is, to lose face. The reporting or acknowledging of a problem is far more serious than the problem itself, for it causes a loss of face for the teller and a loss of morale for the hearer. Thus, when the Thai employees withheld knowledge about plant problems from Ben, they did so to (1) preserve his face *and* (2) not lose face themselves.

Chapter 11

1 Although the fertiliser company did a good deal of scientific research in developing its product, it was woefully lacking in cultural information that would have enabled the company to market it. First, the company tried to convince the village men to accept an agricultural innovation when in fact it was mainly the women who grew crops, as the men worked away from home in larger towns to earn money. That they failed to realise this fact did little for their general credibility. Second, as many of the villagers saw themselves as part of large extended families and clan systems no individual farmer would never participate in any scheme that promised to produce considerably more per hectare than their neighbour. To do so would be seen as not being part of the family and be against the collectivity of the village.

Index